LETTERING -THROUGH THE CREATIVE PROCESS-

Editor, concept, and project director
Anna Minguet

Project's selection, design and layout
Carolina Amell (Monsa Publications)
Cover design
Carolina Amell (Monsa Publications)
Introduction and text edition
Monsa Publications
Translation by SomosTraductores

Cover image by Gemma O'Brien
Back cover by Sammie Ho

INSTITUTO MONSA DE EDICIONES
Gravina 43 (08930)
Sant Adrià de Besòs
Barcelona (Spain)
Tlf. +34 93 381 00 50
www.monsa.com
monsa@monsa.com

Visit our official online store!
www.monsashop.com

Follow us!
Facebook: @monsashop
Instagram: @monsapublications

ISBN: 978-84-16500-63-5
D.L. B 23412-2017
Printed by Impuls

BY CAROLINA AMELL

LETTERING

- THROUGH THE CREATIVE PROCESS -

monsa

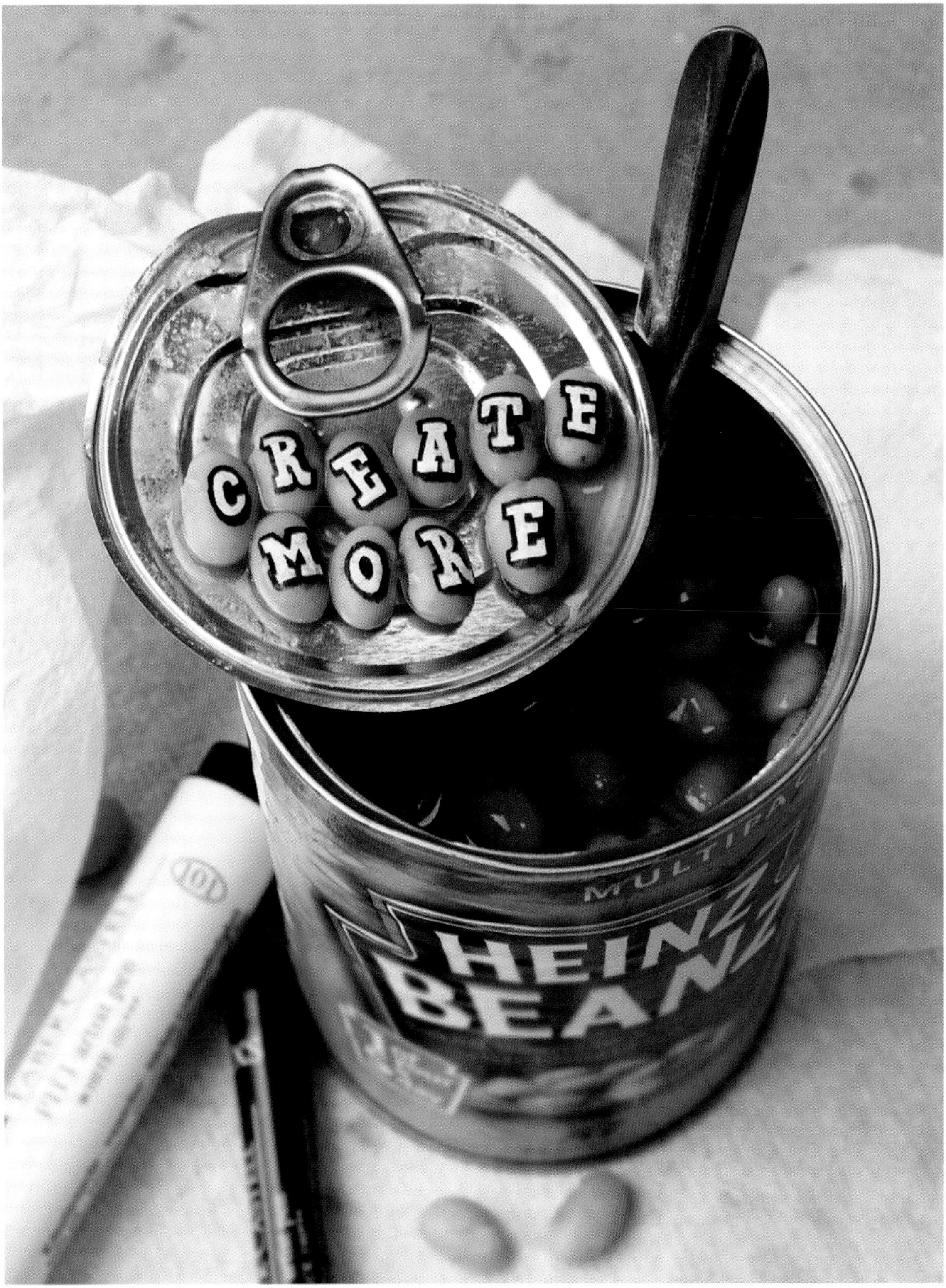
CREATE
MORE
HEINZ

INTRO

This is not just another lettering book. We live in a time in which words have become highly relevant. Everything is labeled and marked. The need to emphasize a text over others has led us to experiment and create images with letters themselves.

At present, this art has been performed for several decades. It enjoys a high level of popularity due to the possibilities, uses, and techniques that give you the opportunity to experience, play, and enjoy while you create. There are more people now than ever who understand its potential and are dedicated to making "letters" full of beauty and individual style.

Following the hand of authentic masters of the art of lettering from around the world, you can enter into their fascinating worlds full of unique letters and learn their techniques, tips and tricks from each artist.

Este no es un libro más de Lettering, vivimos un momento en que las palabras han cobrado una gran relevancia, todo está etiquetado y rotulado, la necesidad de destacar un texto sobre otros nos ha llevado a experimentar y crear imágenes con las propias letras.

En la actualidad, este arte que se lleva empleando desde hace ya varias décadas, está gozando de un alto nivel de popularidad, debido a las posibilidades, usos y técnicas que te dan la oportunidad de poder experimentar, jugar y disfrutar mientras creas. Hay más gente que nunca que comprende su potencial, y se dedica a hacer "letras" llenas de belleza y estilo propio.

A continuación, de la mano de auténticos maestros del arte del lettering de todo el mundo, os podréis introducir en sus fascinantes mundos llenos de letras únicas y aprender sus técnicas, trucos y consejos.

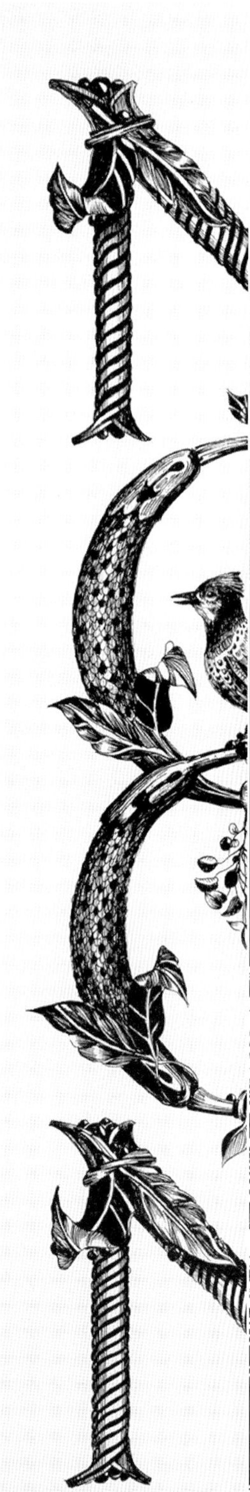

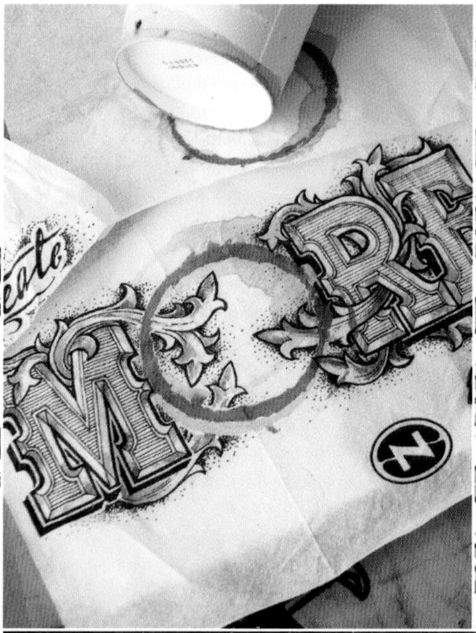

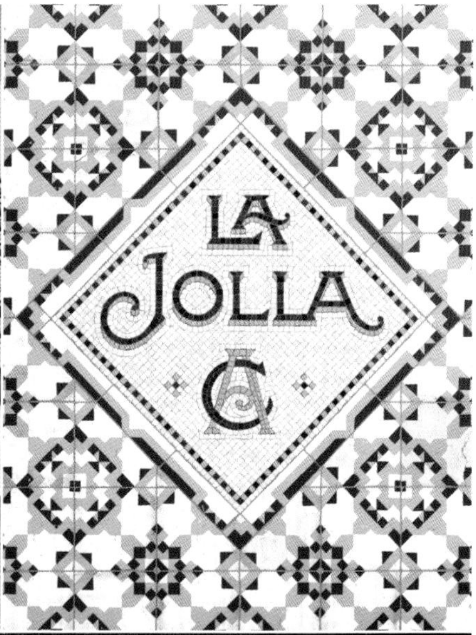
LA
JOLLA

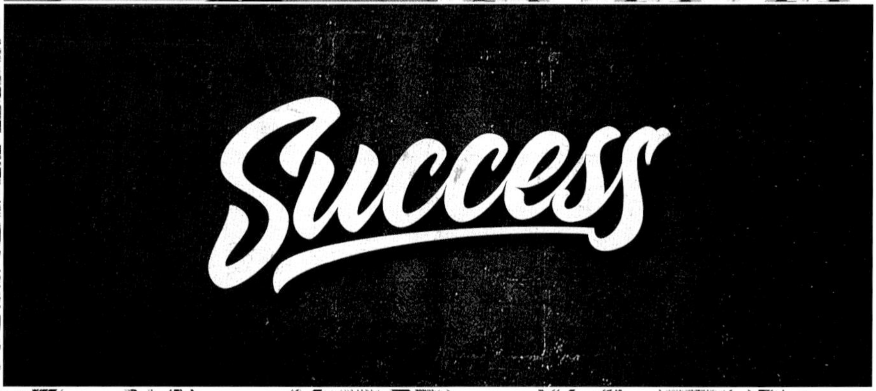
Success

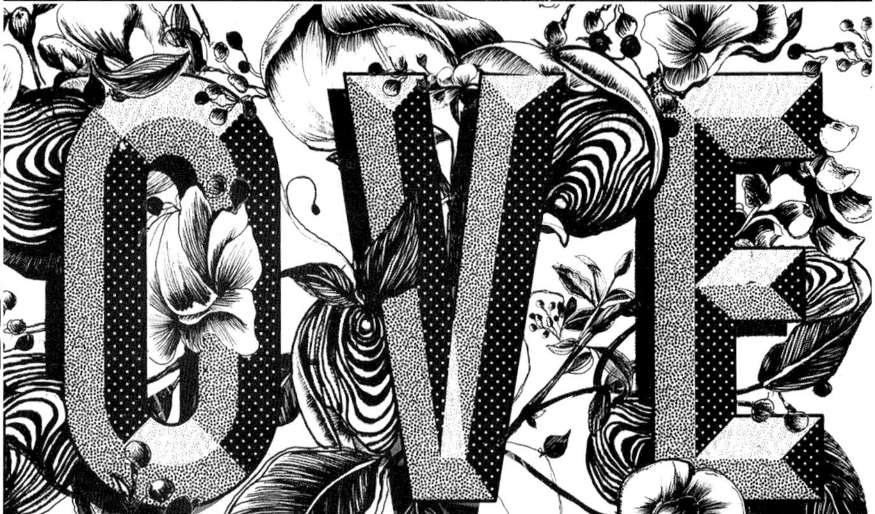

INDEX

NICHOLAS MISANI

www.fauxsaics.com
www.misani.com

Nicholas Misani is a designer and letterer based in New York City. He started his formal training by studying architecture and industrial design in Italy, where he was born. After a brief period living and working in Japan, he relocated to the United States and obtained an MFA in Communications Design from the Pratt Institute in New York City. After being an in-house book cover designer at Penguin Random House, he became the senior designer at Louise Fili Ltd: a boutique studio that offers elegant, high-end solutions to all things related to food, books, and culture. Nick is now a freelance designer and is passionate about period typography, decorative arts, and old crafts - especially when reimagined in contemporary, unexpected ways.

Most recently, Nick has combined his love for lettering, interior design, and decorative arts to create a self-initiated series of typographic mosaic illustrations - called Fauxsaics - where the form is dictated by the limitations of traditional mosaic technique.

His work has been featured on a variety of online and print publications including Print Magazine, Fast Company, The Dieline, Wired, Quipsologies, Adobe, and Designboom. In 2014, He was named a Young Gun by the Art Directors Club and has received recognition from both the Type Directors Club and the AIGA.

Nicholas Misani es un diseñador y rotulador de Nueva York. Inició su formación estudiando arquitectura y diseño industrial en Italia, su país de nacimiento. Tras una breve experiencia laboral en Japón, se trasladó a Estados Unidos, donde estudió un Máster en Diseño de Comunicaciones en el Instituto Pratt de Nueva York. Tras formar parte de la plantilla de Penguin Random House como diseñador de portadas de libros, se convirtió en diseñador sénior de Louise Fili Ltd, un estudio boutique que ofrece productos elegantes y lujosos para todo aquello relacionado con la alimentación, los libros y la cultura. Actualmente, Nick es diseñador autónomo, apasionado de la tipografía, las artes decorativas y la artesanía antigua, especialmente cuando esta se reimagina de forma moderna e inesperada.

Recientemente, Nick ha combinado su pasión por la rotulación, el diseño de interiores y las artes decorativas para crear una serie de ilustraciones tipográficas con estructura de mosaico, llamadas Fauxsaics, cuya forma se ve condicionada por las limitaciones de la técnica del mosaico tradicional.

Sus obras han aparecido en diversas publicaciones impresas y online como la revista Print, Fast Company, The Dieline, Wired, Quipsologies, Adobe o Designboom. In 2014, Nick fue nombrado Young Gun por el Club de Directores de Arte y ha sido galardonado por el Club de Directores Tipográficos y la AIGA.

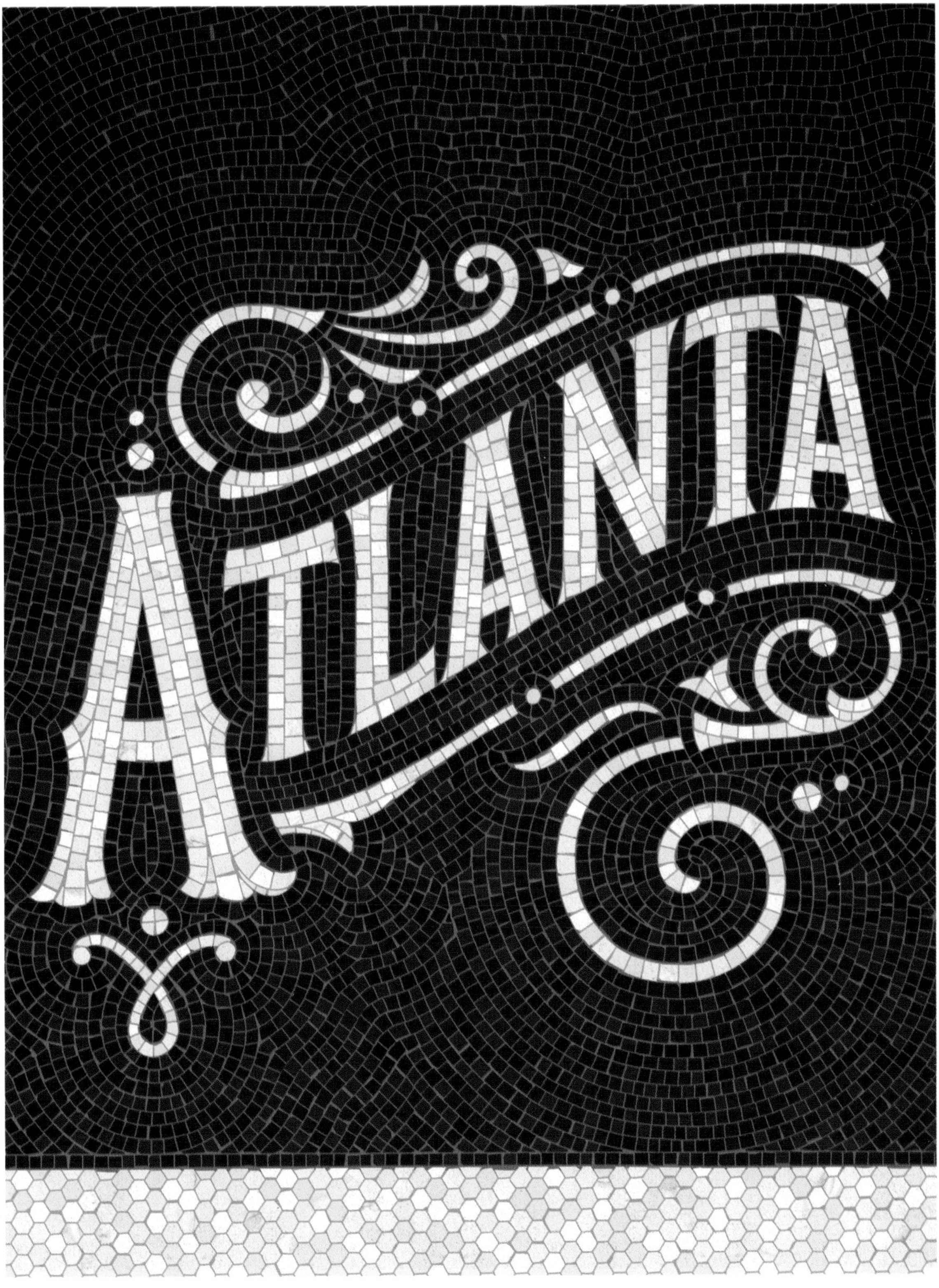
ATLANTA

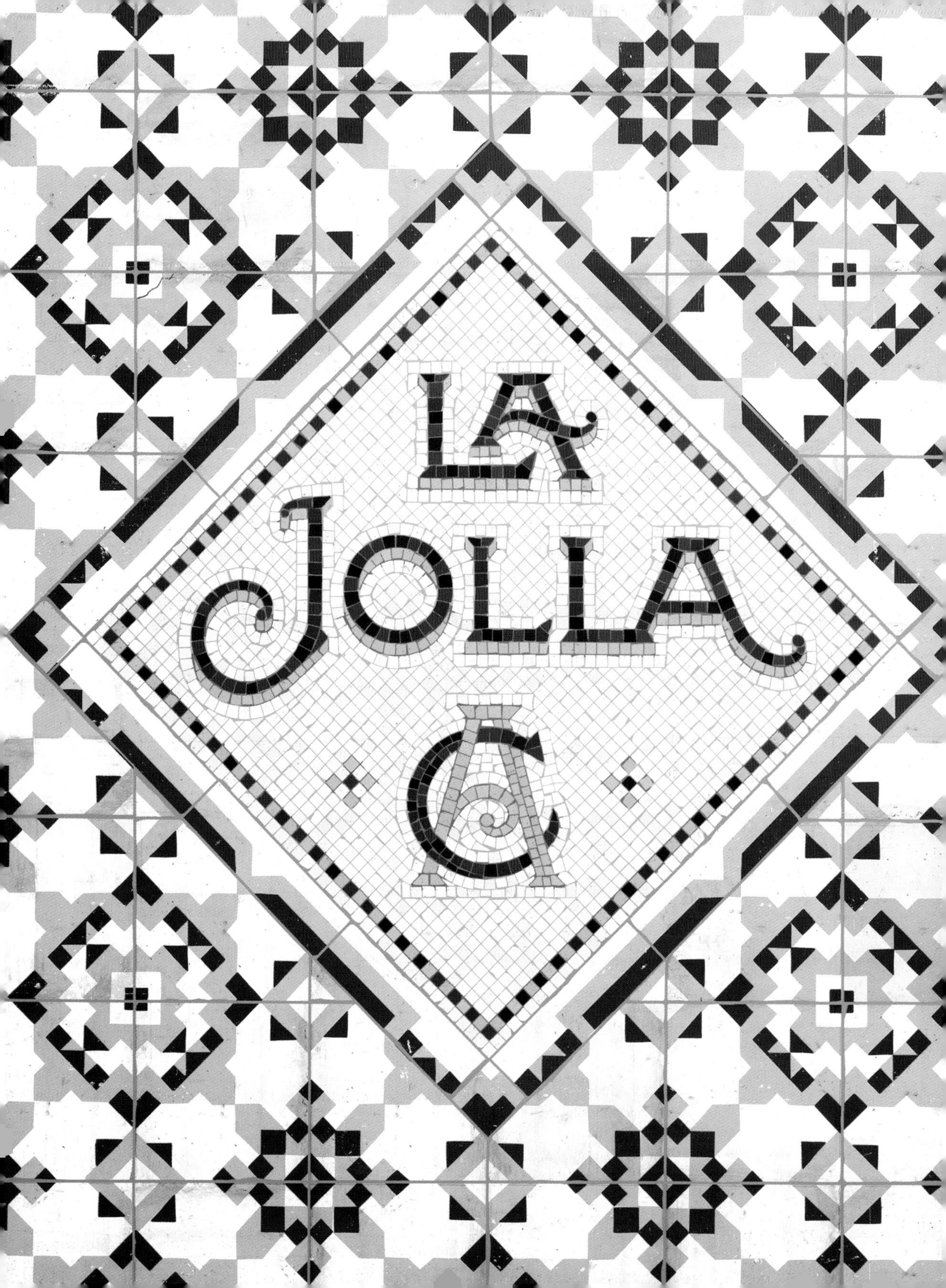
LA
JOLLA

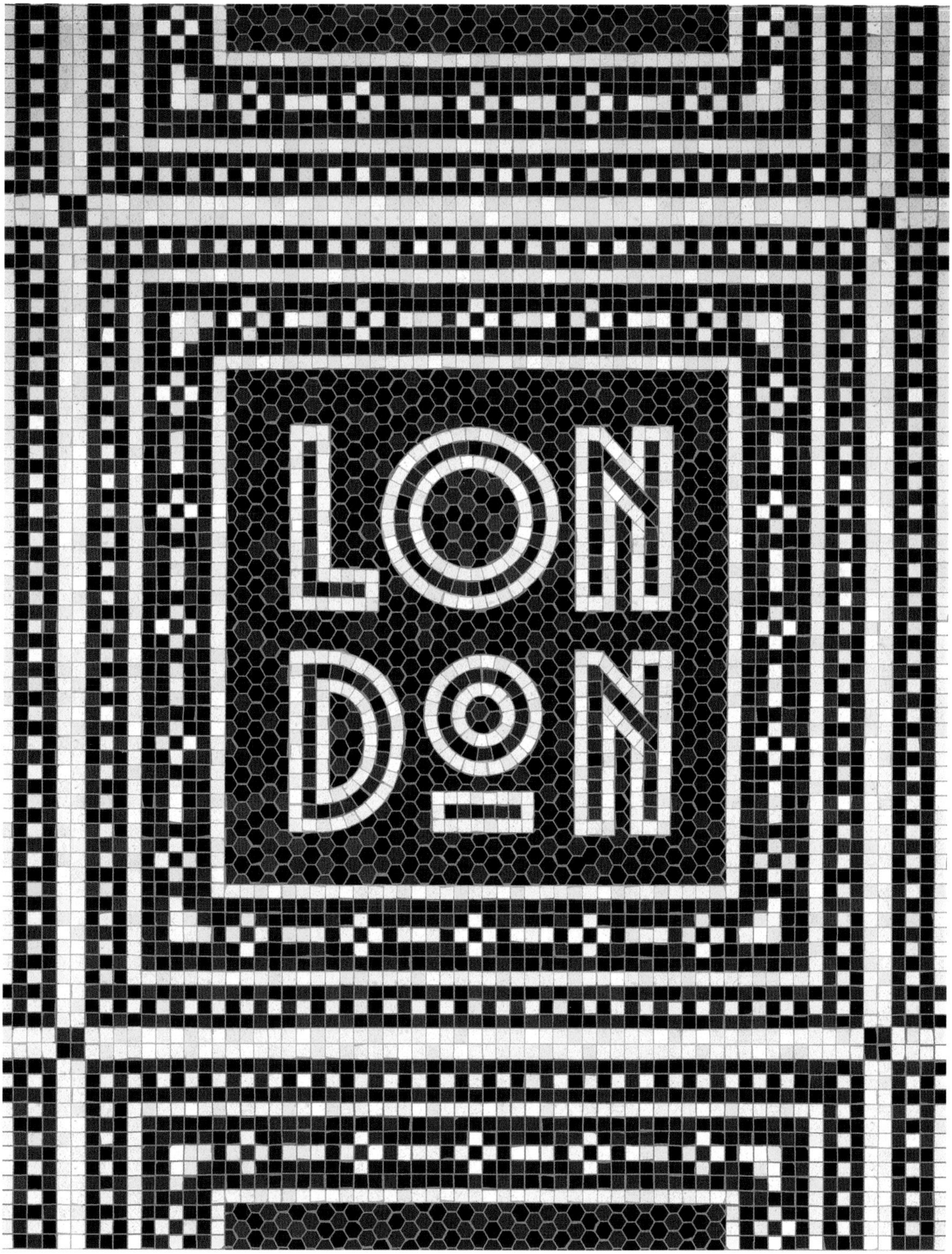
LONDON

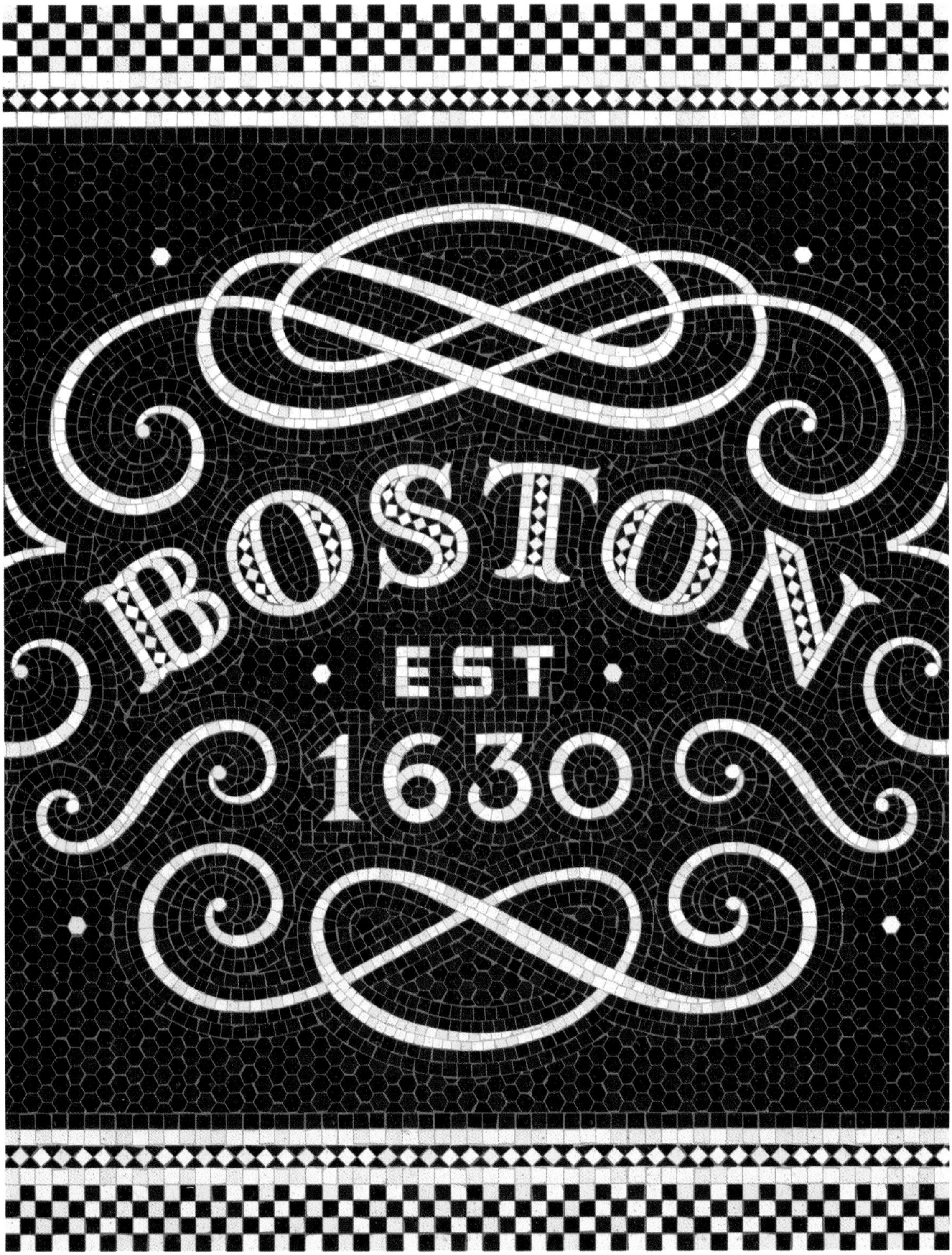
BOSTON
EST
1630

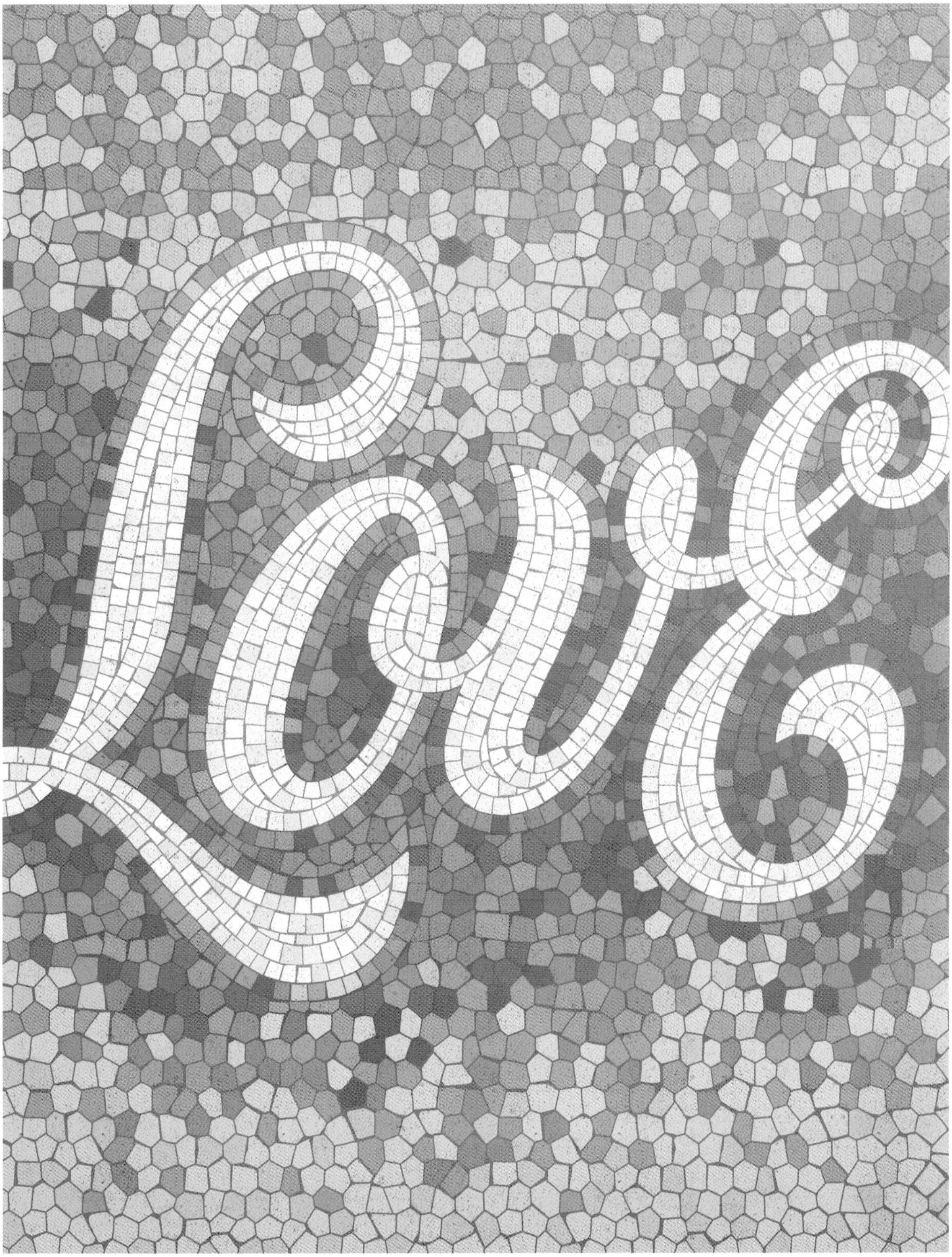
Love

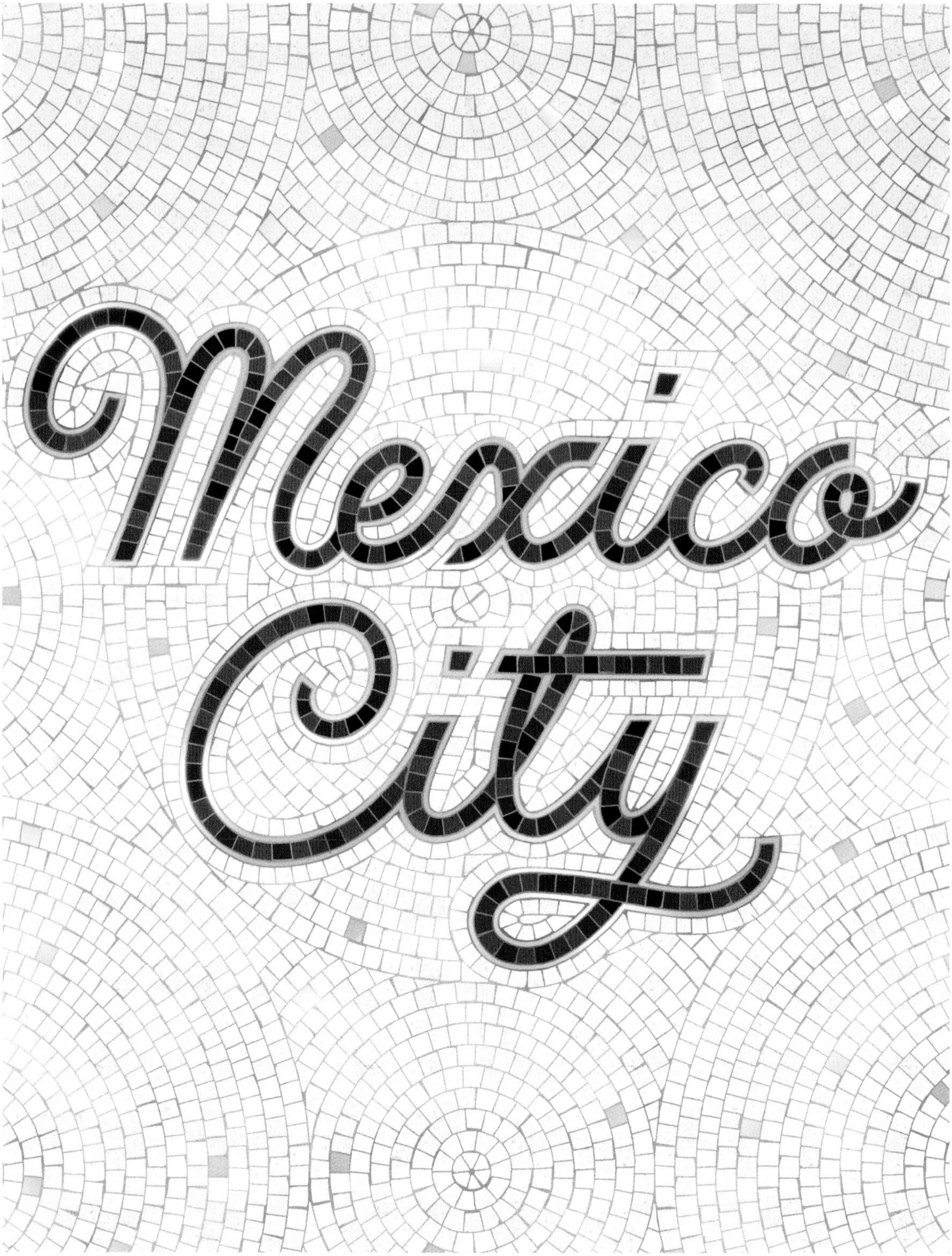
Mexico
City

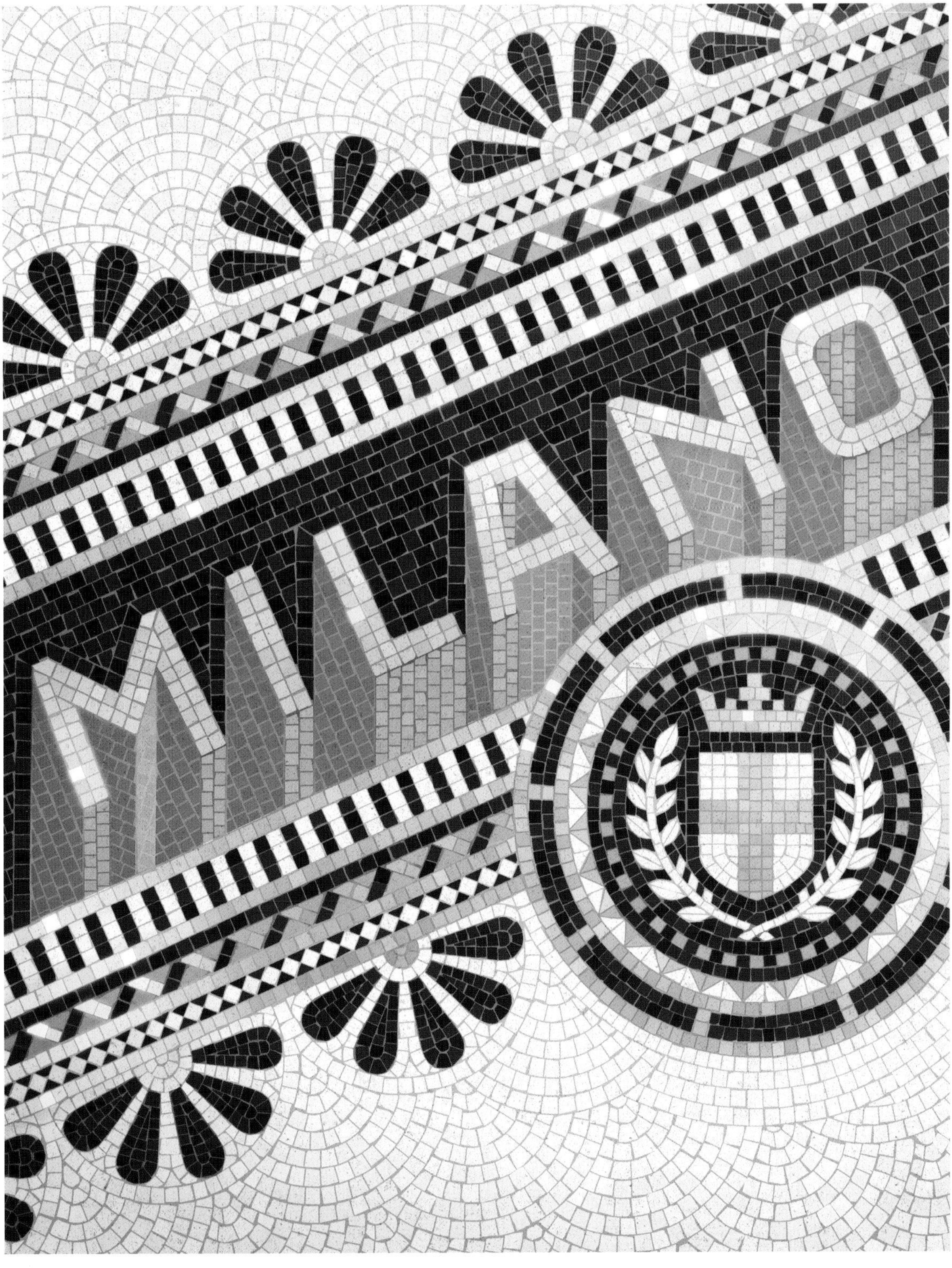
MILANO

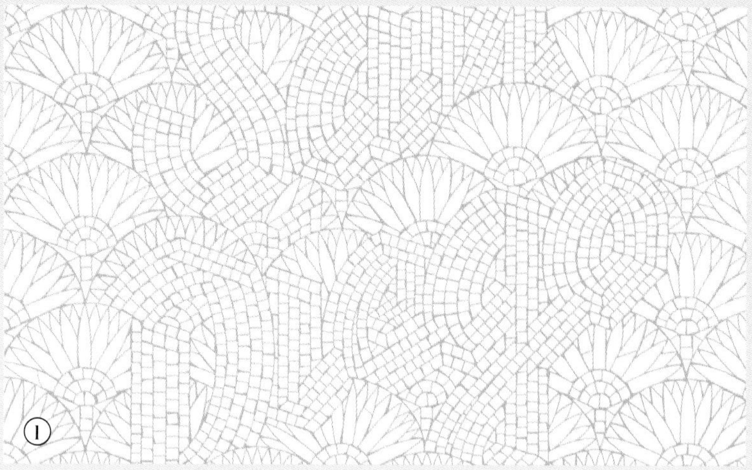
①

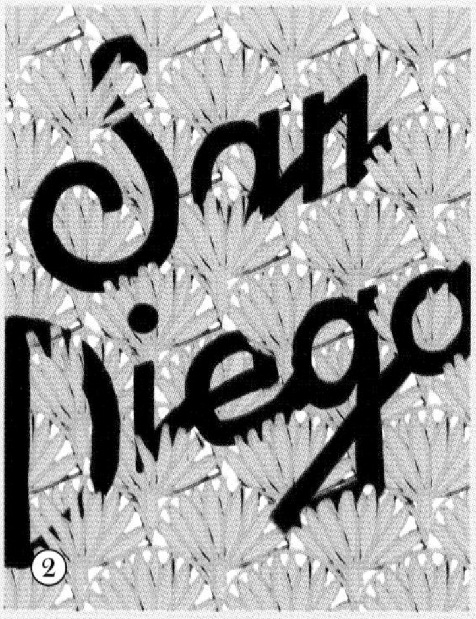

②

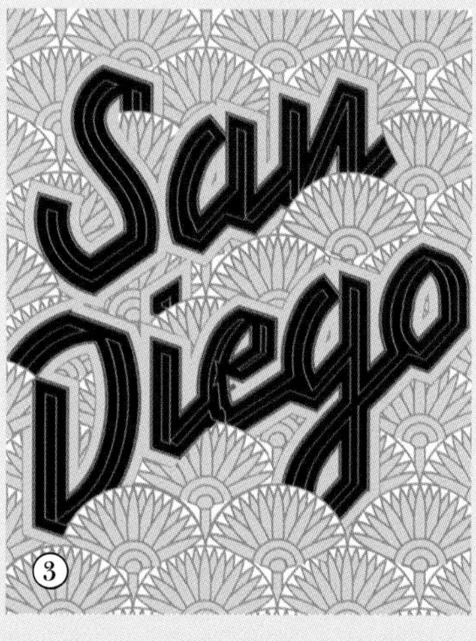

③

Making my mosaic illustrations

I begin the process by sketching and planing the design of a new mosaic by hand, I then use Illustrator to clean up the illustration and prepare it for the grouting phase. This is where I establish the tile size and shape as well as the different tiling patterns I plan on using. The "grouting" also happens by hand, with the aid of my iPad Pro. Afterwards, every tile is individually colored in Photoshop. Considering each illustration has between 6,000 and 10,000 tiles, this phase takes quite a while. I stay in Photoshop and finish the piece by adding one or two textures and some subtle lighting. Metallic effects take quite a bit longer, but the process is essentially the same. The last phase involves selecting some shoes that complement the colors and patterns of the particular piece, photographing them with my iPhone, and Photoshopping them in place. I love this last stage because it transforms the mosaic into a space, giving it a sense of scale and place.

Creando mi mosaico ilustrado

Empecé el proceso diseñando el boceto, planificando el diseño de un nuevo mosaico a mano, y luego utilizando Illustrator para limpiar la ilustración y prepararla para la fase de empastado. Ahí es donde establezco el tamaño y la forma de los cuadros, así como los distintos patrones que tengo previsto utilizar. El "empastado" también se realiza a mano, con ayuda de un iPad Pro. A continuación, cada cuadro se colorea por separado con Photoshop. Esta fase lleva bastante tiempo, sobre todo teniendo en cuenta que cada ilustración tiene entre 6000 y 10 000 cuadros. Sigo utilizando el Photoshop y finalizo la pieza añadiendo una o dos texturas y una iluminación sutil. Los efectos metálicos llevan algo más de tiempo, pero el proceso es, en esencia, el mismo. La última fase consiste en seleccionar unos segmentos que complementen los colores y patrones de la pieza en cuestión, fotografiándolos con el iPhone, y aplicándoles Photoshop sobre el terreno. Esta última fase me encanta porque transforma el mosaico en un espacio, confiriéndole un sentido de escala y lugar.

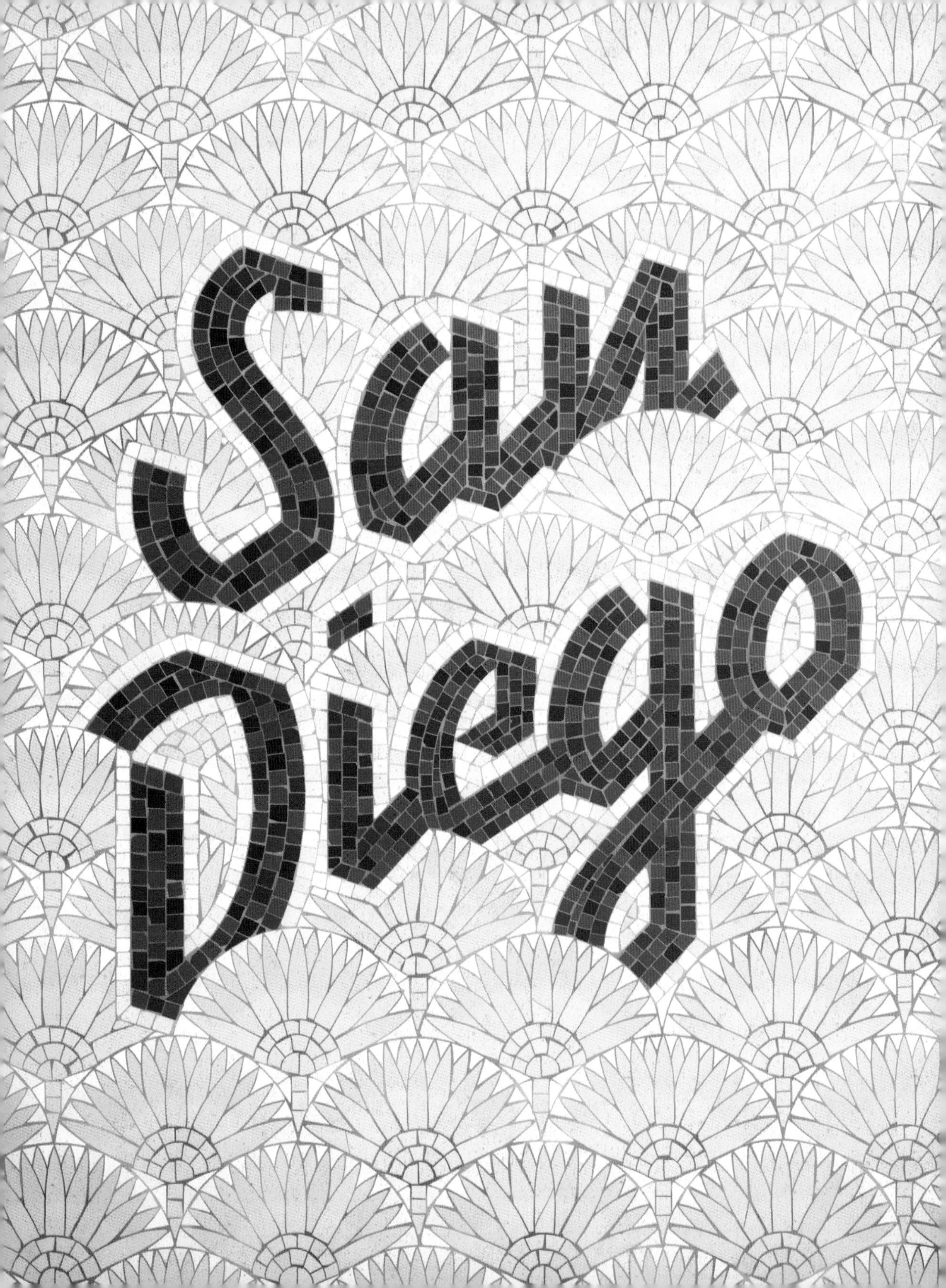
San
Diego

DALIBASS

www.behance.net/Dalibass

Dalibor Momčilović (Dalibass) is a self-thought graphic designer located in Novi Sad, Serbia. Main focus of his work is on hand-drawn lettering logo design. In over 5 years of experience, he has produced over a hundred lettering logo design solutions for satisfied clients worldwide. Enjoying the process of creation, Dalibor is continuously striving for excellence in his work and is always happy to accept the next challenge.

Dalibor Momčilović (Dalibass) es un diseñador gráfico autodidacta de Novi Sad, Serbia, especializado en el diseño de rotulaciones de logos a mano. En sus más de 5 años de trayectoria, ha producido más de 100 diseños de rotulaciones de logos para clientes de todo el mundo, quienes han quedado totalmente satisfechos. Dalibor, que disfruta del proceso de creación, no deja de buscar la excelencia en el trabajo y siempre está dispuesto a aceptar un nuevo reto.

Rolloe™

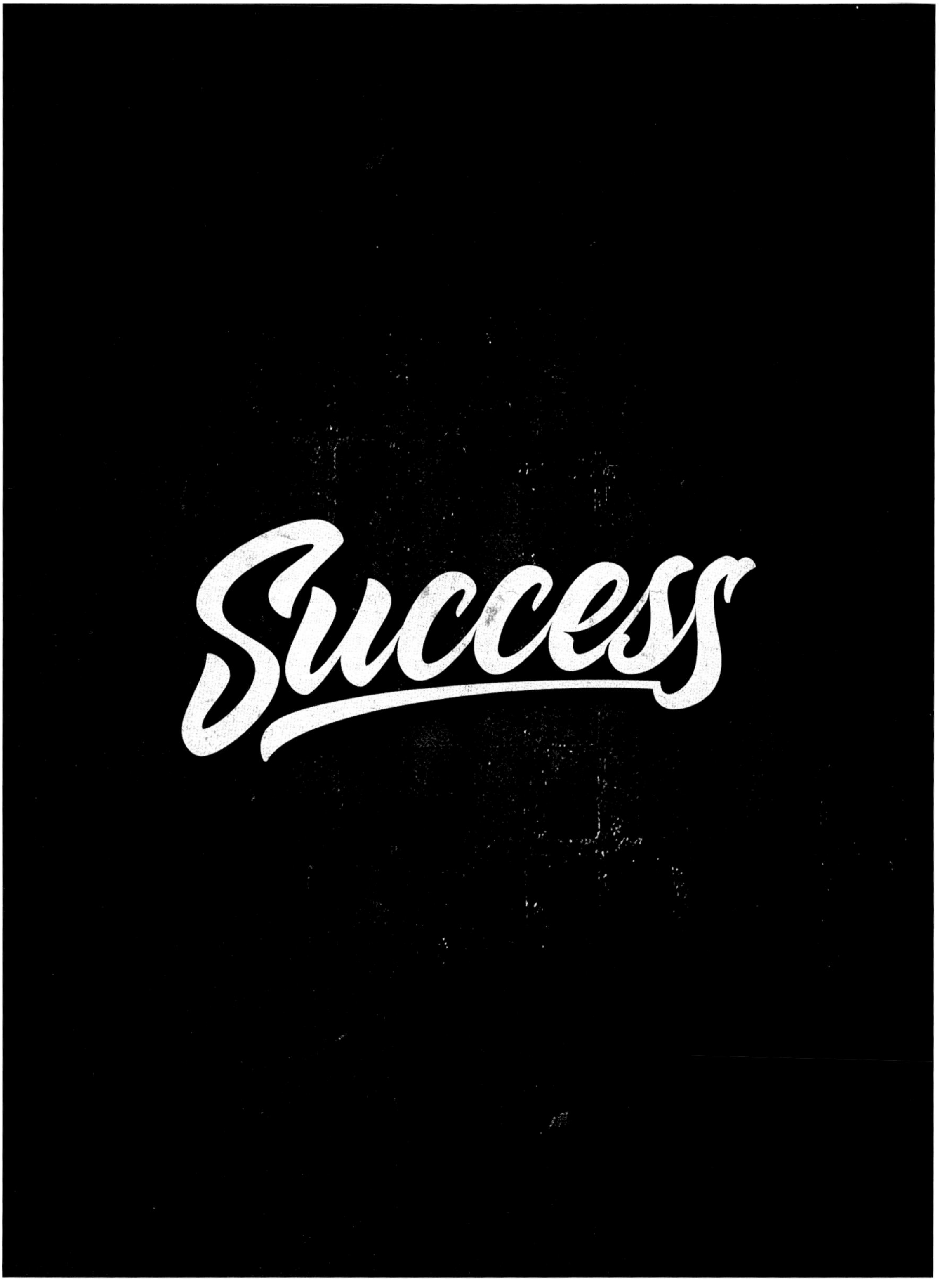
Success

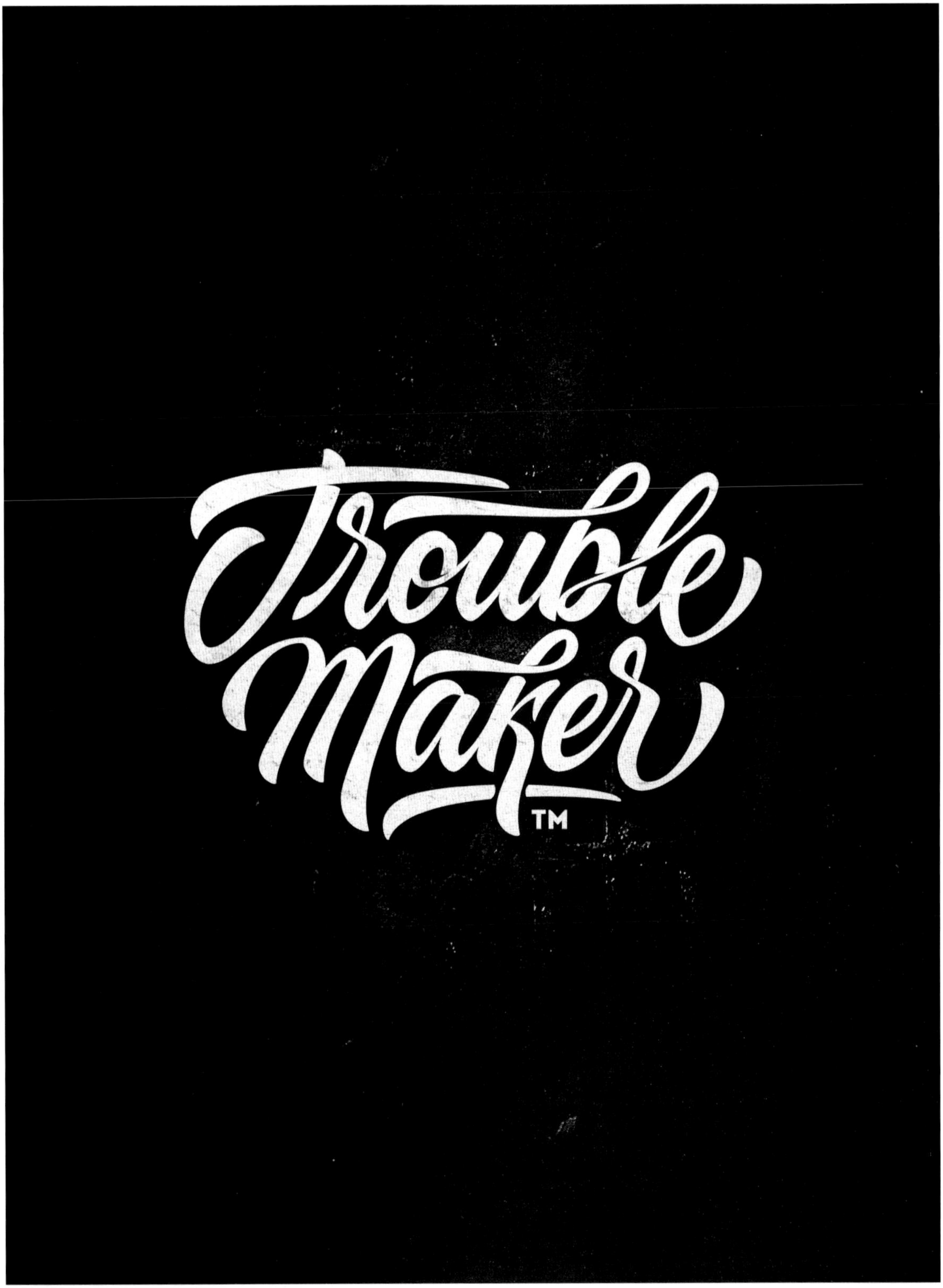
Trouble
Maker
TM

WELL Zoe's ESTD

PATIO

• GOOD EATS • GOOD BEATS •

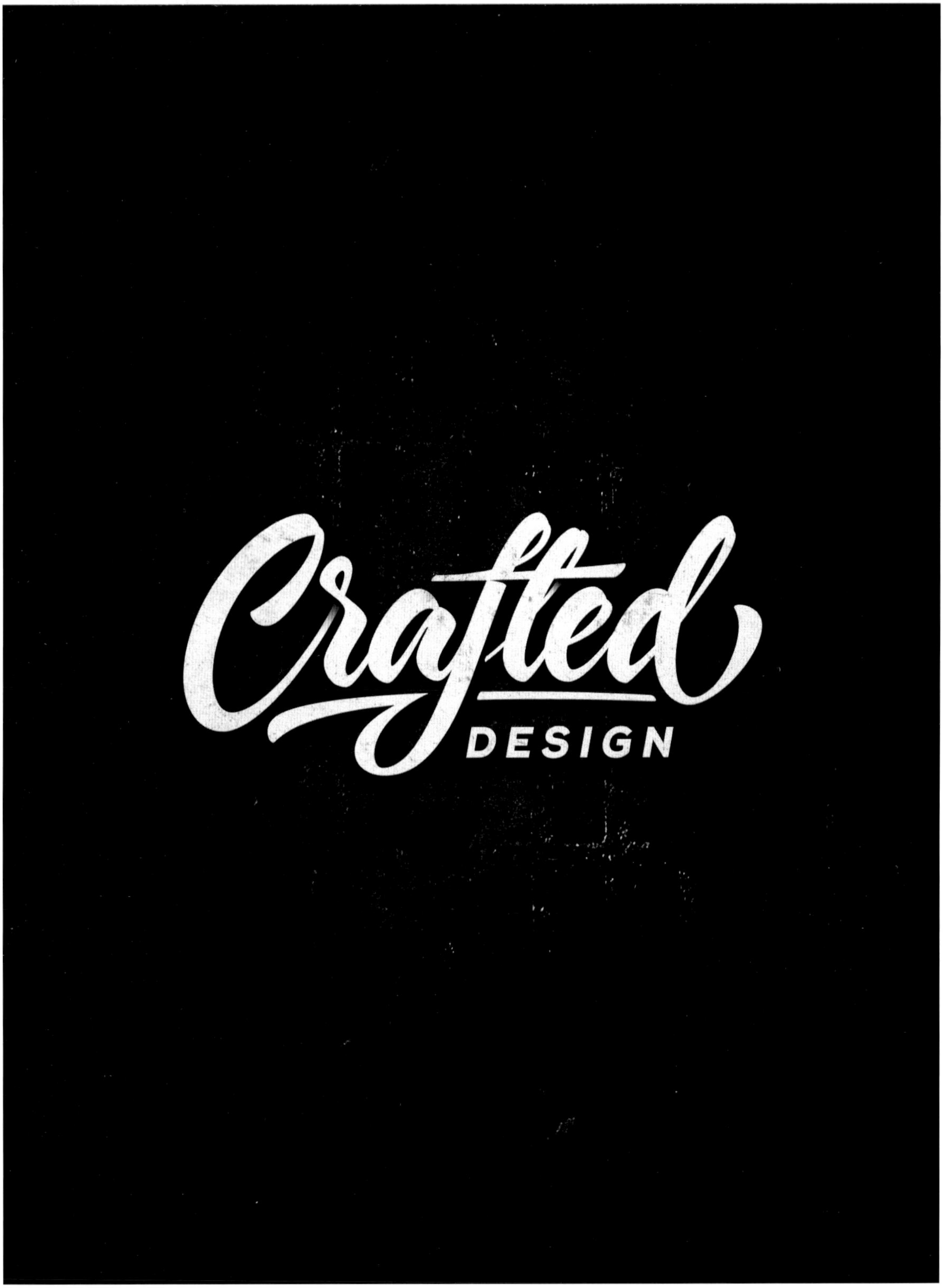
Crafted
DESIGN

Ateliers Jouffre

CONCEPTION & CRÉATION

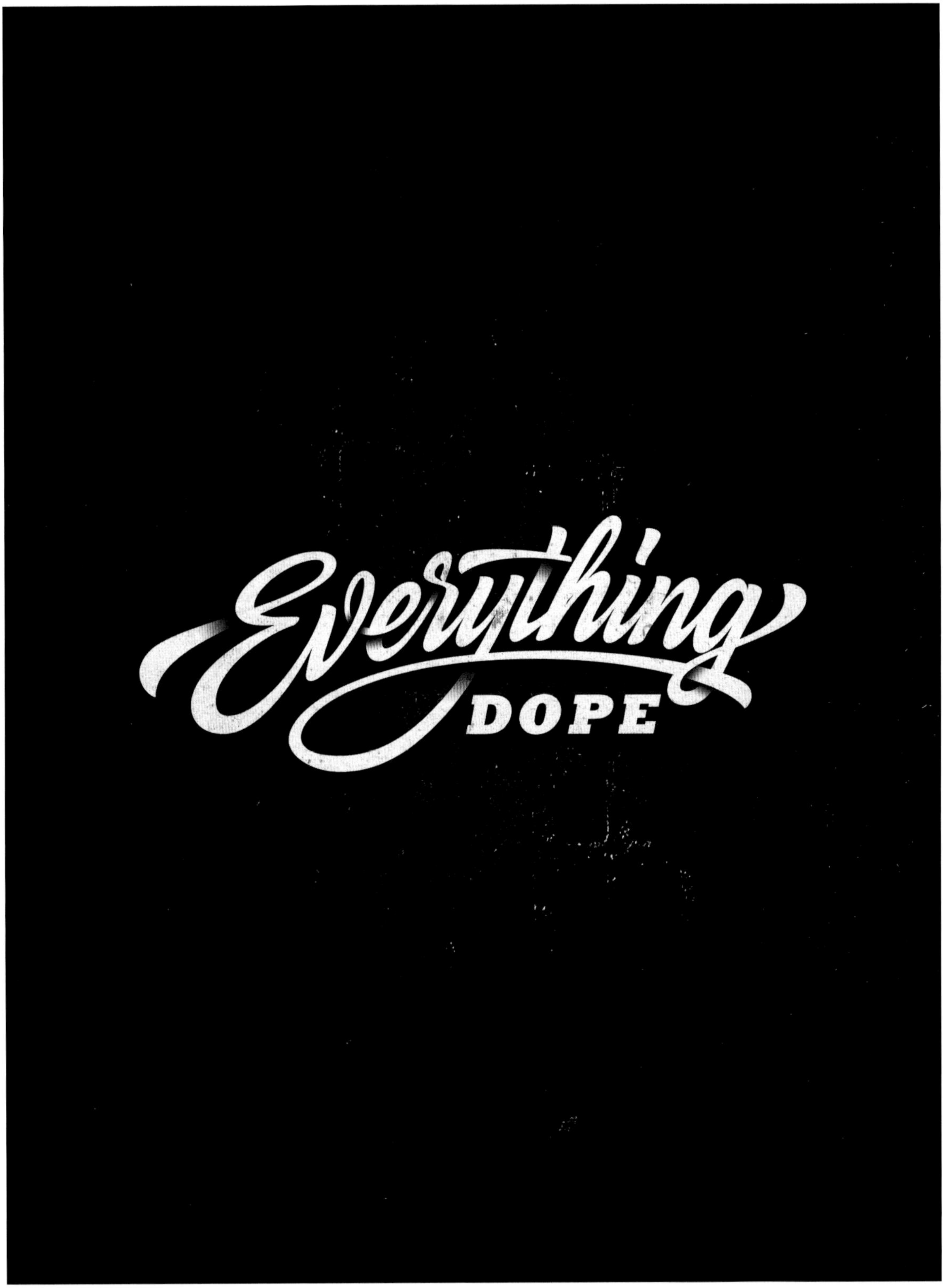
Everything
DOPE

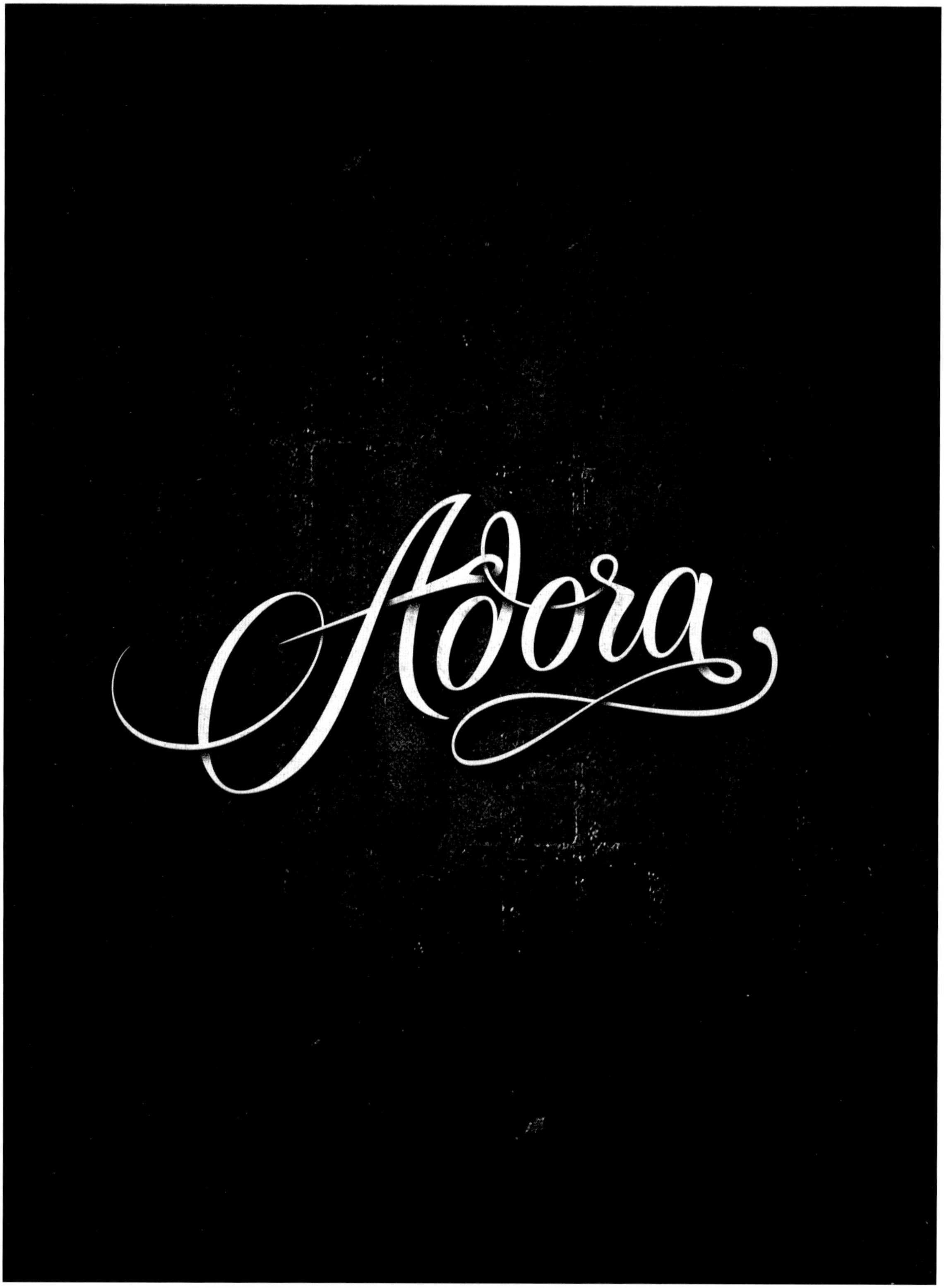
Adora

Rockbox
PHOTO

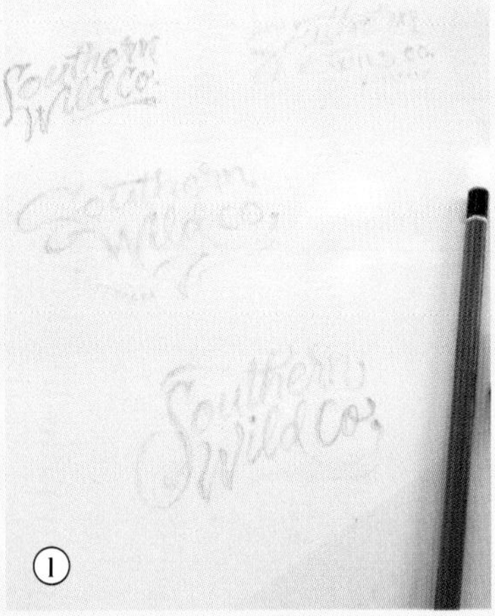

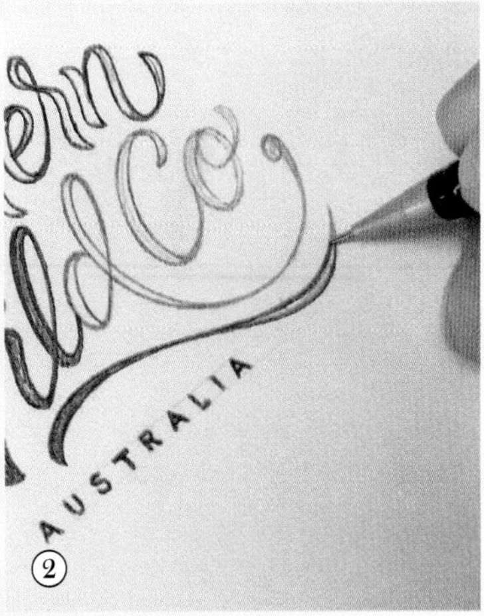

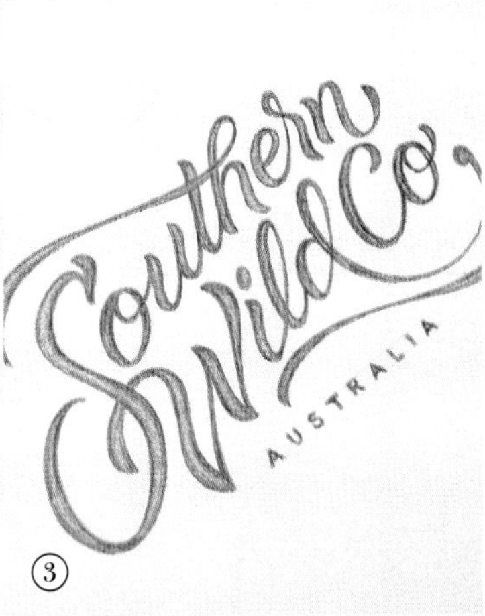

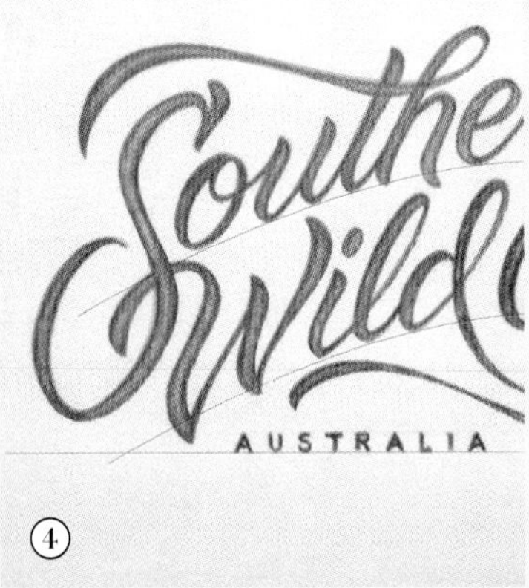

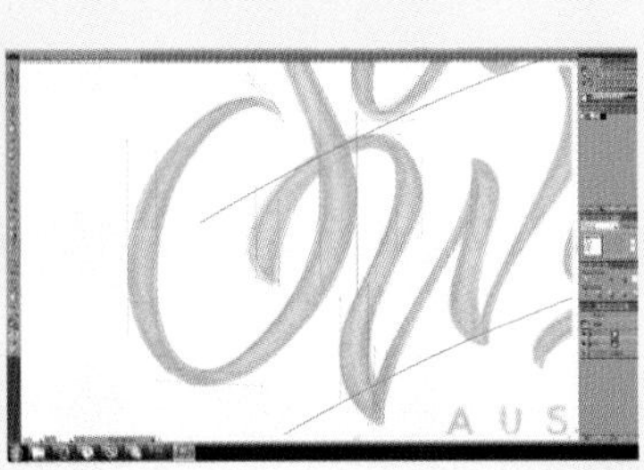

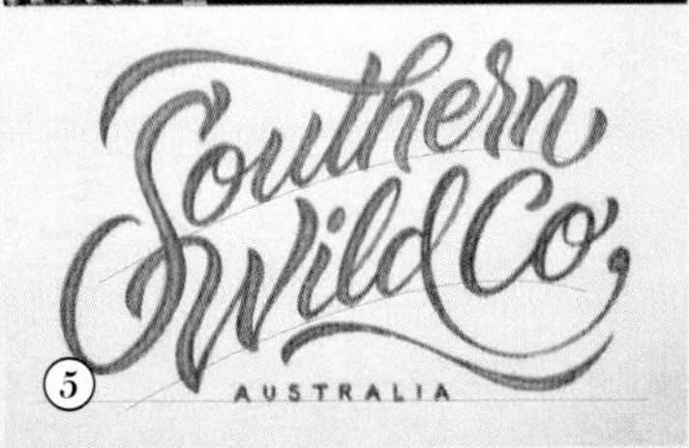

Making my lettering

1. Sketching, of course, means searching the right look, coherence and flow of the letters. In the picture above you can see several different sketches for "Southern Wild Co." Sometimes it takes much more sketches. In this case these were enough. Upper three sketches allowed me to see what the solution could look like and that is what I sketched in the fourth one.

2. Having the right style in head and in sketch led me to clean paper and I've started drawing final version. Usually I use ruler to define the scale, centers, angle guides, etc...

3. When I finalize the drawing that I find to be suitable and responds well to my clients wishes, I transfer the drawing (through scanning or taking a photo) to my computer and the process of creating vector art starts.

4. Using a simple pen tool, I draw around letter lines to get to the final, vectorized art.

5. This pretty much encapsulates my process of creating lettering designs.

Creando mi lettering

1. Hacer un boceto implica, evidentemente, buscar el aspecto, la coherencia y el fluir adecuado de las letras. En la imagen de arriba aparecen varios bocetos para "Southern Wild Co". Y aunque a veces hacen falta muchos más, en este caso fueron suficientes. Los tres bocetos de arriba me permitieron hacerme una idea de cómo quedaría el resultado final, que reflejé en el cuarto boceto.

2. Tener el estilo correcto en la mente y en el boceto me ayuda a empezar a dibujar en limpio la versión final, para la cual suelo utilizar una regla para definir la escala, los centros, las guías de ángulos, etc.

3. Cuando finalizo el dibujo (después de que me haya parecido adecuado y de que comprobar que responde bien a los deseos de mis clientes), lo paso al ordenador (escaneándolo o haciéndole una foto); ahí es donde empieza el proceso de creación de arte vectorial.

4. Con un simple boli, voy dibujando alrededor de los trazos de las letras para conseguir el producto final vectorizado.

5. Ese es más o menos el proceso que sigo a la hora de crear diseños de rotulación.

Southern Wild Co

AUSTRALIA

GEMMA O'BRIEN

www.gemmaobrien.com

Gemma O'Brien is an Australian artist specialising in lettering, illustration and typography. After studying design at the College of Fine Arts in Sydney, Gemma worked as an art director at Animal Logic, Fuel VFX and Toby and Pete before deciding to fly solo as a commercial illustrator in 2012. She is currently represented by the Jacky Winter Group and splits her time between advertising commissions, gallery shows, speaking engagements and hosting hand-lettering workshops around the world. Her typography work takes on a variety of forms, from calligraphic brushwork, illustrated letterforms and digital type to large scale hand-painted murals. Her clients include Adobe, Volcom, Heineken, Kirin Cider, QANTAS, Heinz, Smirnoff and The New York Times. A number of her projects have been recognised by the New York The Type Directors Club with Awards of Typographic Excellence. In her spare time she travels and draws puke puns on barf bags for the Spew Bag Challenge.

Gemma O'Brien es una artista australiana especializada en rotulación, ilustración y tipografía. Después de estudiar diseño en la Escuela de Bellas Artes de Sídney, Gemma trabajó como directora artística en Animal Logic, Fuel VFX y Toby and Pete antes de emprender en solitario una aventura como ilustradora comercial en el año 2012. Representada actualmente por el Grupo Jacky Winter, Gemma forma parte de comisiones publicitarias, expone en galerías, da conferencias y celebra talleres de rotulación manual por todo el mundo. Sus obras tipográficas adquieren diversas formas, desde pinceladas de caligrafía, formas de letras ilustradas y tipografía digital a murales de gran tamaño pintados a mano. Entre sus clientes figuran Adobe, Volcom, Heineken, Kirin Cider, QANTAS, Heinz, Smirnoff o el New York Times. Varios de sus proyectos han recibido galardones por parte del Club de Directores Tipográficos de Nueva York a la excelencia tipográfica. En su tiempo libre le gusta viajar y dibujar imágenes divertidas de regurgitaciones en bolsas para vómitos para the Spew Bag Challenge.

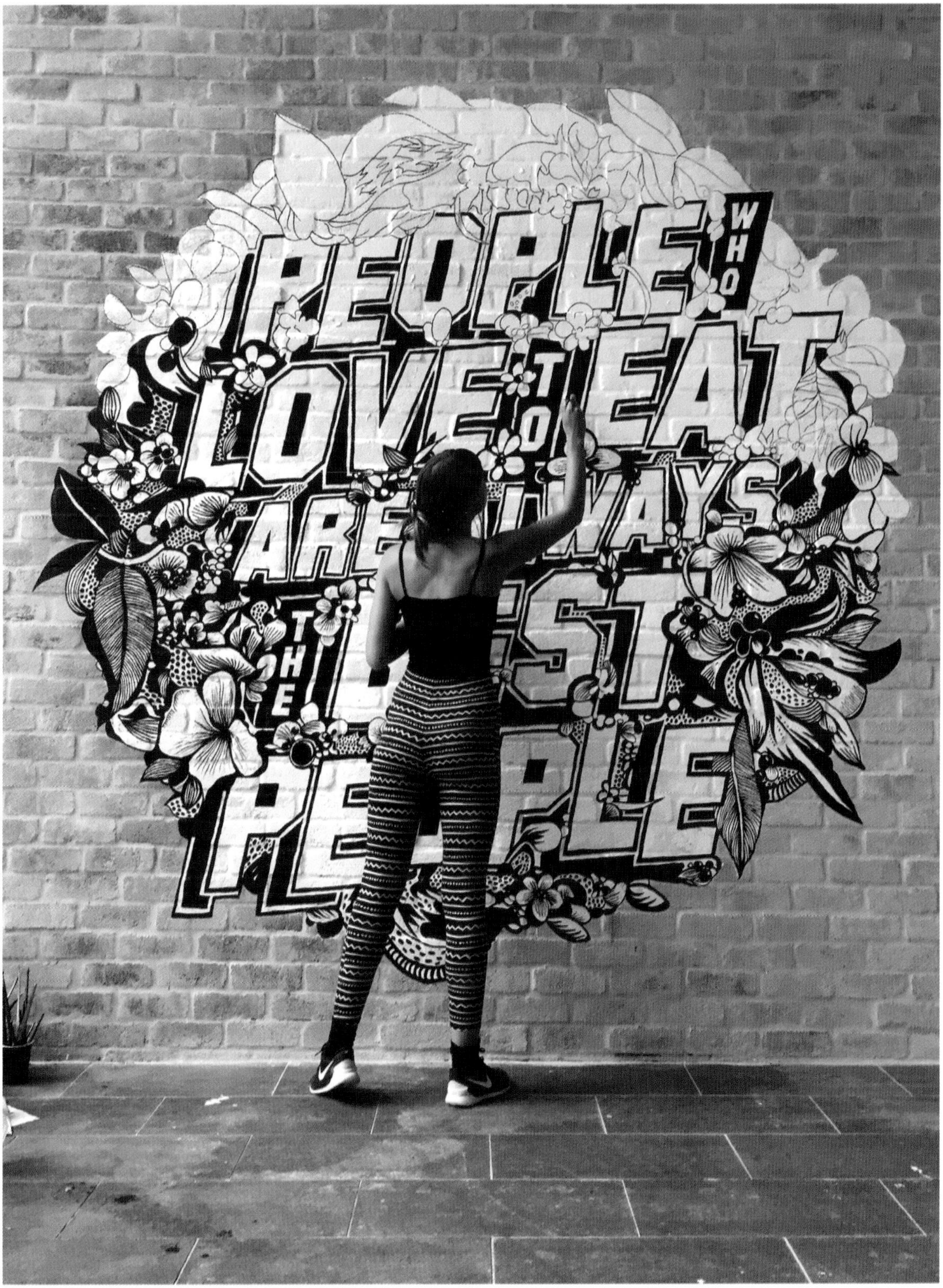
PEOPLE WHO
LOVE TO EAT
ARE
WAYS
THE
ST
PLE

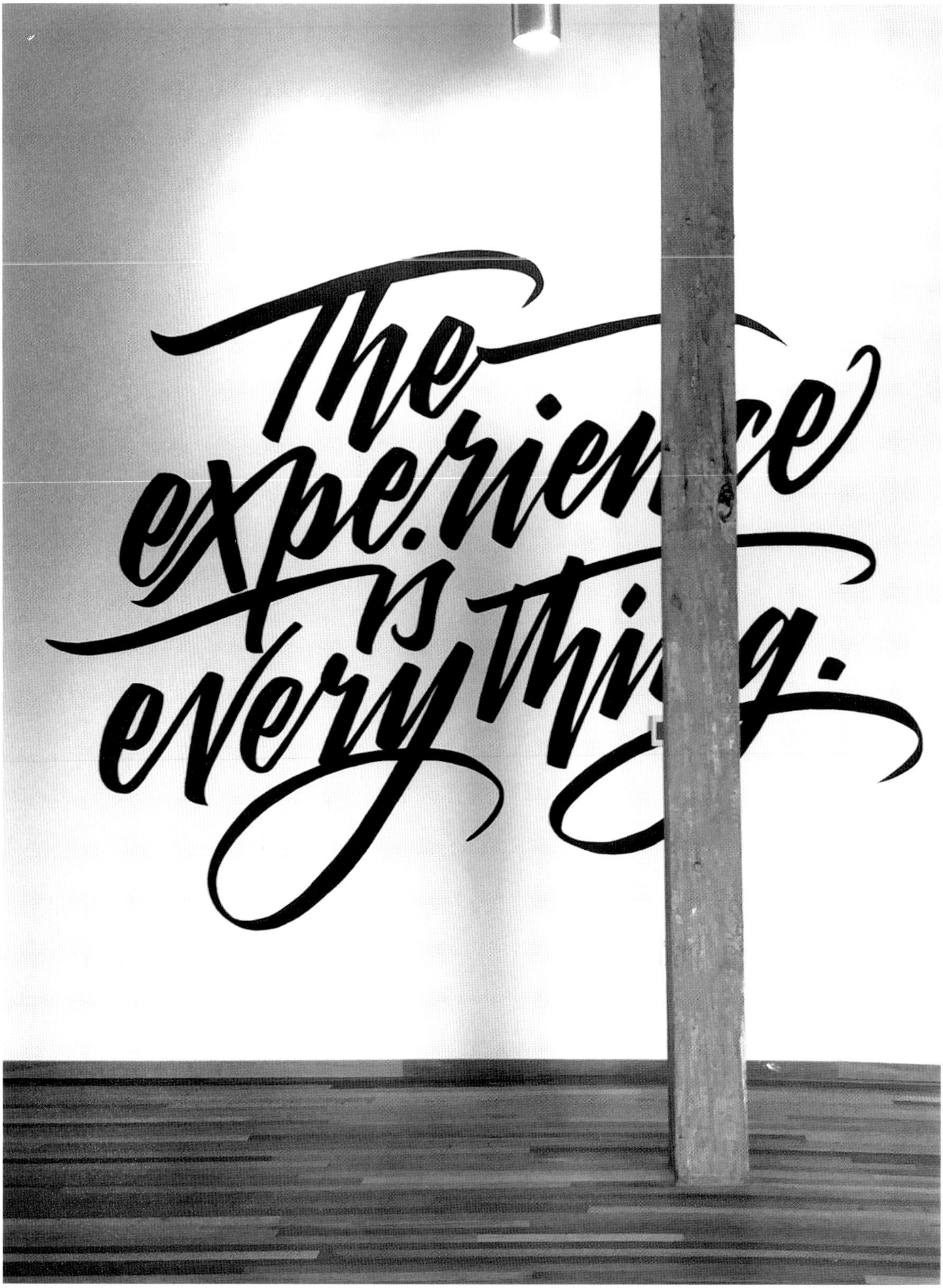
The
is

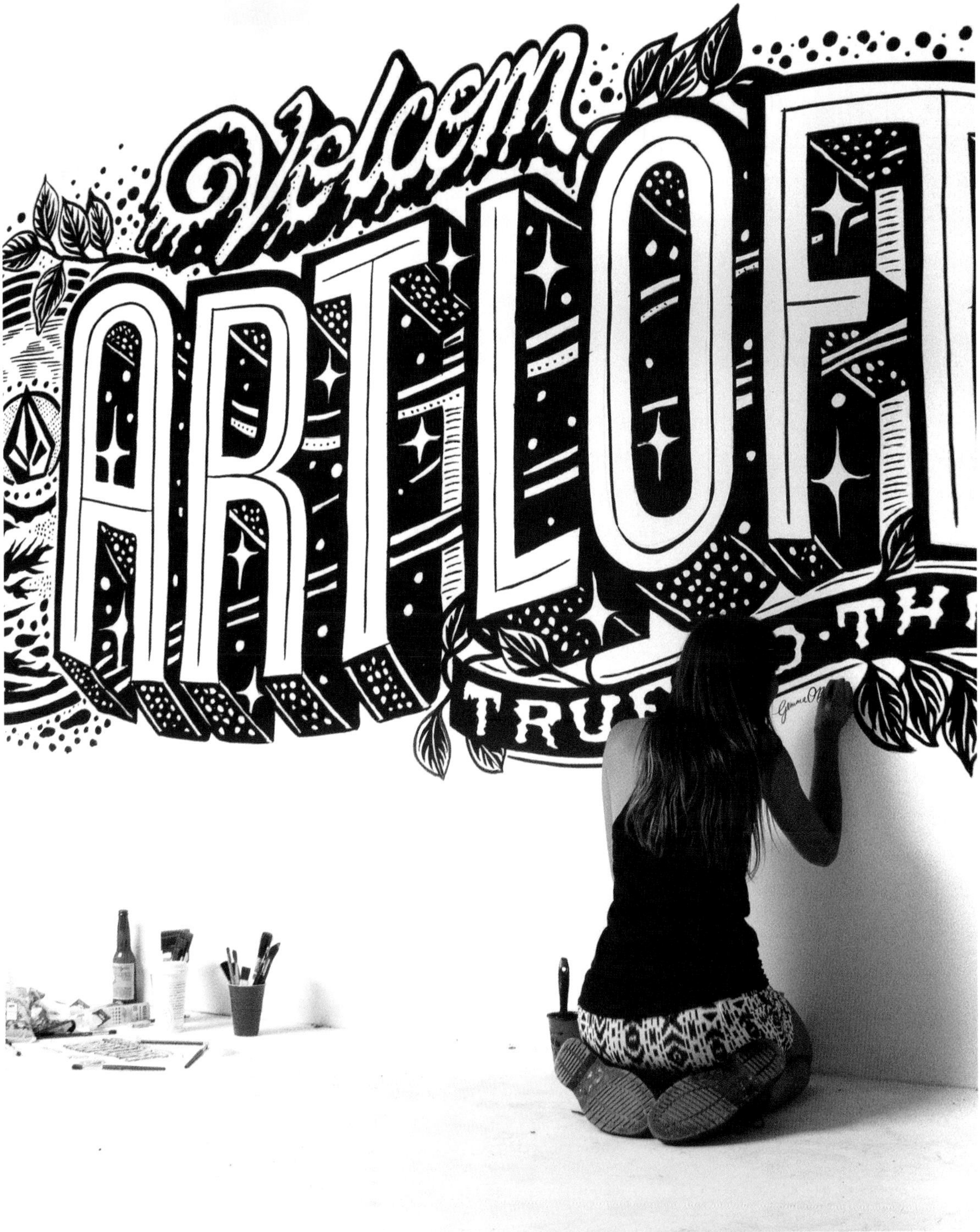
Volcom
ARTLOF
TRU
TH

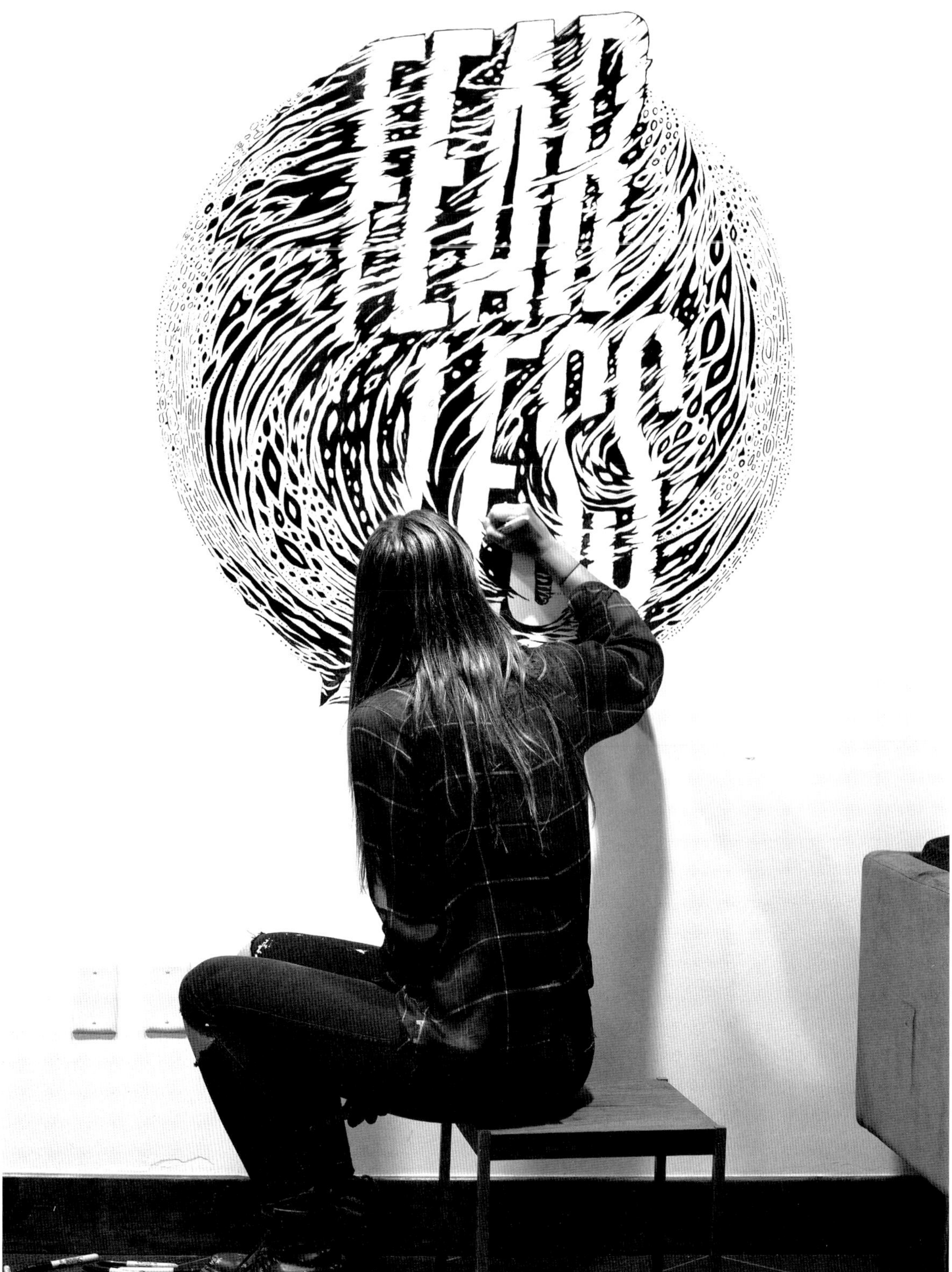

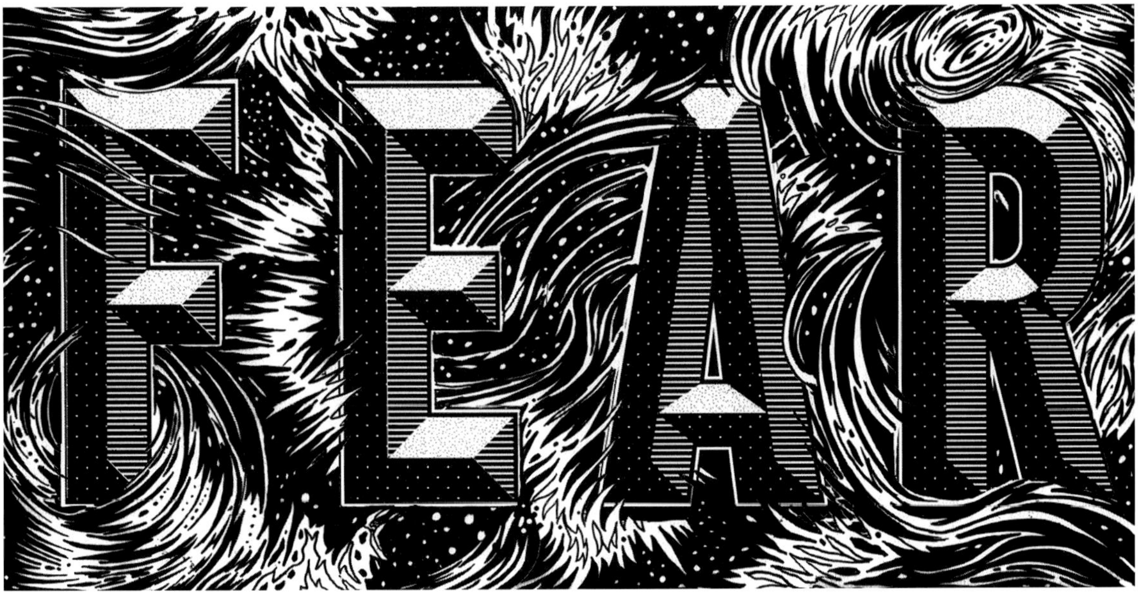
FEAR

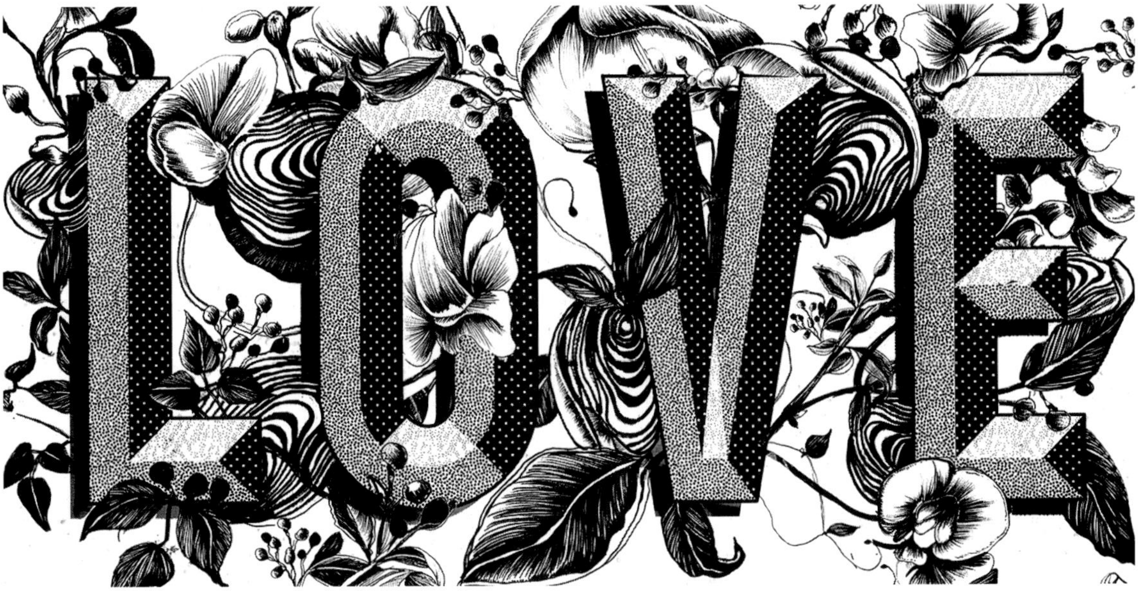
LOVE

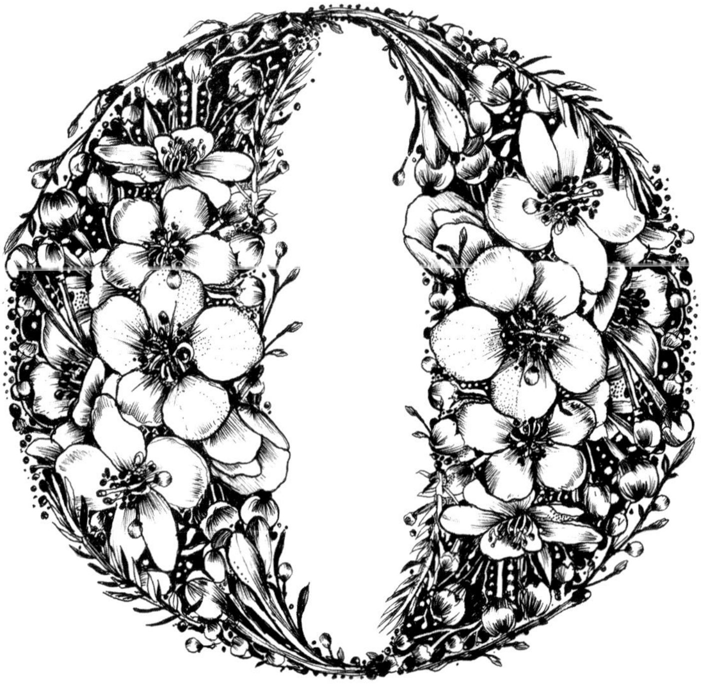

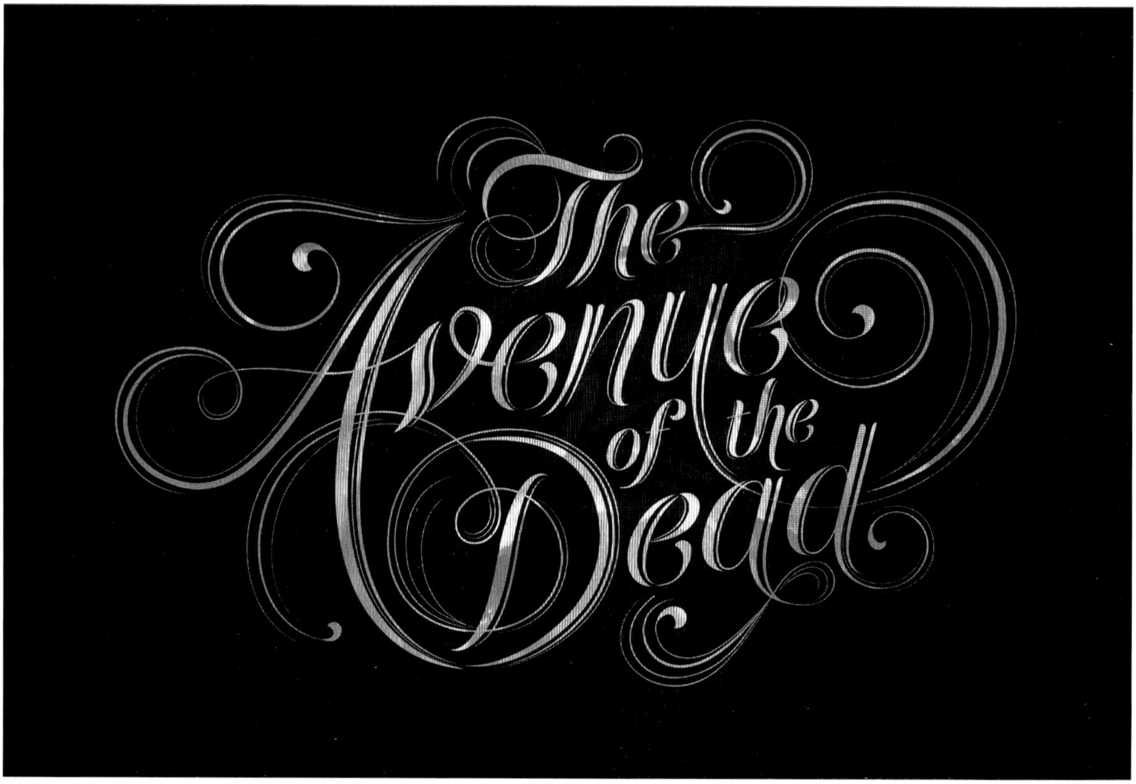
The Avenue of the Dead

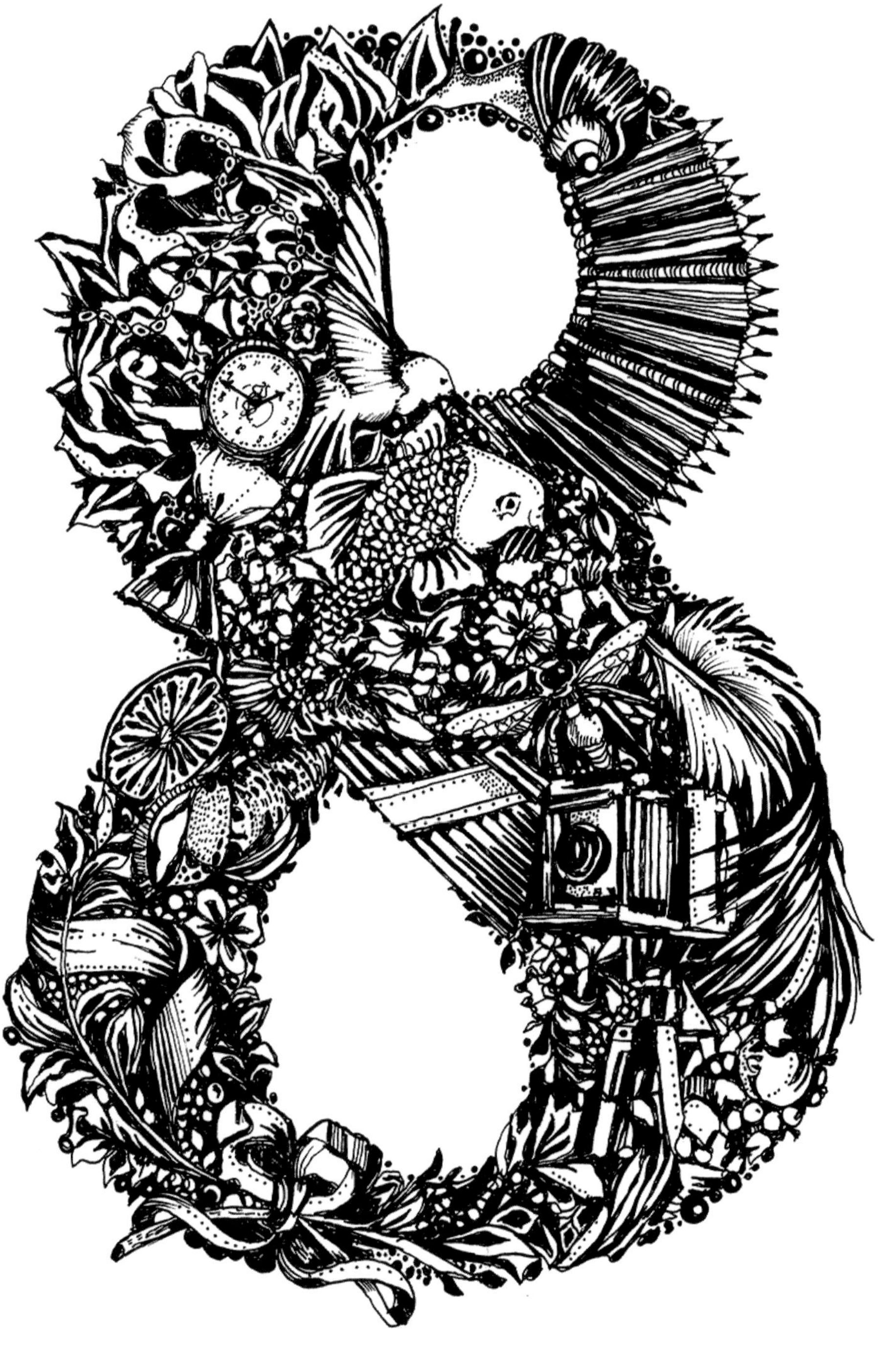

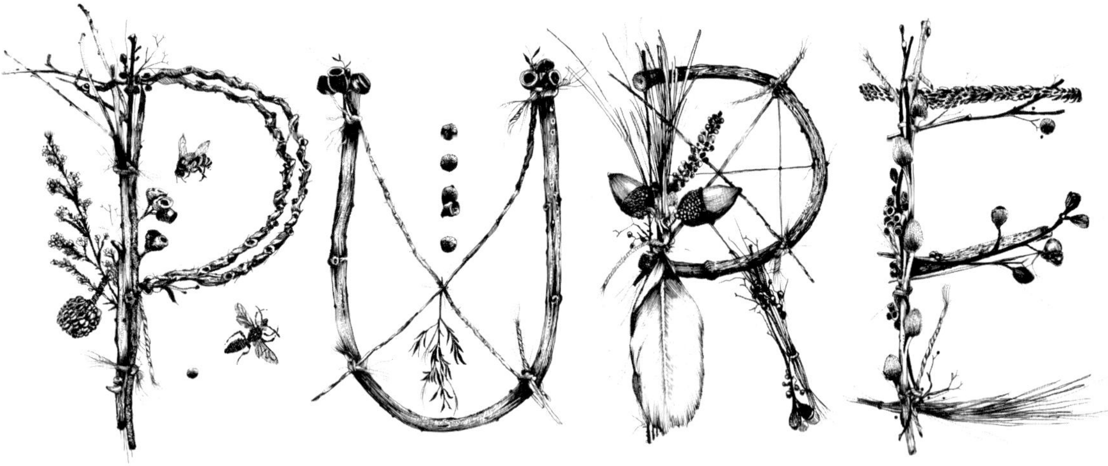
PURE

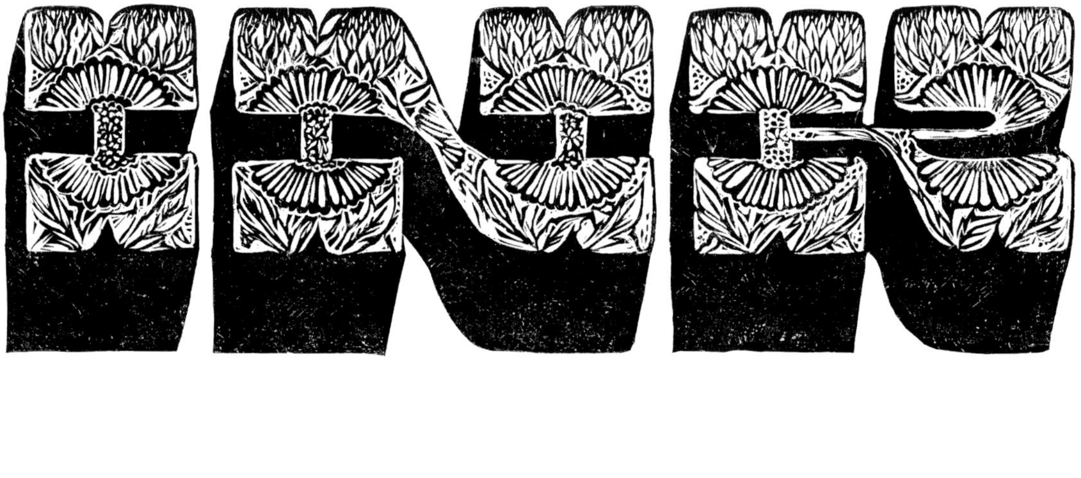

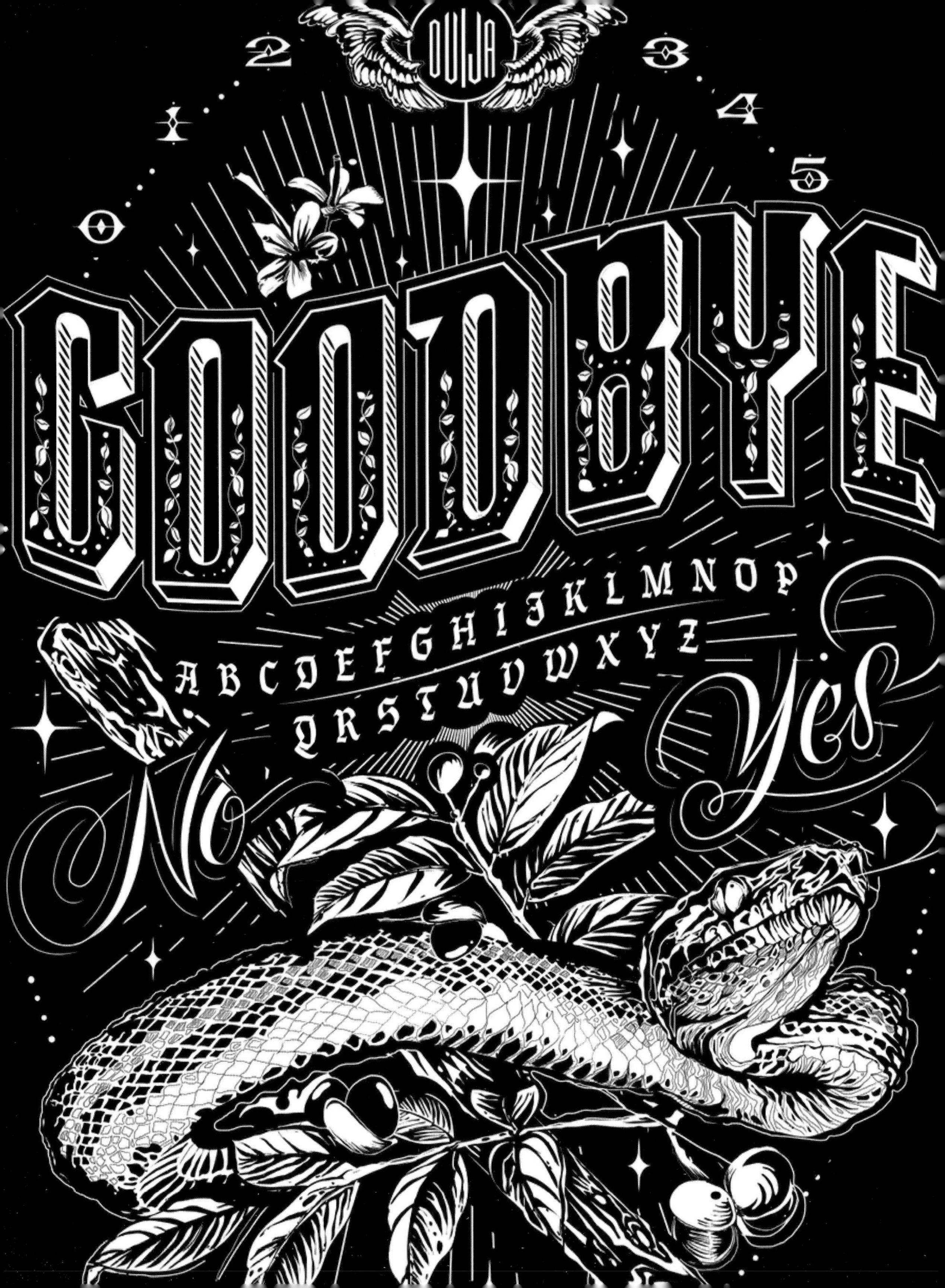

OUIJA
1 2 3 4 5 0
GOODBYE
ABCDEFGHIJKLMNOP
QRSTUVWXYZ
No
Yes

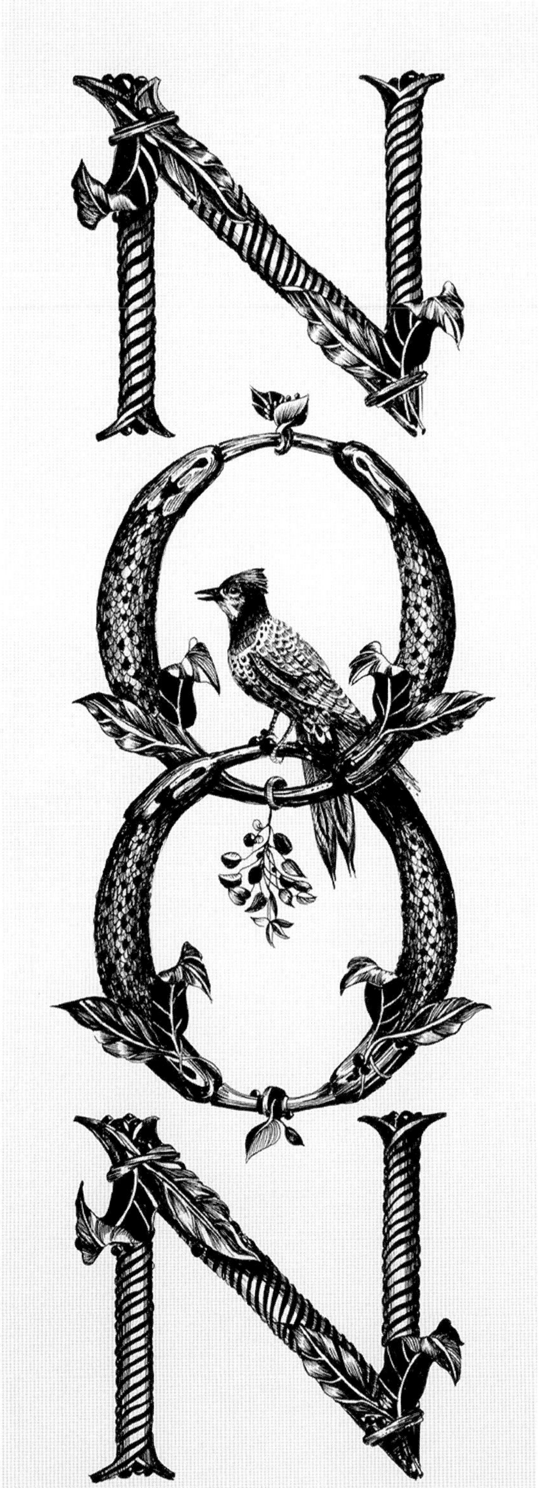

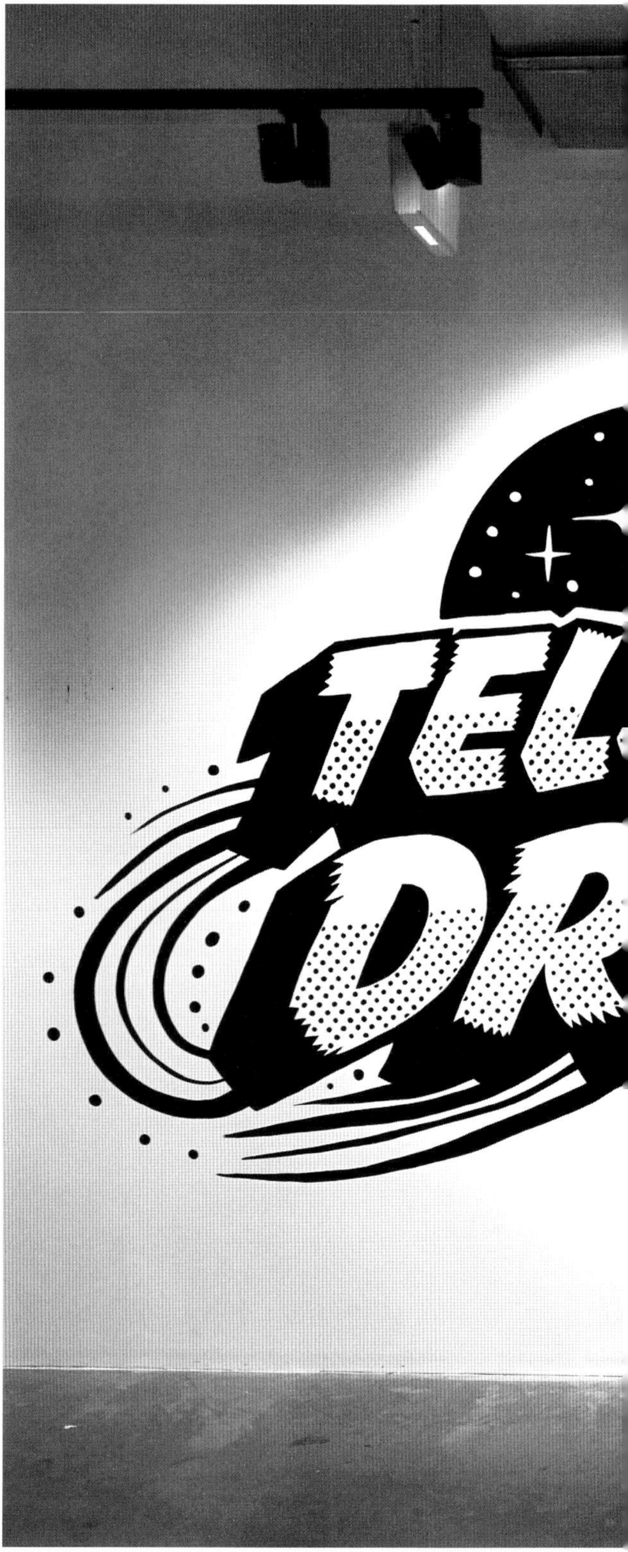

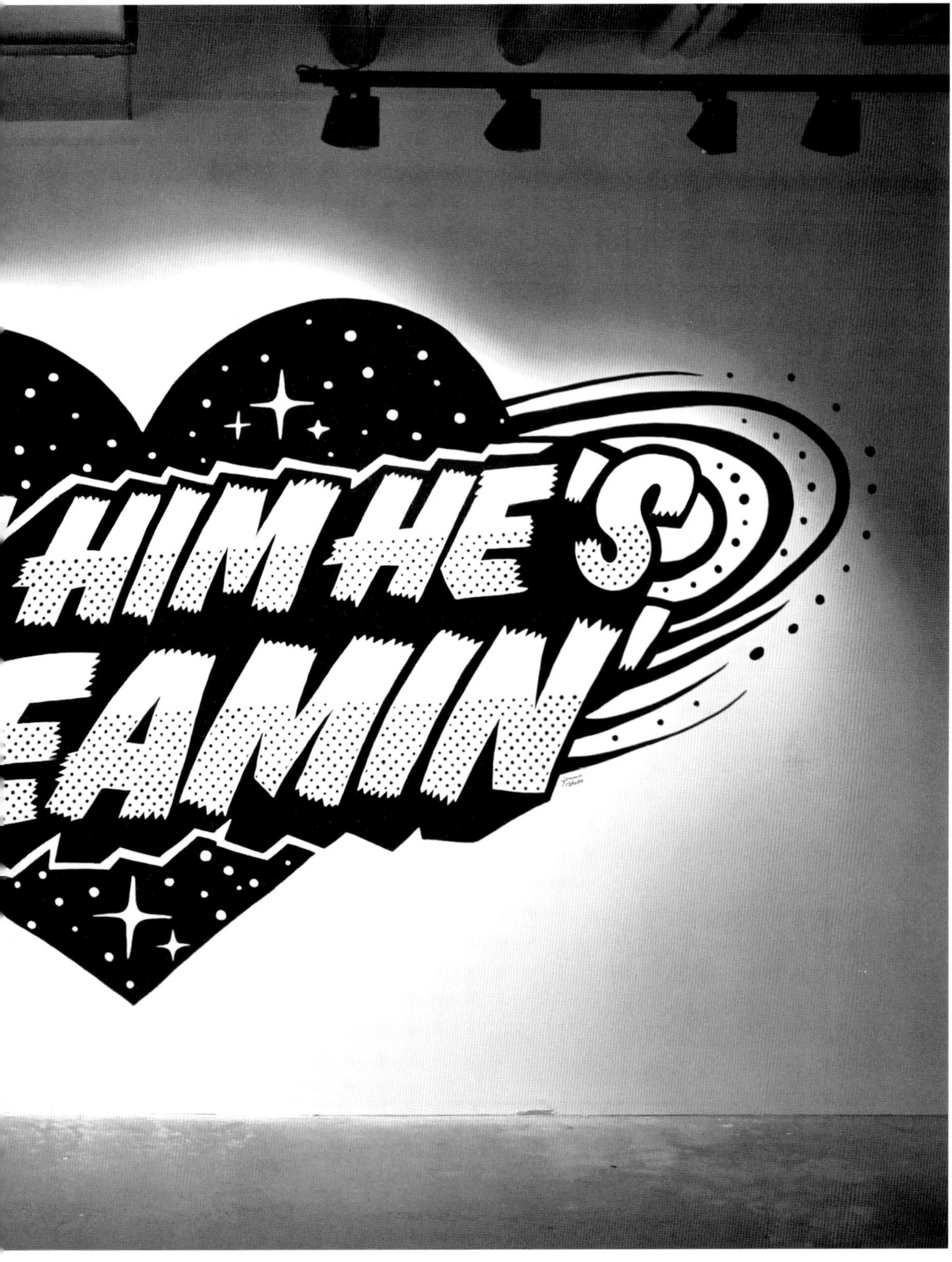
HIM HE'S
EAMIN'

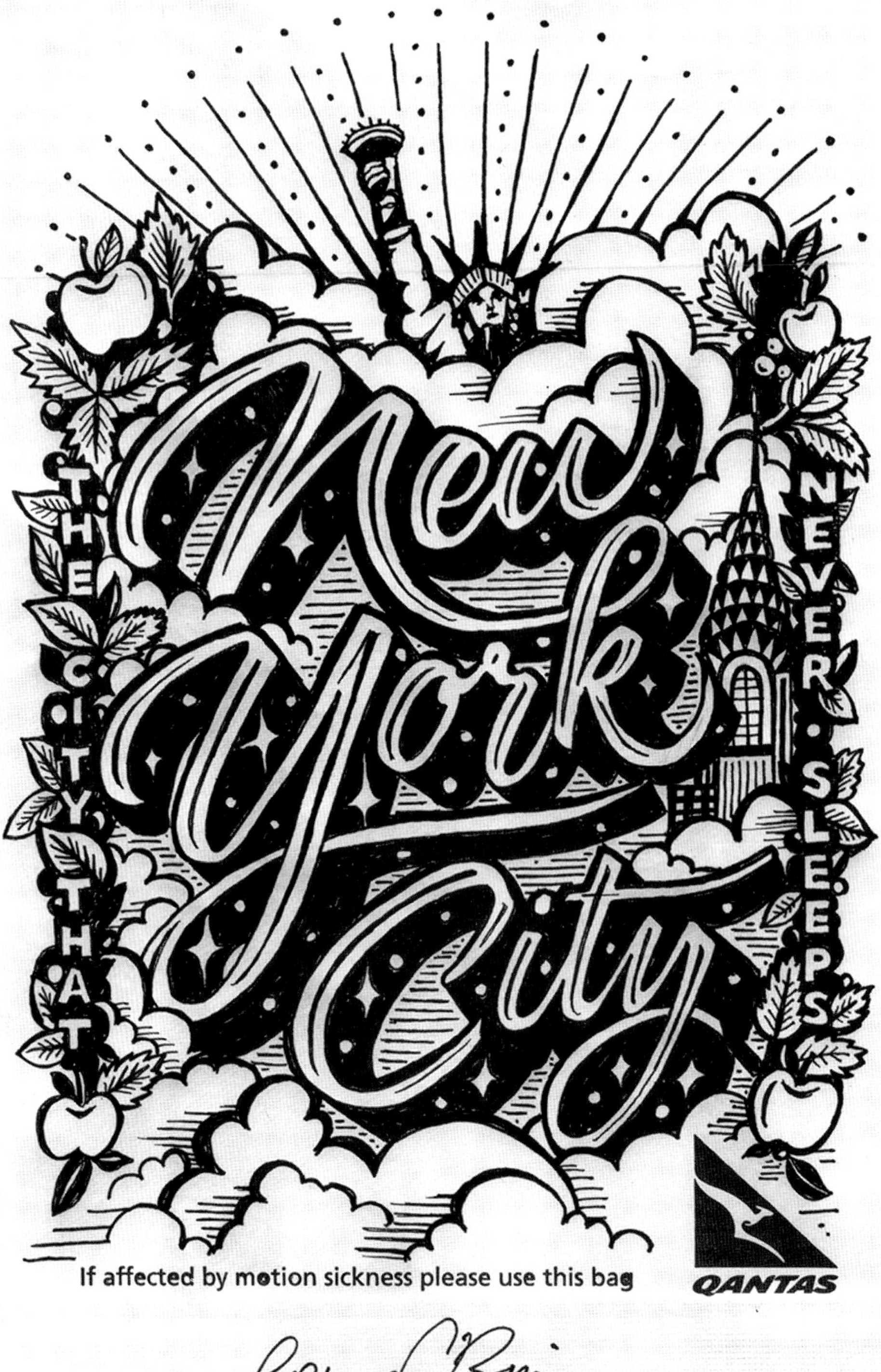
New York City
THE CITY THAT
NEVER SLEEPS
If affected by motion sickness please use this bag
QANTAS

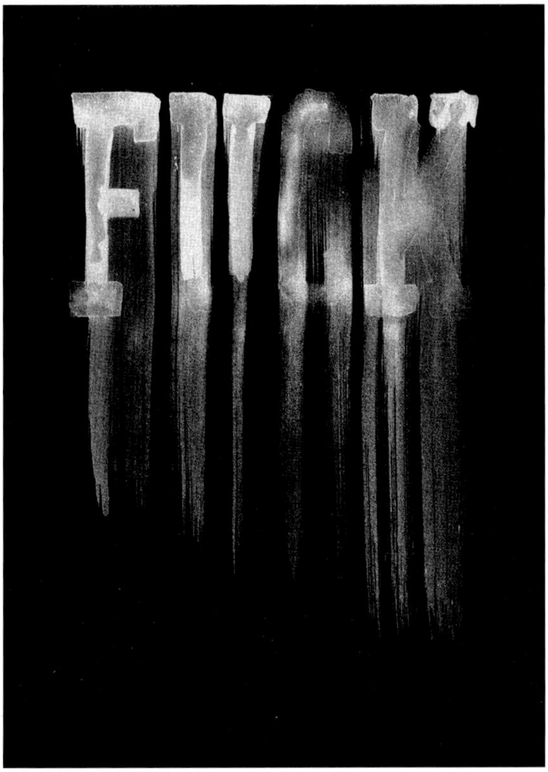
FIGHT

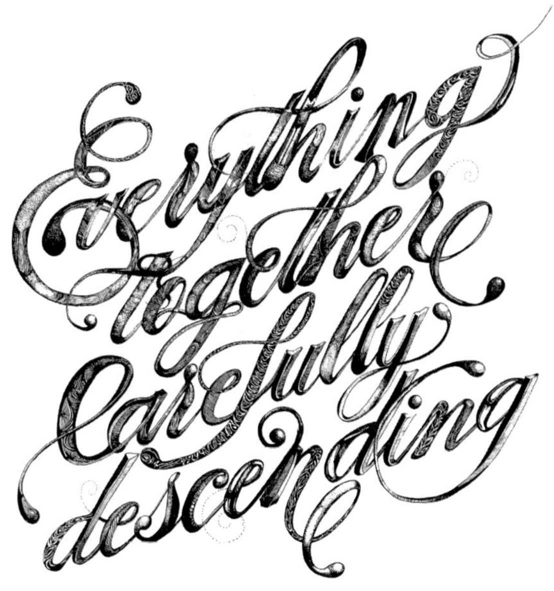
Everything
together
carefully
descending

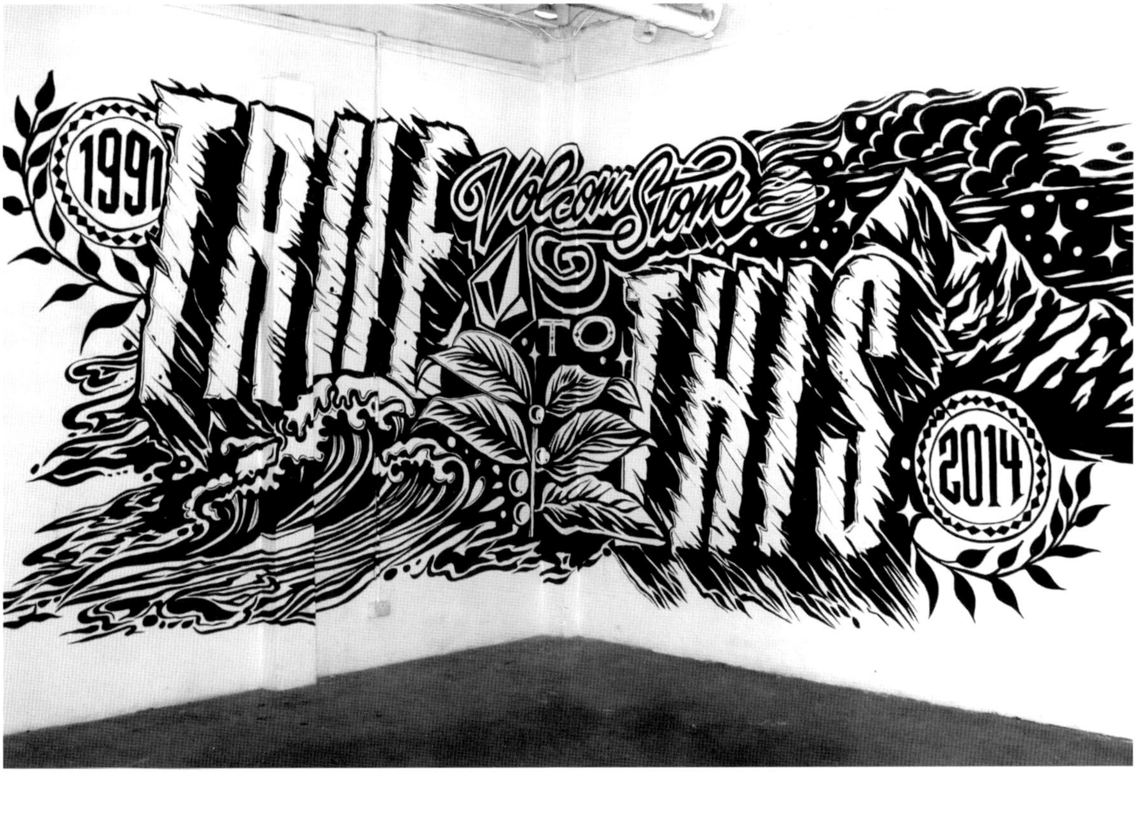
1991
TRUE
Volcom Stone
TO
THIS
2014

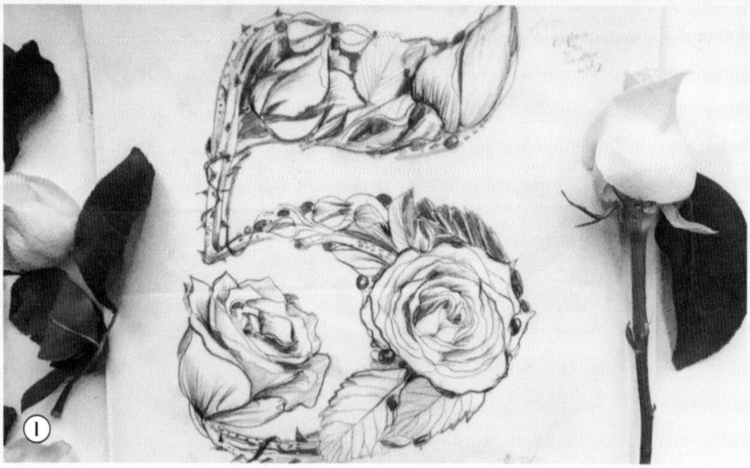

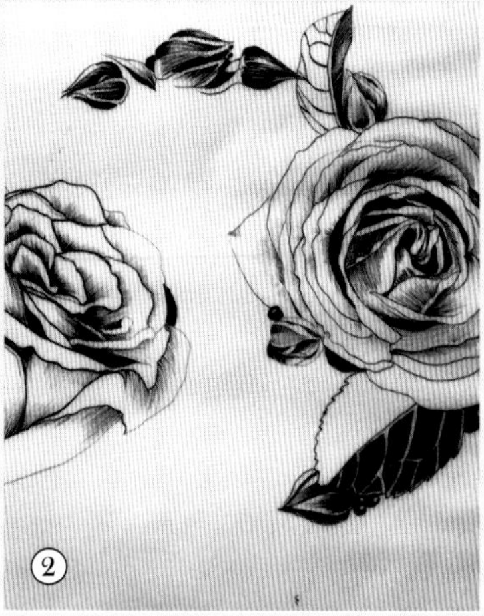

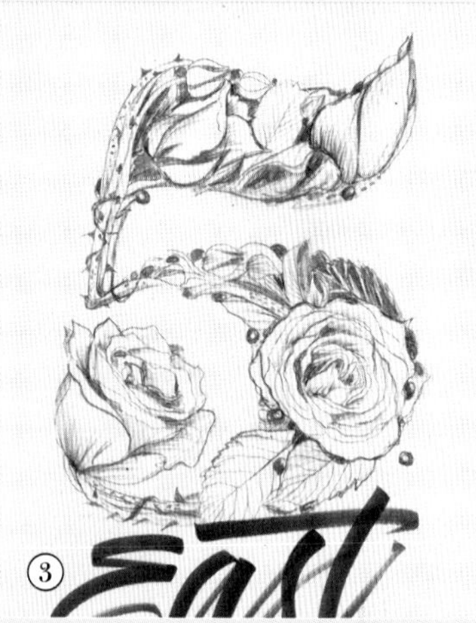

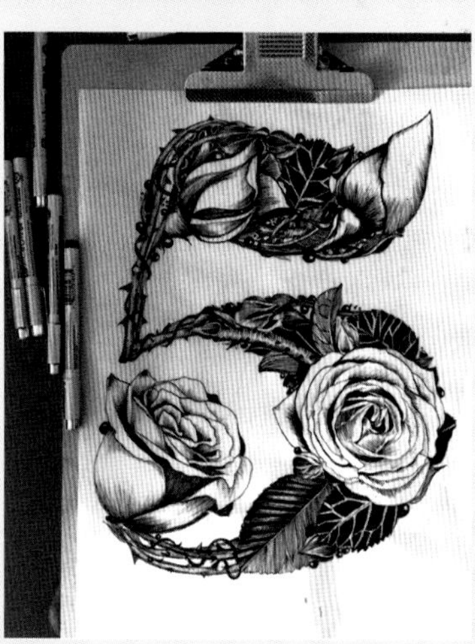

Making my lettering

The creative process for each project is slightly different for me, but most begin with gathering reference material followed by pencil sketching. Sometimes I will use physical references – such as roses and foliage in this particular project. I will arrange the flowers in various shapes that fit within my desired letterform or numeral and begin sketching. Once I have a refined pencil sketch, I move into working with black ink fineliner pens. I will use tracing paper on top of my original sketch and finesse the final details with intricate lifework, dots and and patterning. For the complimentary text in this project I used a Tombow brush pen in an expressive style. I will then scan these two elements and do any final tweaks in Photoshop.

Creando mi lettering

El proceso creativo de cada proyecto suele variar ligeramente, aunque la mayoría empieza con la recogida del material de referencia para el posterior diseño a lápiz de los bocetos. A veces empleo referencias físicas, como las rosas y el follaje en este proyecto concreto. Dispongo las flores en formas distintas que encajen con la forma de las letras y los números que deseo, y empiezo a hacer el boceto. Cuando ya tengo un boceto a lápiz más o menos consistente, empiezo a trabajar con bolígrafos negros de punta fina. Utilizo papel de calco sobre el boceto original y perfecciono los acabados con detalles complejos, puntos y patrones. Para el texto complementario de este proyecto utilicé un boli de punta fina Tombow con un estilo expresivo. Luego escanearé los dos elementos y haré los retoques finales que haga falta con Photoshop.

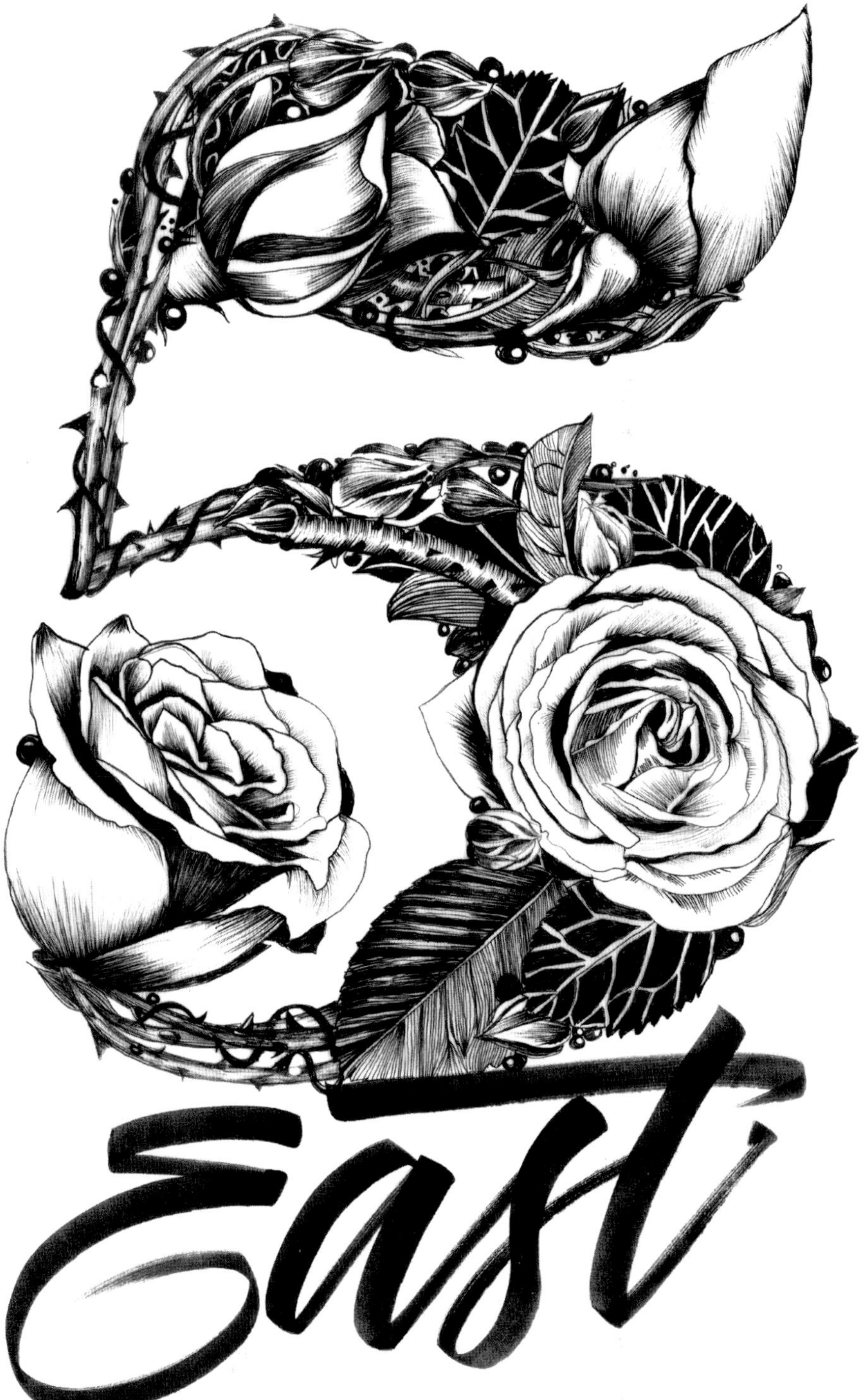
East

MARTIN SCHMETZER

martinschmetzer.com
@schmetzer

Martin Schmetzer is a award winning designer based in Stockholm. He specializes in hand-drawn typography with a high lever of detail and diligence. His style is a fusion of old and new, vintage 1900's-era feel to a full-blown street graffiti temperament. Martin was born in 1984 and came in contact with hand draw typography through graffiti in the mid nineties. His style has evolved into what it is today through many years of development but you can still hint the graffiti background in most of his designs.

Curves, symmetry and balance have always been appealing to Martin and he appreciates the laser sharp execution of detailed vector graphics.

Martin Schmetzer es un galardonado diseñador de Estocolmo especializado en tipografía a mano con una gran diligencia y atención al detalle. Su estilo fusiona lo antiguo y lo nuevo, la sensación vintage de la década de 1900 con el temperamento avanzado de los grafitis callejeros. Martin nació en 1984 y se adentró en el mundo de la tipografía a mano a mediados de los 90 gracias a los grafitis. Y aunque su estilo ha evolucionado hasta sus características actuales tras muchos años de desarrollo, aún pueden verse en la mayoría de sus diseños indicios de su pasado grafitero.

Las curvas, la simetría y el equilibrio siempre han atraído a Martin, que aprecia la ejecución con precisión láser de los gráficos vectoriales detallados.

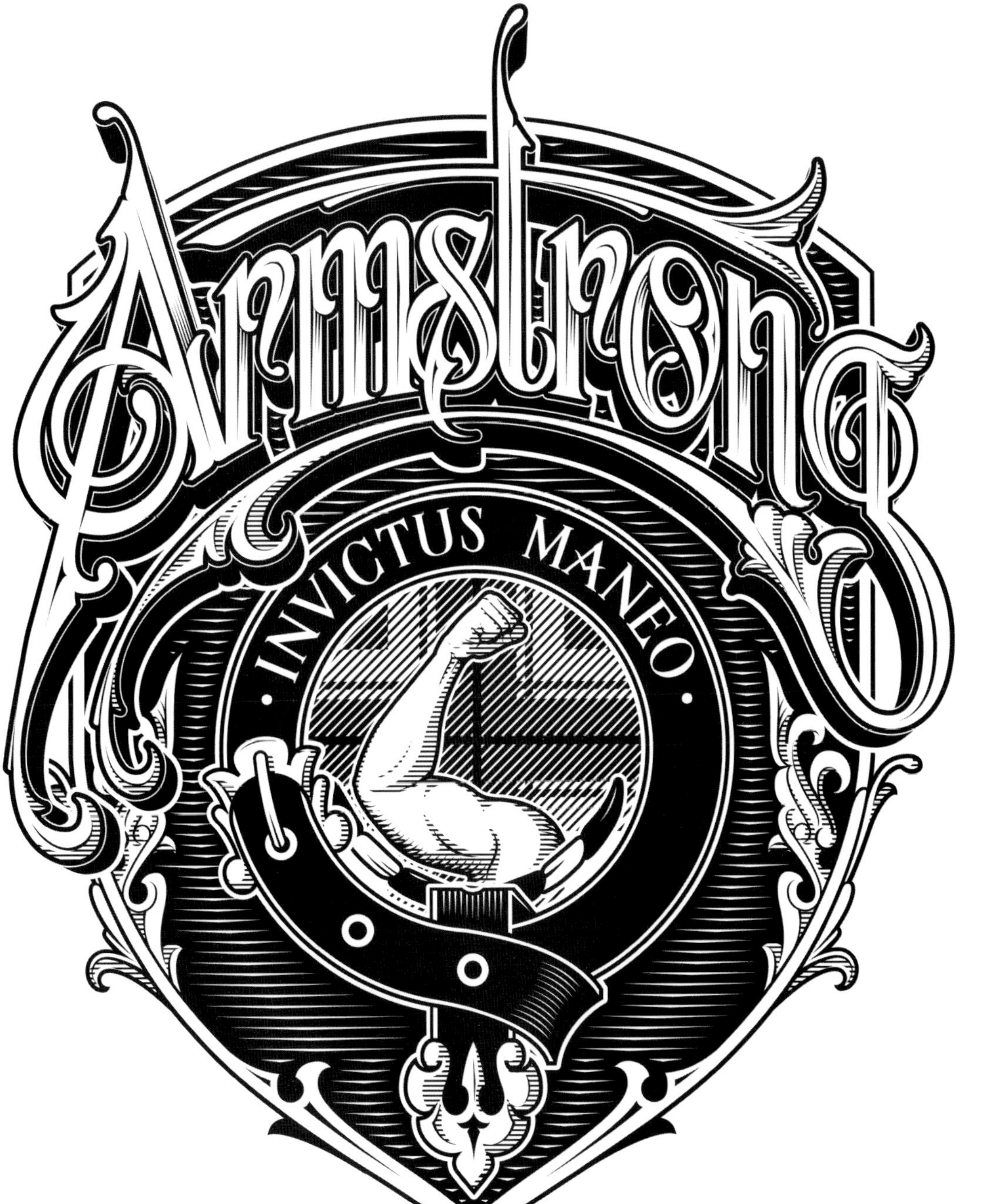
Armstrong
INVICTUS MANEO

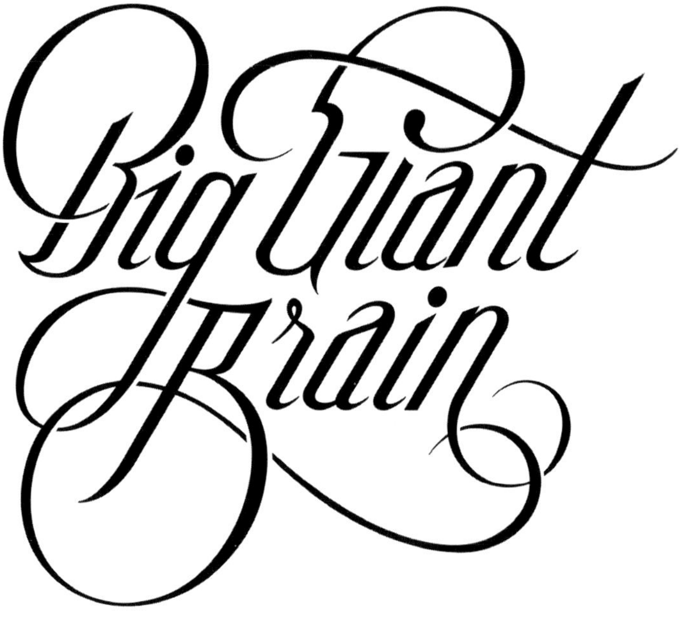
Big Giant
Brain

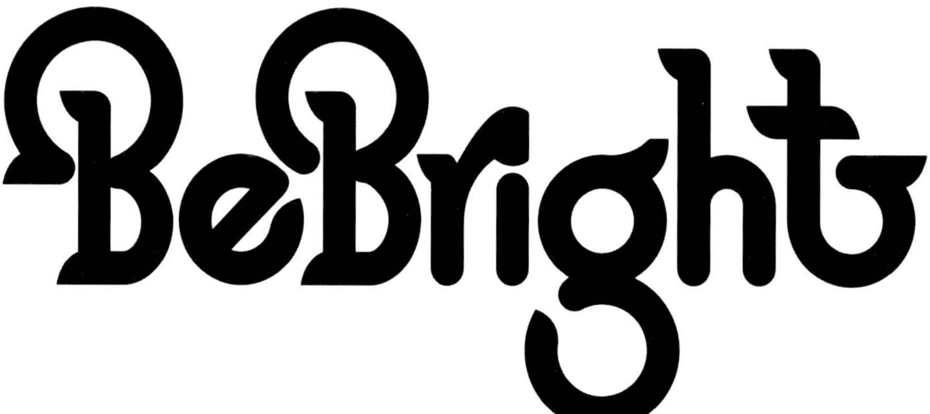
BeBright

TONGUE SPANK
SPICE COMPANY

Gangsta·Wrapper

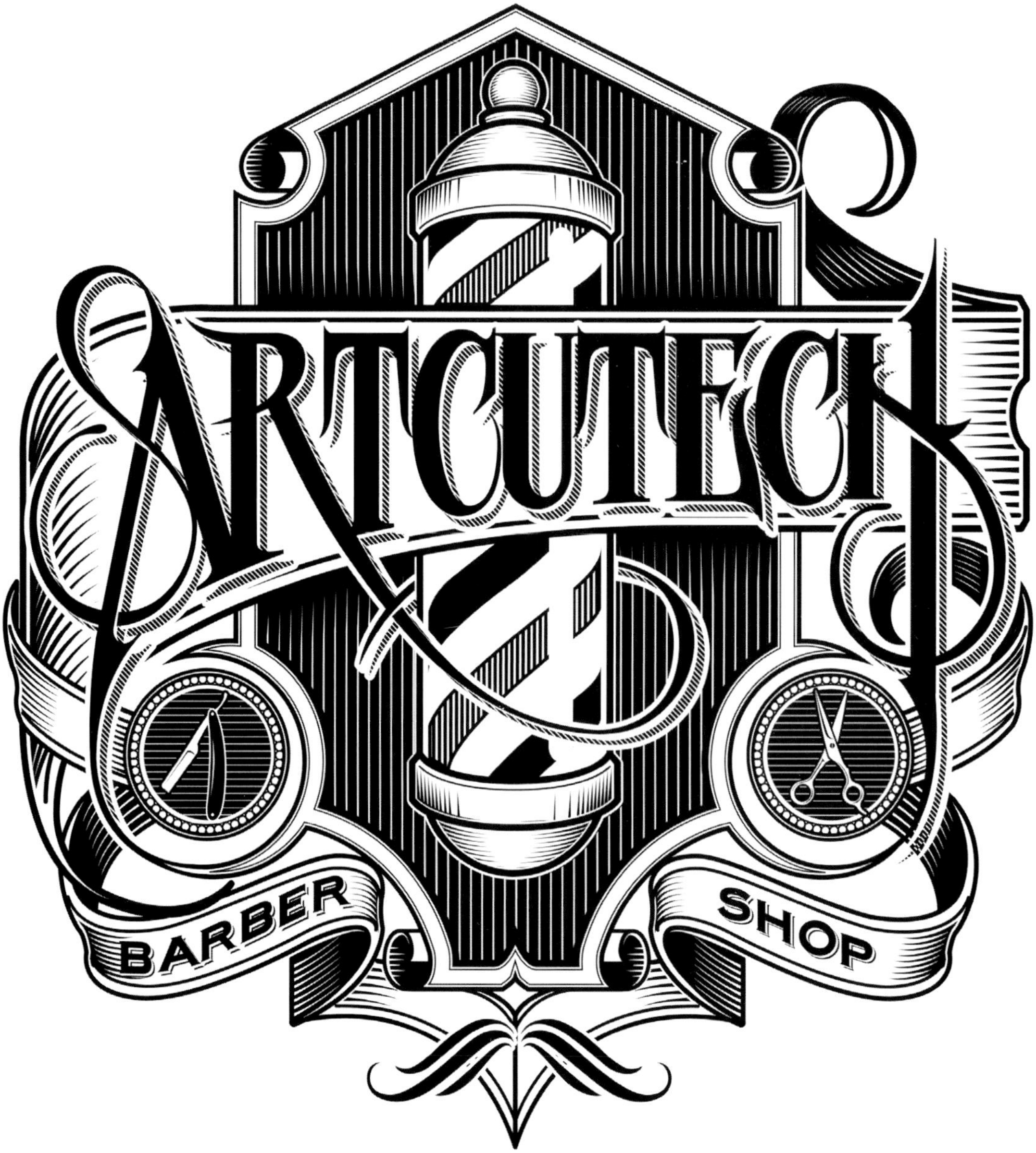
ARTCUTECH
BARBER
SHOP

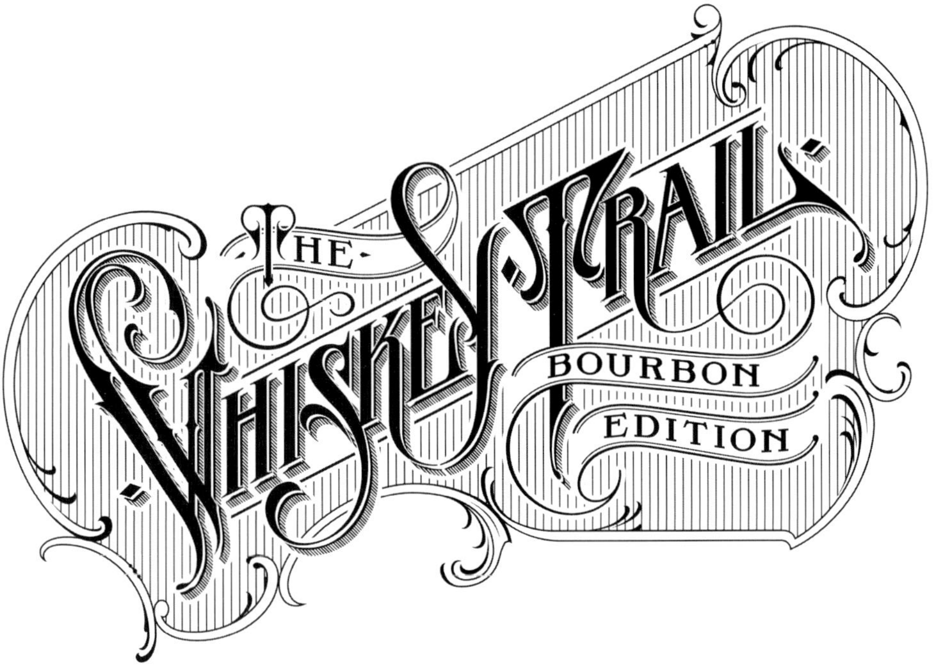
THE
WHISKEY TRAIL
BOURBON
EDITION

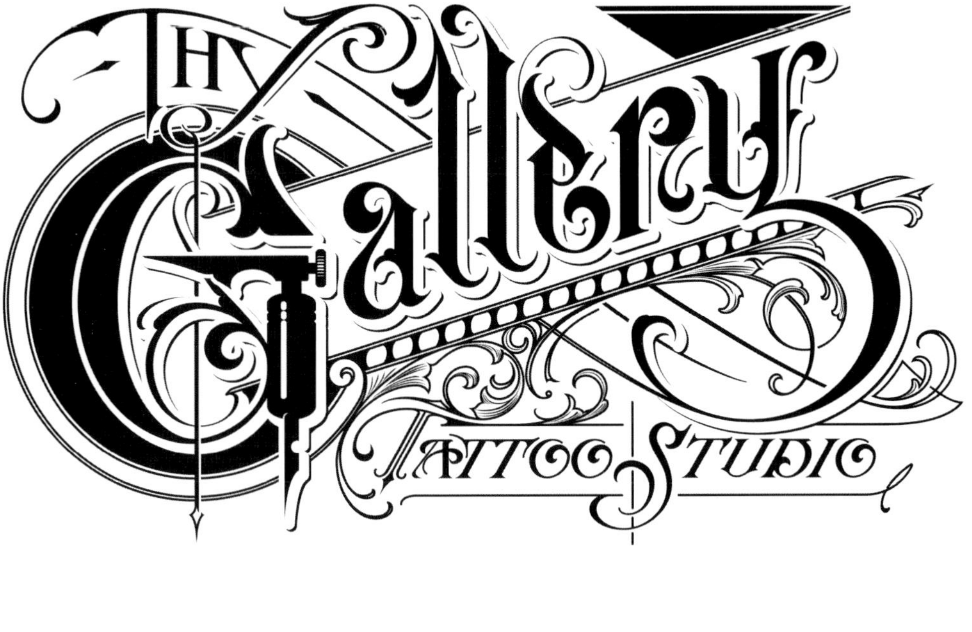
Gallery
TATTOO STUDIO

Ekensdal

ETABL. 1917

ÅTER-ETABL. 2007

STUDIO

Blanco

TATTOO

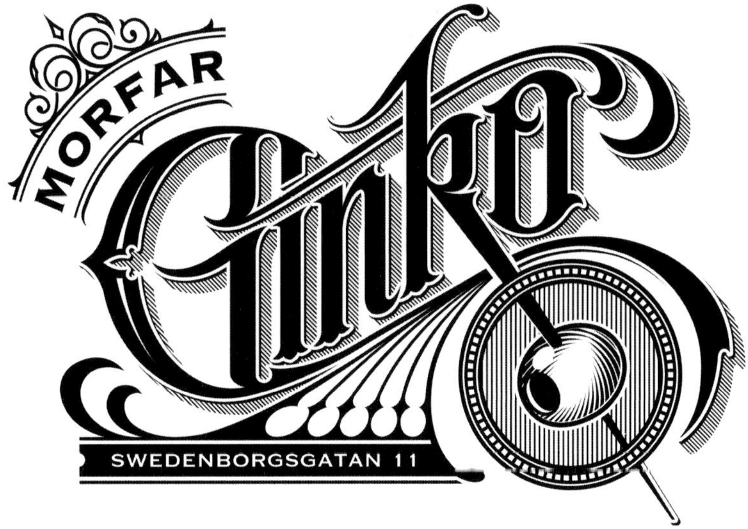
MORFAR
Ginko
SWEDENBORGSGATAN 11

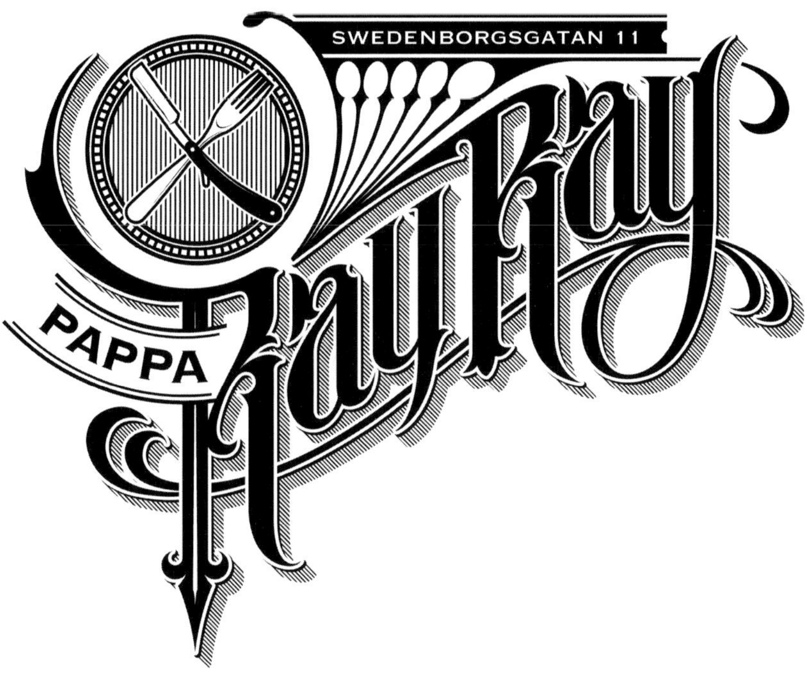
SWEDENBORGSGATAN 11
PAPPA
RayRay

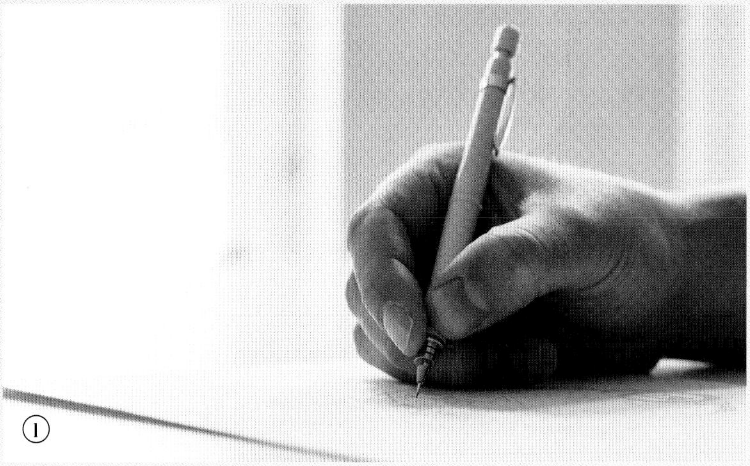

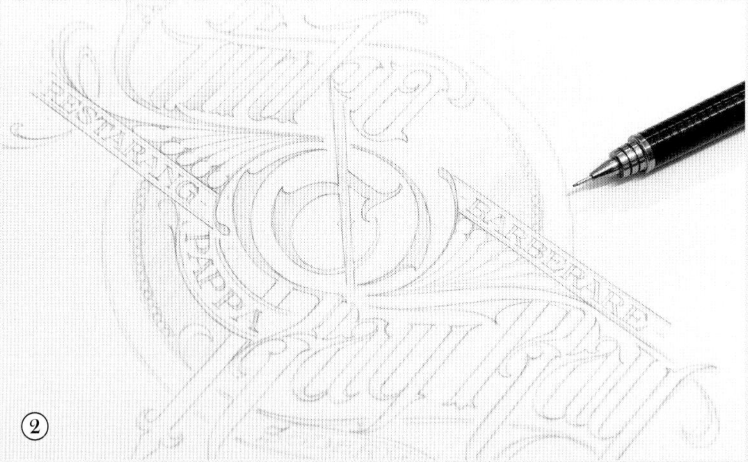

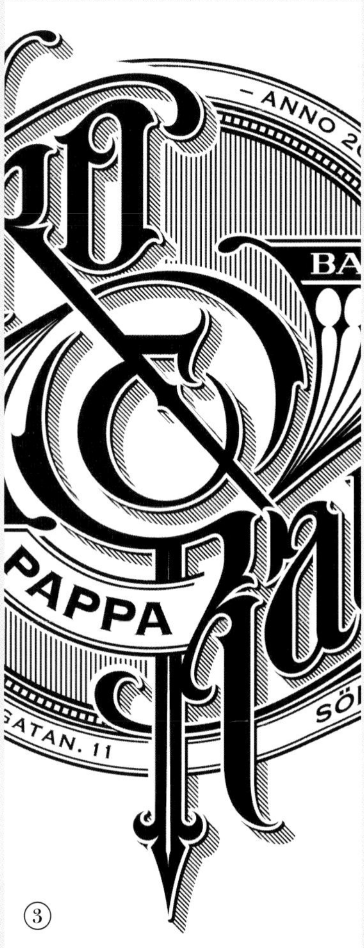

Making my lettering

The process of my work is very valuable to me and I always start with a pen and paper before turning to the computer.

The computer is a fantastic finalizing tool but I believe it also limits my shapes and composition if I do not start first by hand where I can go the whole hog.

Creando mi lettering

El proceso de mis obras me resulta muy valioso; siempre empiezo con papel y lápiz antes de recurrir al ordenador.

El ordenador es una estupenda herramienta de perfeccionamiento, pero creo que, si no empiezo a mano, no voy hasta el fondo de la cuestión y mis formas y la composición quedan limitadas.

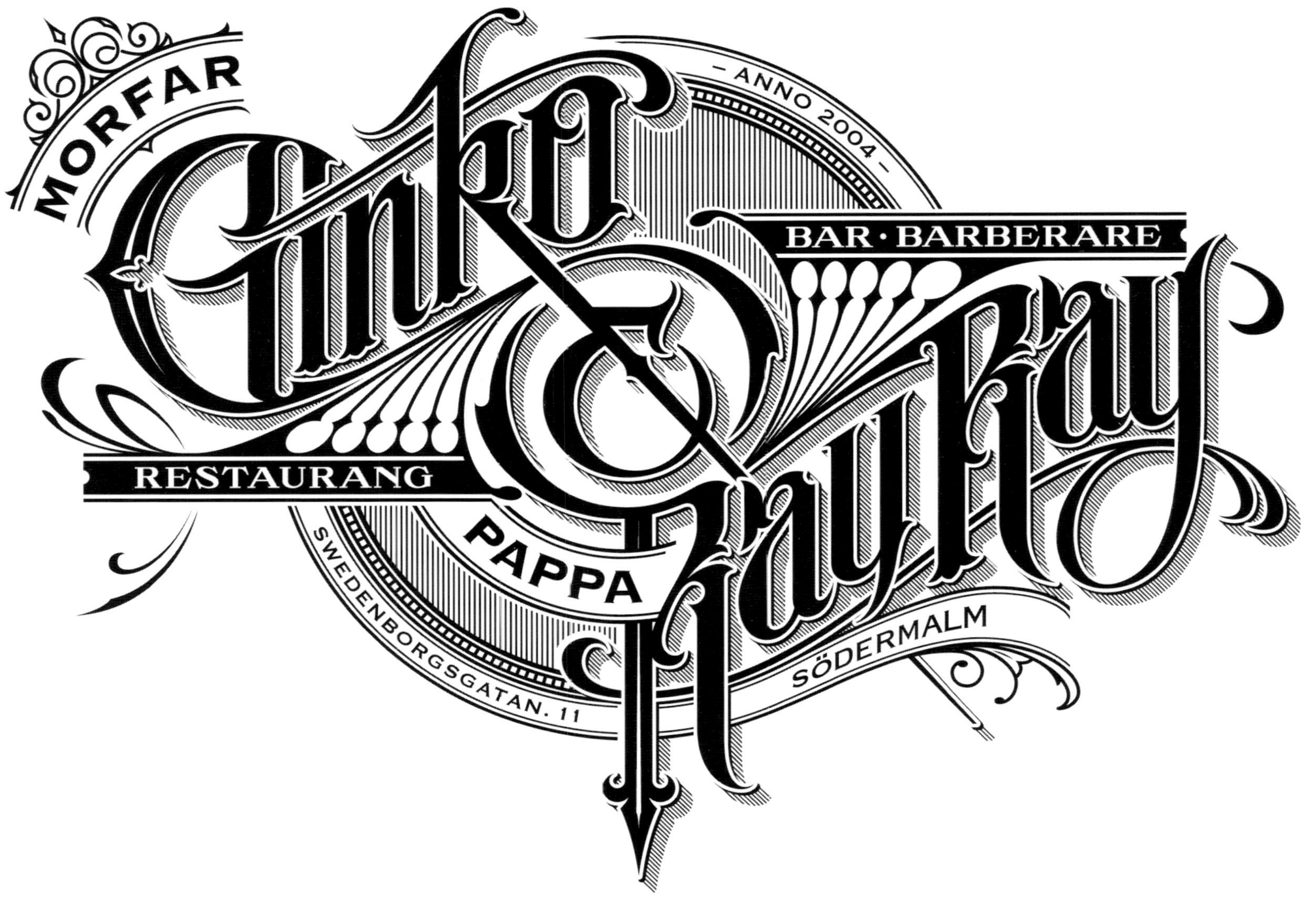

MORFAR
Ginko
&
Ray Ray
– ANNO 2004 –
BAR · BARBERARE
RESTAURANG
PAPPA
SWEDENBORGSGATAN. 11
SÖDERMALM

SR. SLEEPLESS

srsleepless.com
@sr_sleepless

Mr. Sleepless is the scribbled mask behind which hides the Málaga illustrator and designer Agu Méndez.

His work chock-full of small details where one stroke tells the story of another stroke. All his illustrations make recurrent references to traditional tattoos, the wonderful world of Walter Lantz, Egon Schiele, space, flies and the sea. Portraits - his favourite format - are plentiful since they can deform, through his private vision of the world, the people and characters he admires or loves.

Pencils, watercolours, vectors, patterns, textures, analog and digital... mixing, creating, dreaming. Anything goes for drawing someone's story.

Sr. Sleepless es la mascara tras la que se esconde el ilustrador y diseñador Agu Méndez.

Su obra está llena de pequeños detalles donde un trazo cuenta la historia de otro trazo. El tatuaje tradicional, el maravilloso mundo de Walter Lantz, Egon Schiele, el espacio, las moscas y el mar, aparecen de forma recurrente en todas sus ilustraciones, donde abundan los retratos (su formato favorito) ya que pueden deformar, a través de su particular visión del mundo, a las personas y personajes que admira o quiere.

Lápices, acuarelas, vectores, tramas, texturas, analógico y digital… Mezclar, crear, soñar. Todo vale para dibujar la historia de alguien.

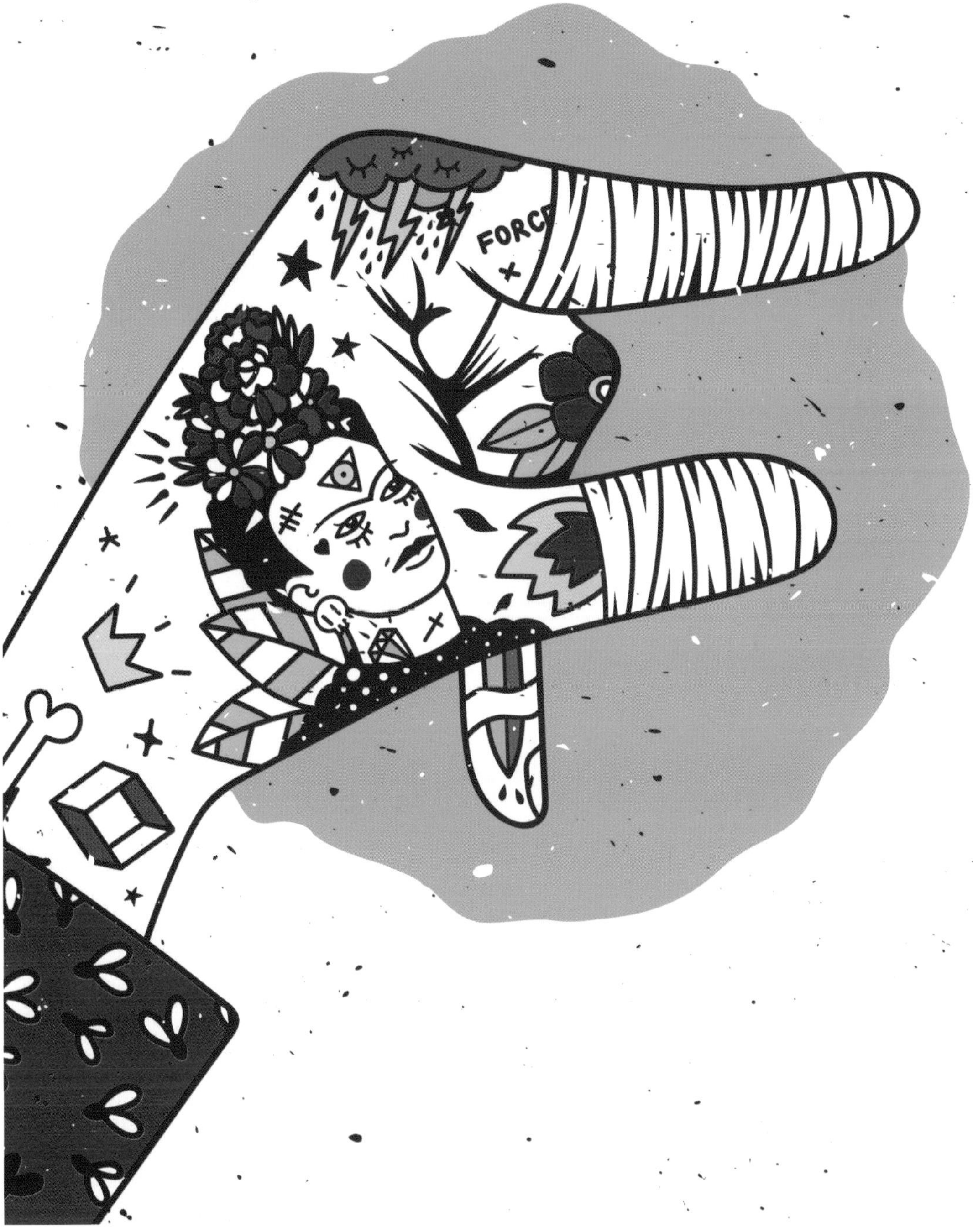
FORC

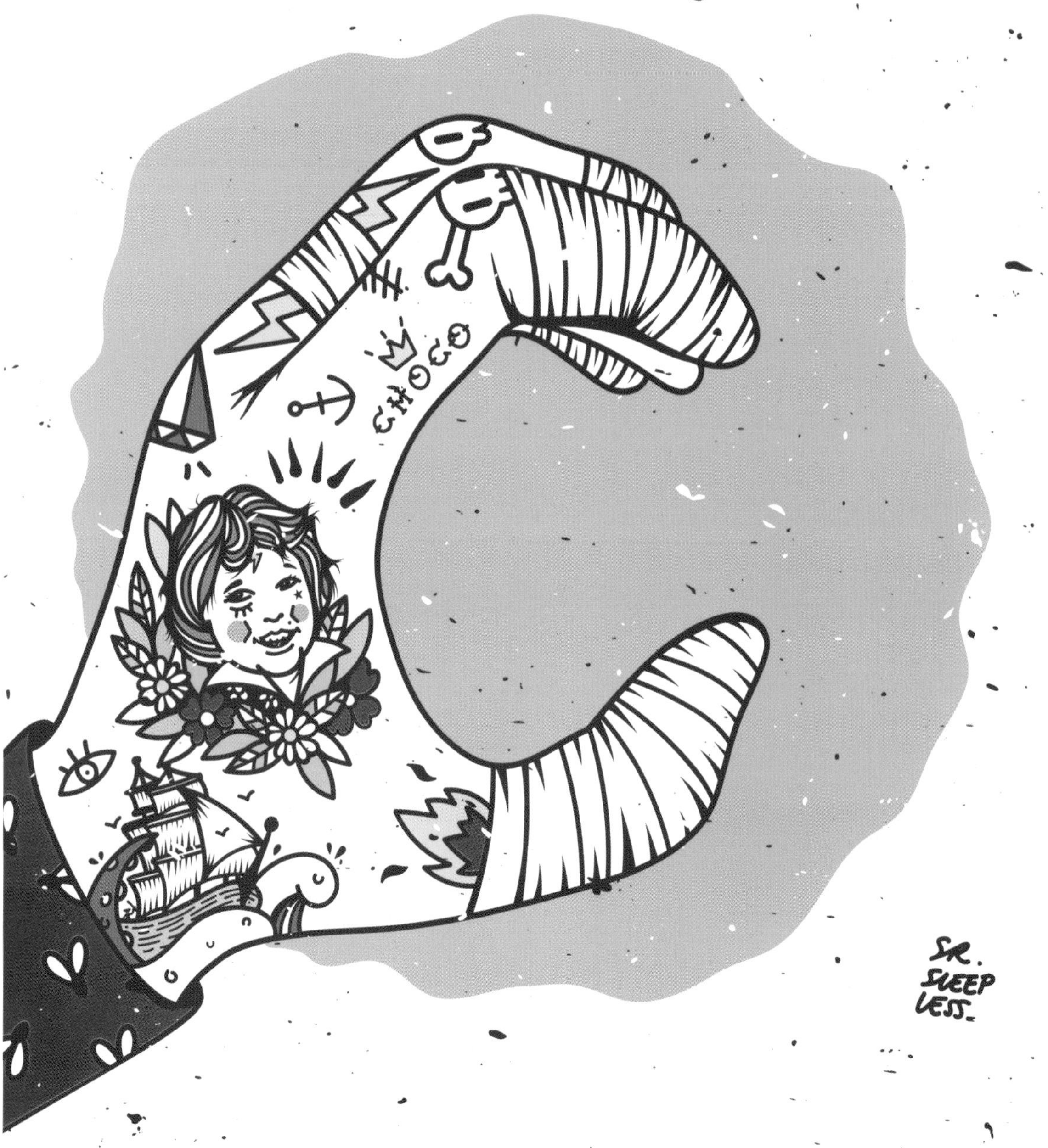
CHOCO
SR.
SLEEP
LESS

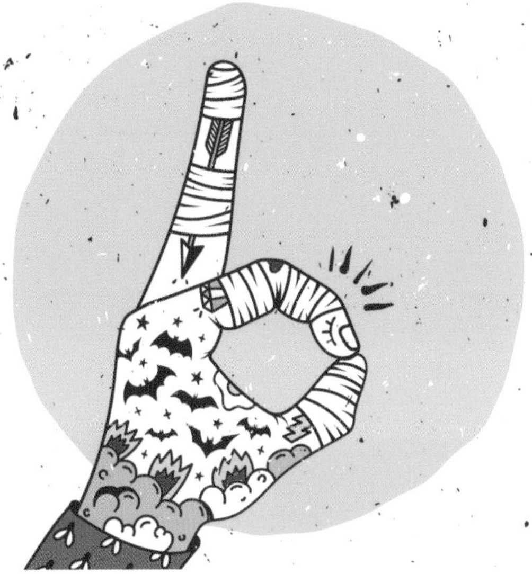

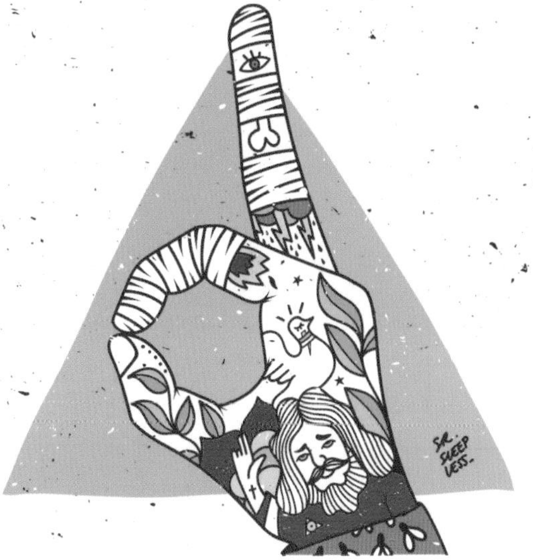
SR.
SLEEP
LESS.

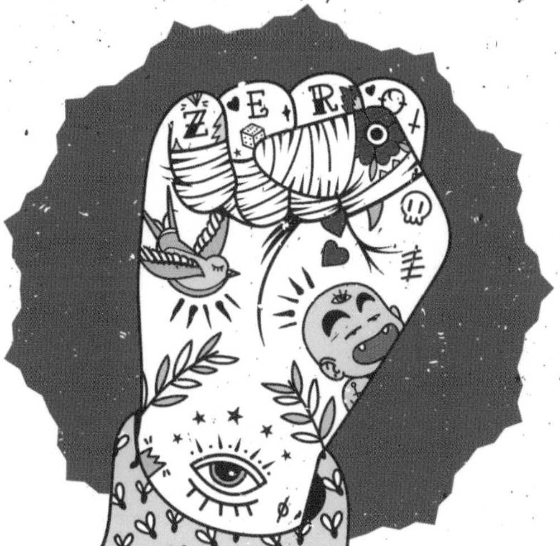
Z E R

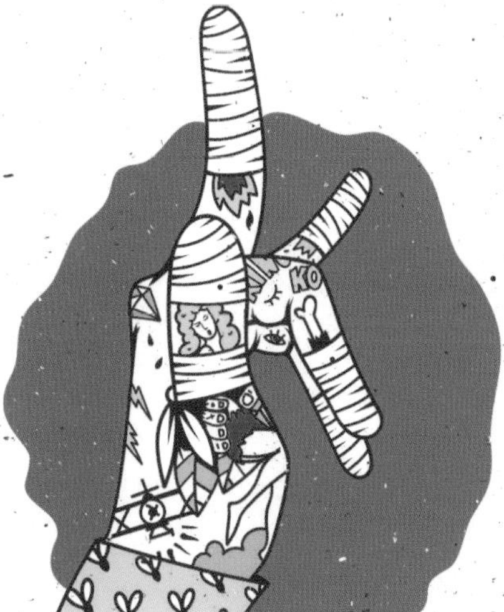
KO

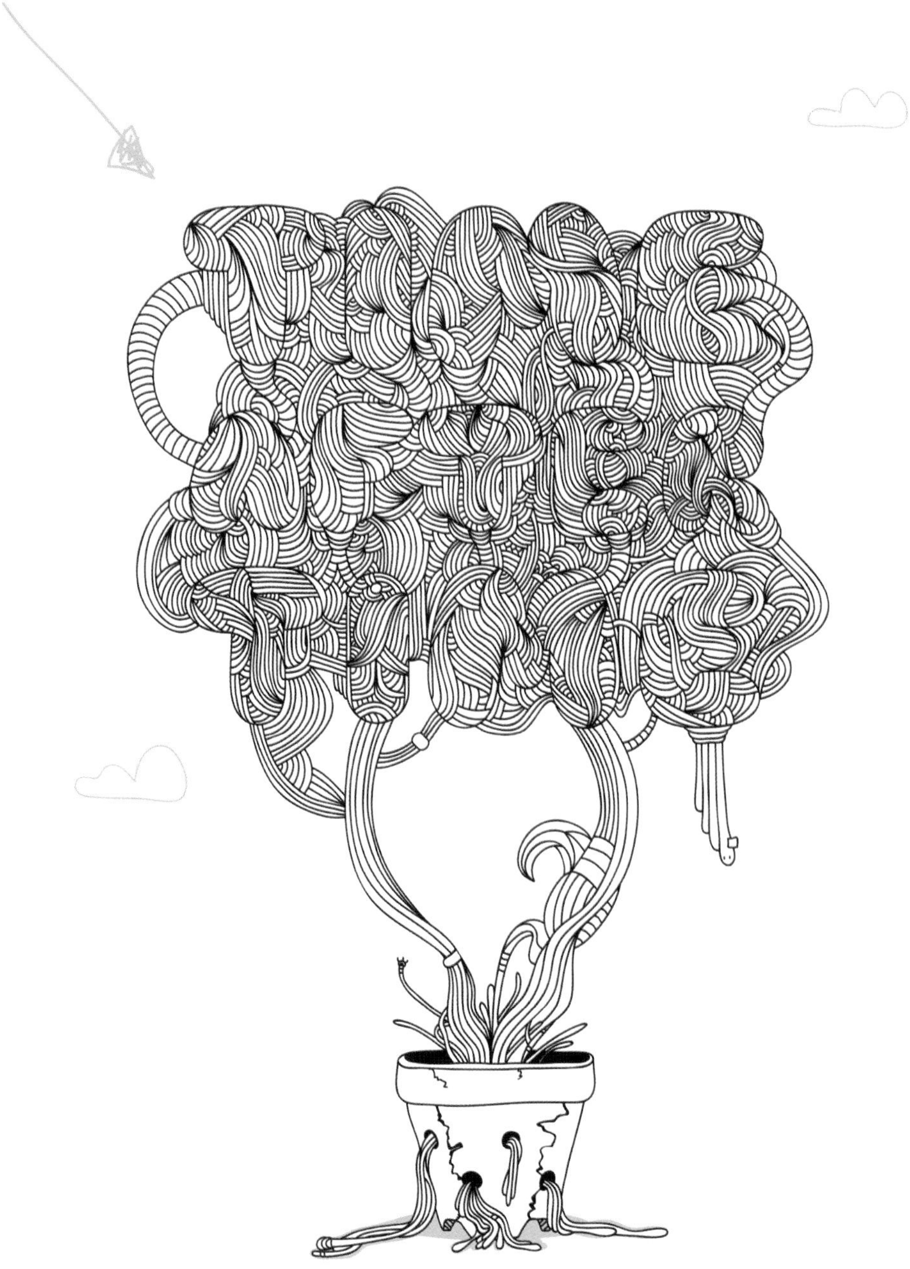

something is growing

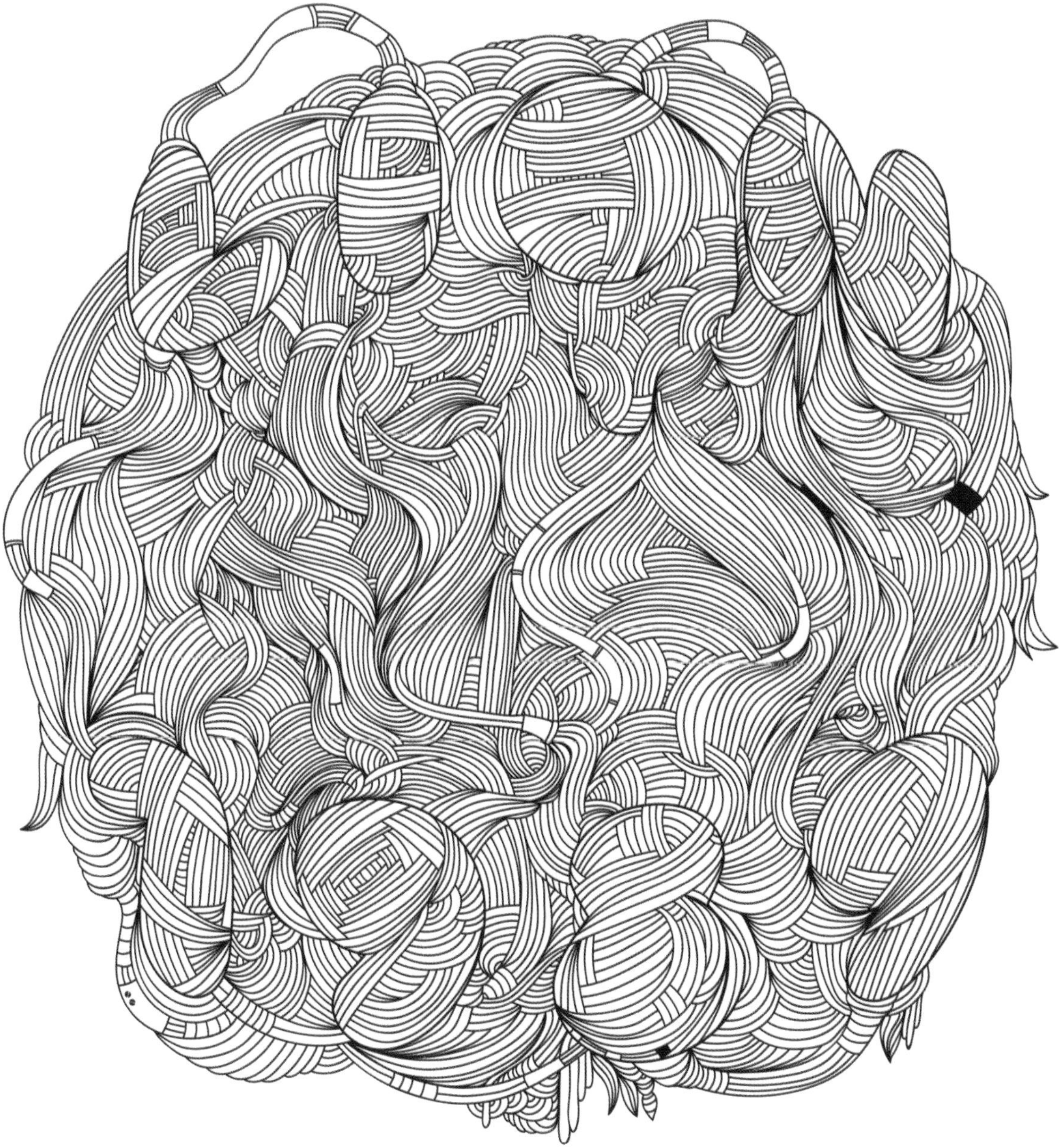

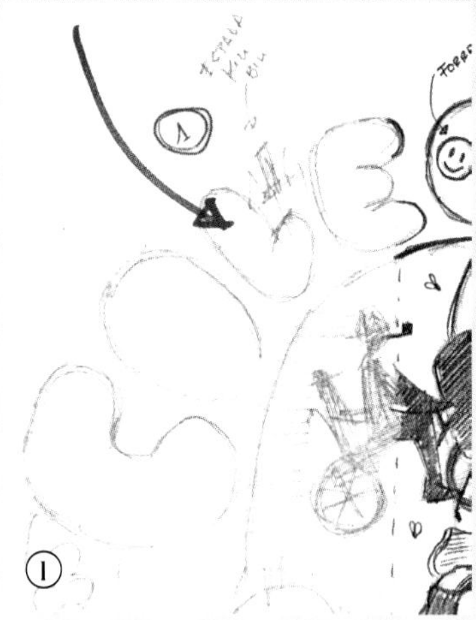

①

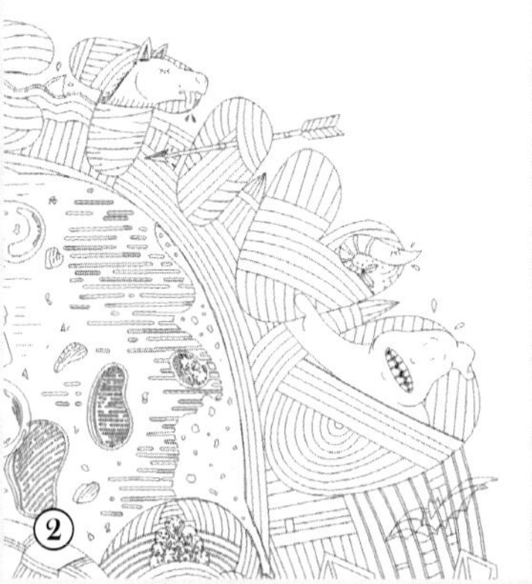

②

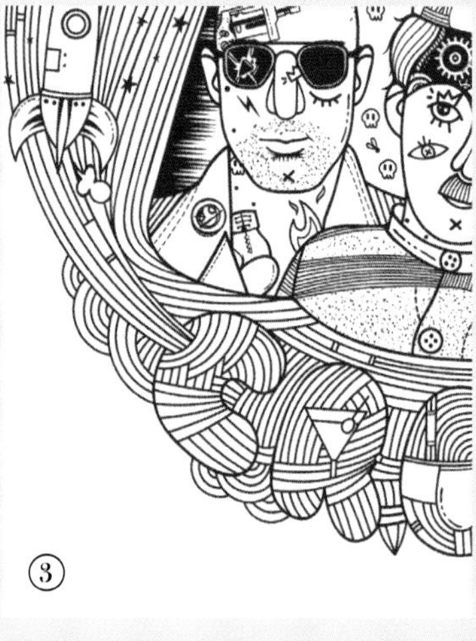

③

Making my lettering illustrations

I do not begin any project if I haven't previously sketched it in a notebook. Sketching has its own life and is the most important stage. It starts off being something very crude. At this point we give the go-ahead to continue. It's at this point where the sketch begins to take shape. I create a few more detailed parts and I fill a small part in with ink in an analogous way. This is what I call a style test. It's essential to perform a part of the work as close as possible to what it later might become.

I scan the sketch. I set some parameters in Photoshop and I open it in Illustrator in order to make a digital inking. In order to do this I use the paintbrush tool. I have a myriad of custom paintbrushes that I have been making over the years. Illustrator has become my Pelikan Case from the 1980s. Once the sketch is done, I expand it and combine all of the resulting shapes into one. I tend to use the combine option. It's marvelous! I color both in Illustrator and Photoshop. In order to choose the color, I always work with the same palette and slight variations. When the job requires it, I like to provide texture with Photoshop. It is one of the most enjoyable stages. I create my own textures and paintbrushes in order provide that hand-made look that is welcomed in some jobs. And in the end, as the great Adrian Johnson used to say, "It's hardly quantum physics." So it all boils down to thinking, painting, and coloring. I don't know if he really said this, but that's not the point.

Creando mi lettering ilustrado

No comienzo ningún proyecto si antes no lo he bocetado en un cuaderno. El boceto tiene su propia vida y es la fase más importante. Nace siendo algo muy bruto. En este punto damos el visto bueno para continuar. Es entonces cuando el boceto empieza a perfilarse. Creo algunas partes más detalladas y una pequeña pieza la entinto de forma analógica. Esto es lo que llamo prueba de estilo. Es básico hacer una parte del trabajo lo más parecido a lo que luego puede resultar.

Escaneo el boceto, ajusto algunos parámetros en Photoshop y lo abro en Illustrator para hacer un entintado digital, para ello me valgo de la herramienta pincel. Tengo un sinfín de pinceles personalizados que me he ido haciendo a lo largo de los años. El Illustrator se ha convertido en mi estuche Pelikan de los 80. Una vez trazado el boceto, lo expando y uno todas las formas resultantes en una única. Suelo usar la opción combinar, ¡es maravilla pura! Coloreo tanto en Illustrator como en Photoshop. Para la elección del color siempre trabajo con la misma paleta y ligeras variaciones. El texturizado en caso de que el trabajo lo requiera me gusta hacerlo con Photoshop. Es de las fases más divertidas. Creo mis propias texturas y pinceles para darle ese punto orgánico que algunos trabajos agradecen. Y al final como decía el gran Adrian Johnson: «no me dedico a la física cuántica», así que, todo se reduce a pensar, pintar y colorear. No sé si decía esto realmente, pero eso no es lo importante.

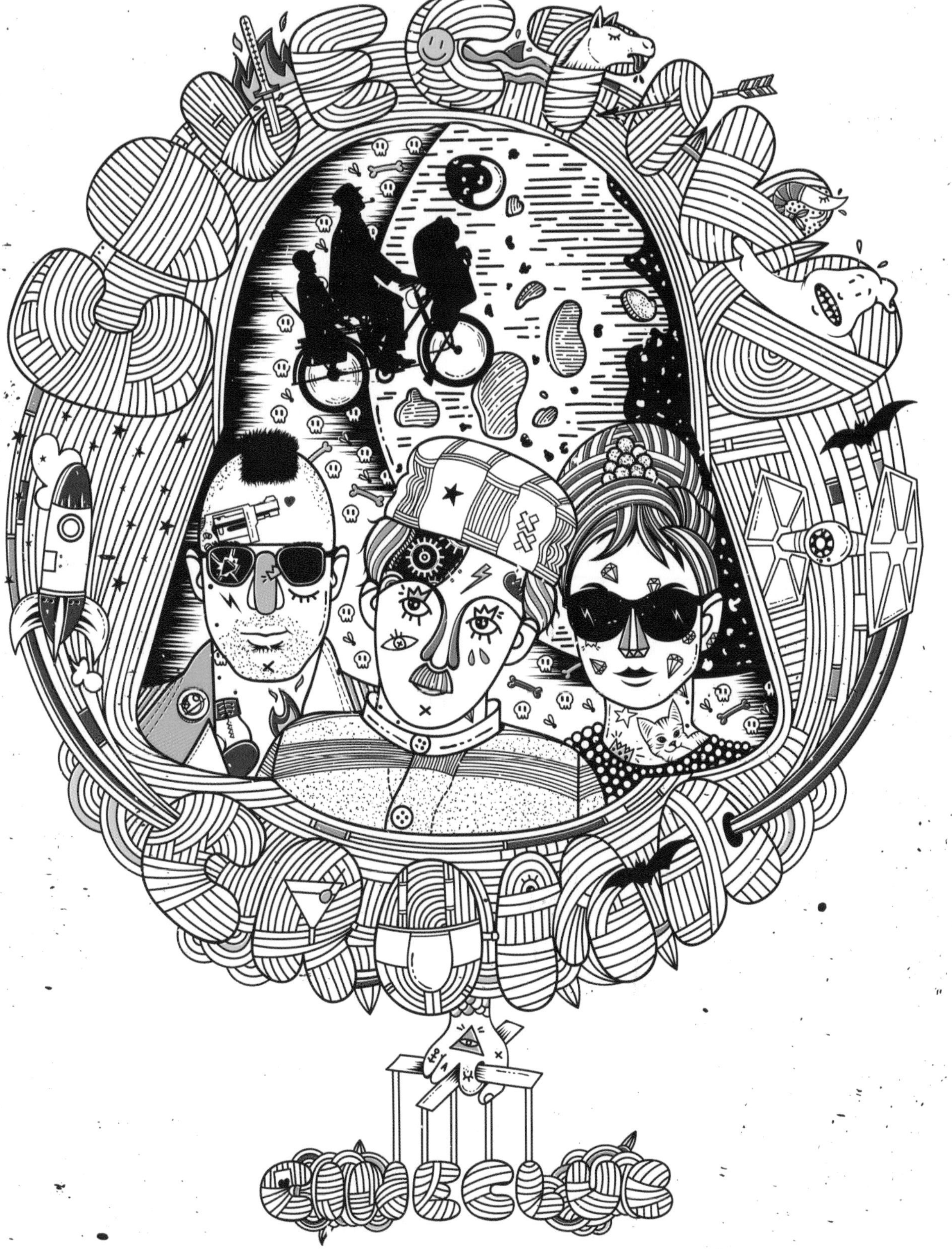

ROB DRAPER

robdraper.co.uk

Rob Draper is an artist and designer based in the UK. He specialises in hand lettering.

Rob worked with a range of worldwide clients including The Golden Globes, Gap, Nike, Penguin Random House, Bartle Bogle & Hegarty, Pentagram, Harper & Collins, WWF, Sustrans, Halfords, MOD Pizza, The Washington Post & Faucet Face.

He has had work featured in worldwide press from IdN International Designers Network Magazine, Design Taxi, UC Quarterly, Thames & Hudsons 'Typography' title, The Design Museum London, The Daily Mail, Shutterstock and has been featured on numerous design/style/creativity blogs.

Rob is passionate about creativity and lettering.

Rob Draper es un artista y diseñador con sede en el Reino Unido. Su especialidad es el lettering hecho a mano.

Rob trabaja con una gama de clientes por todo el mundo, incluyendo The Golden Globes, Gap, Nike, Penguin Random House, Bartle Bogle & Hegarty, Pentagram, Harper & Collins, WWF, Sustrans, Halfords, MOD Pizza, The Washington Post & Faucet Face.

Él ha trabajado para la prensa mundial de IdN International Designers Network Magazine, Design Taxi, UC Quarterly, Thames & Hudsons 'Typography' title, The Design Museum London, The Daily Mail, Shutterstock, ha colaborado en numerosos diseños/estilos/blogs de creatividad.

Rob es un apasionado de la creatividad y las letras.

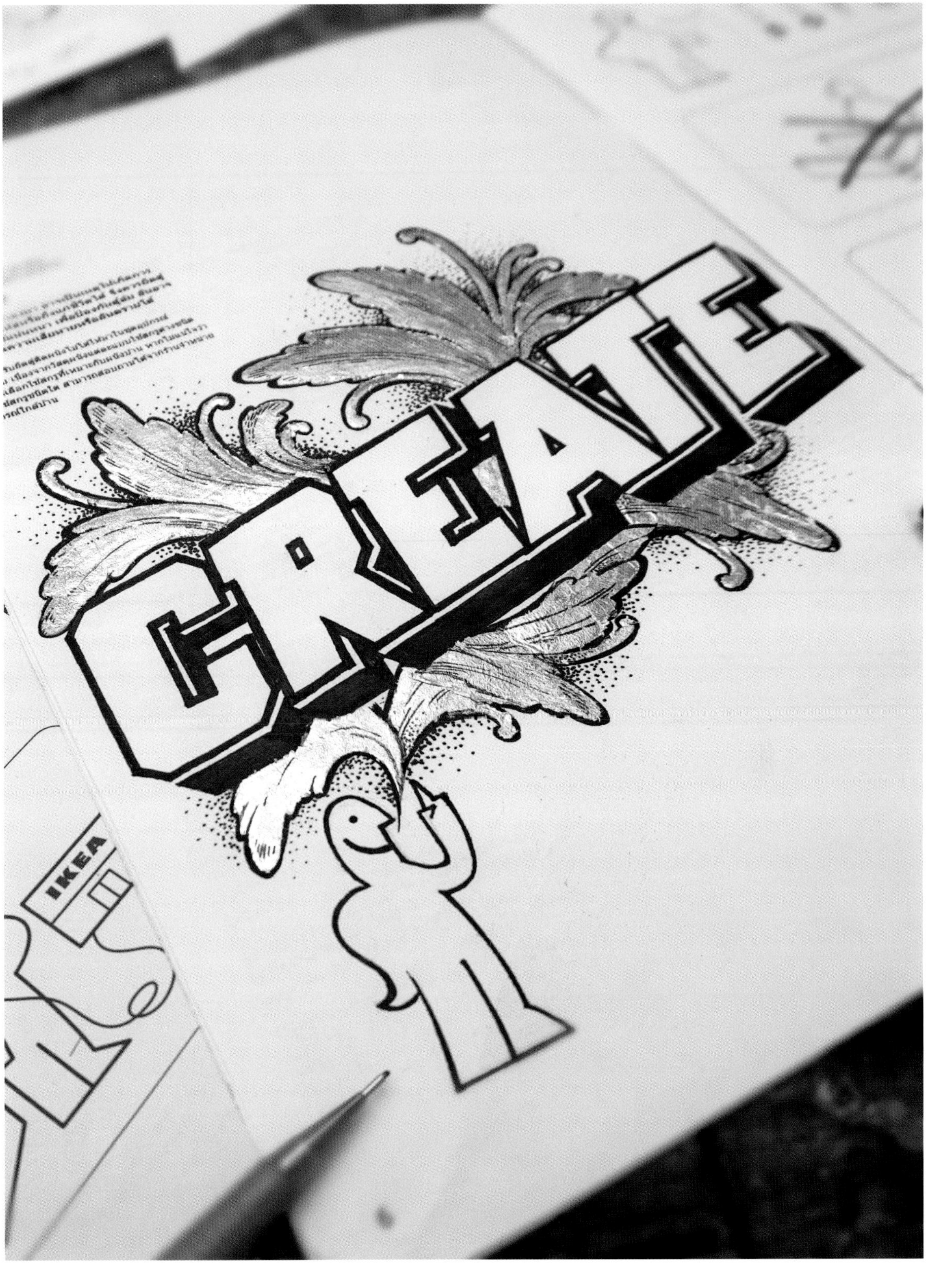
CREATE
IKEA

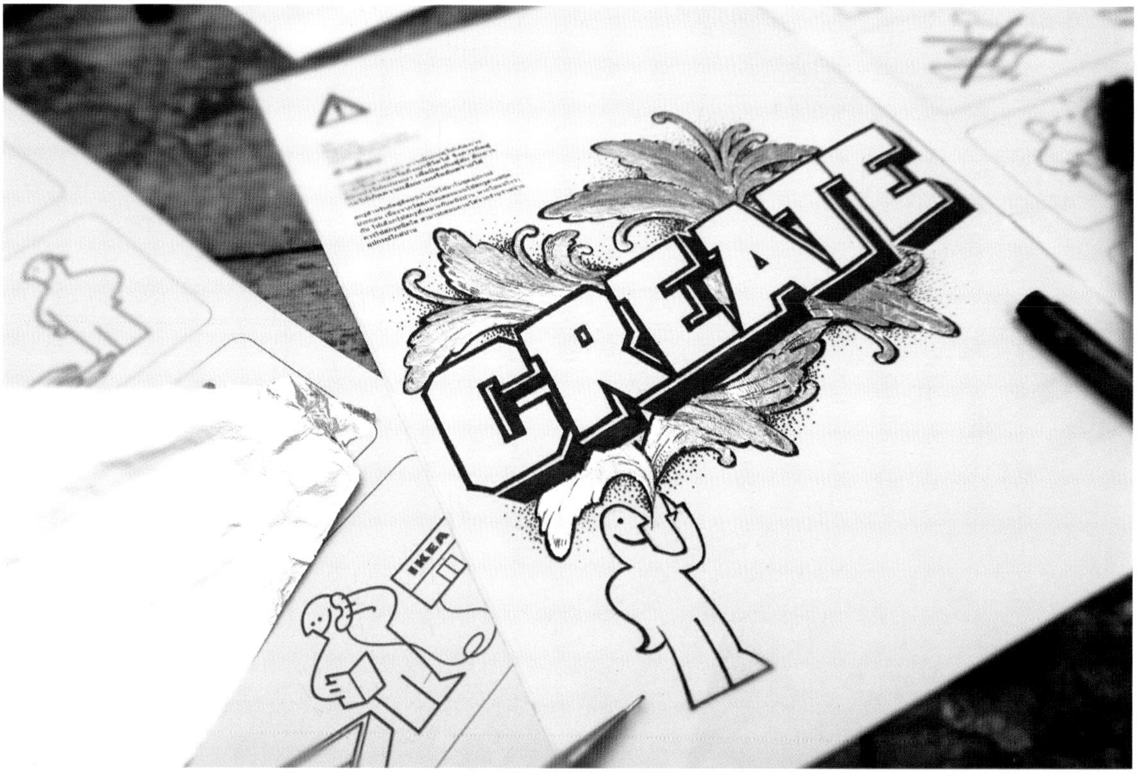
CREATE
IKEA

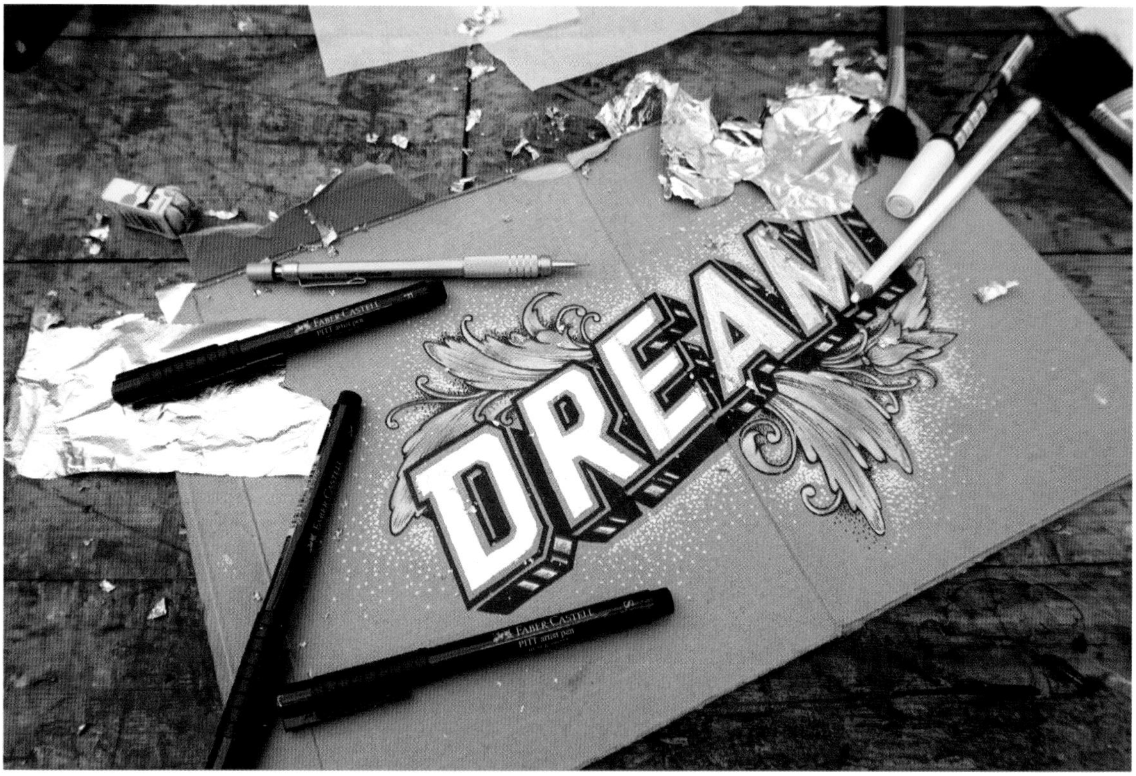
DREAM
FABER-CASTELL
PITT artist pen

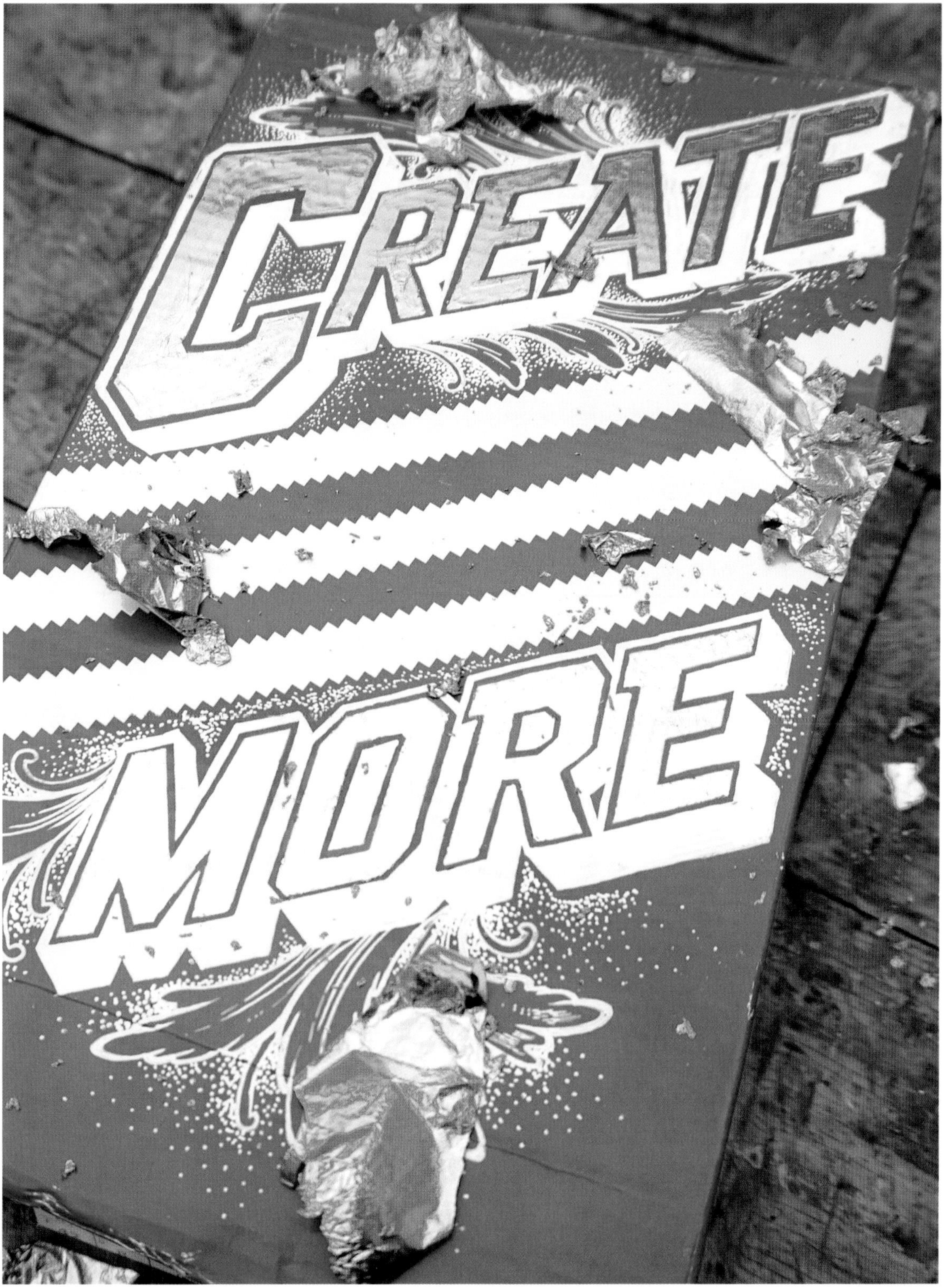
CREATE
MORE

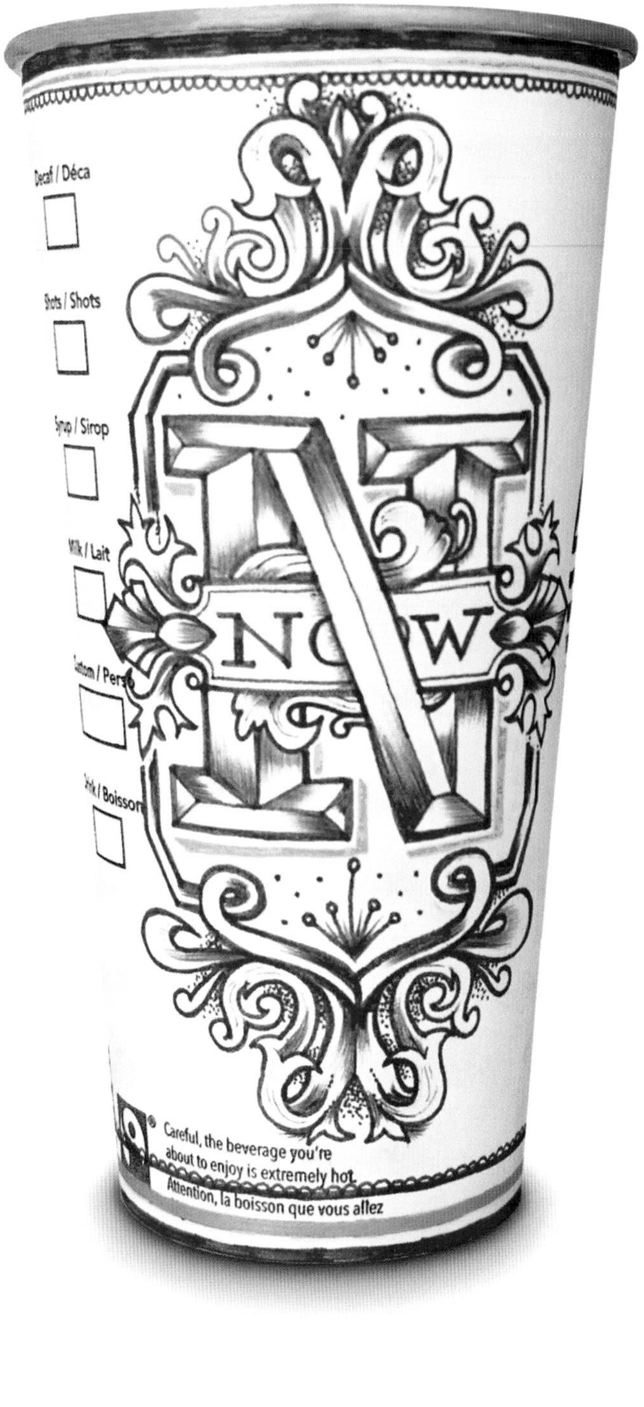
Decaf / Déca
Shots / Shots
Syrup / Sirop
Milk / Lait
NOW
Careful, the beverage you're
about to enjoy is extremely hot
Attention, la boisson que vous allez

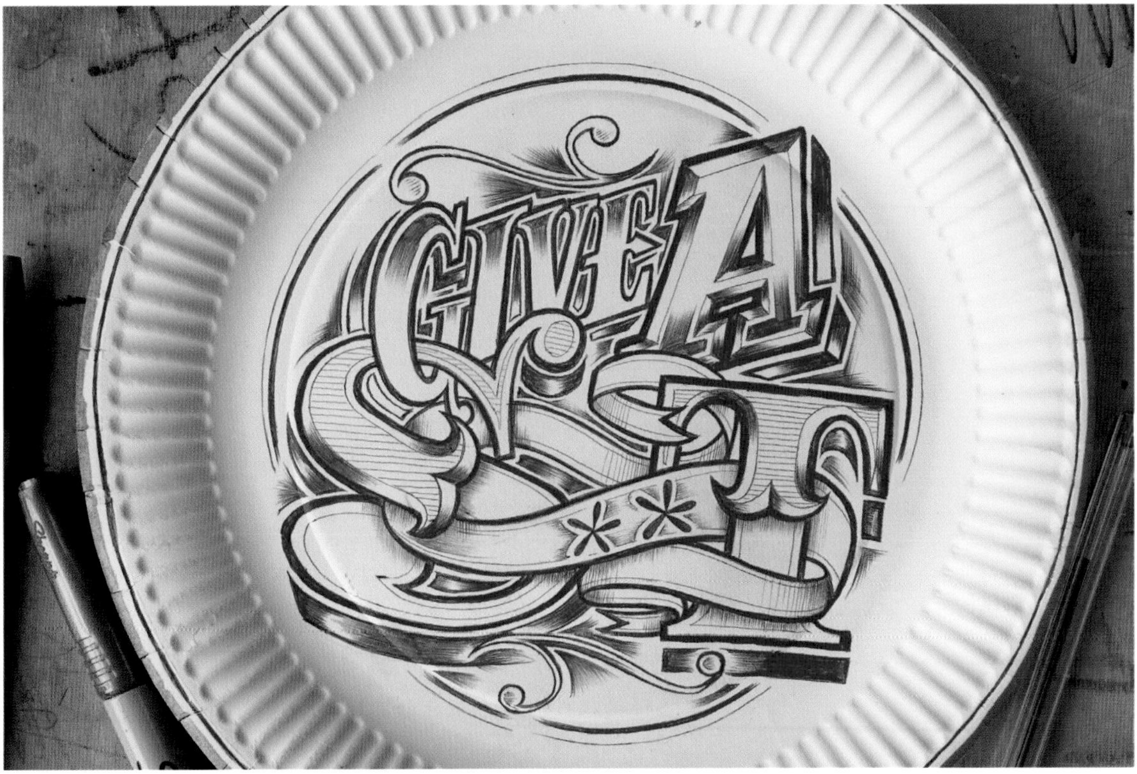
GIVE A
S**T

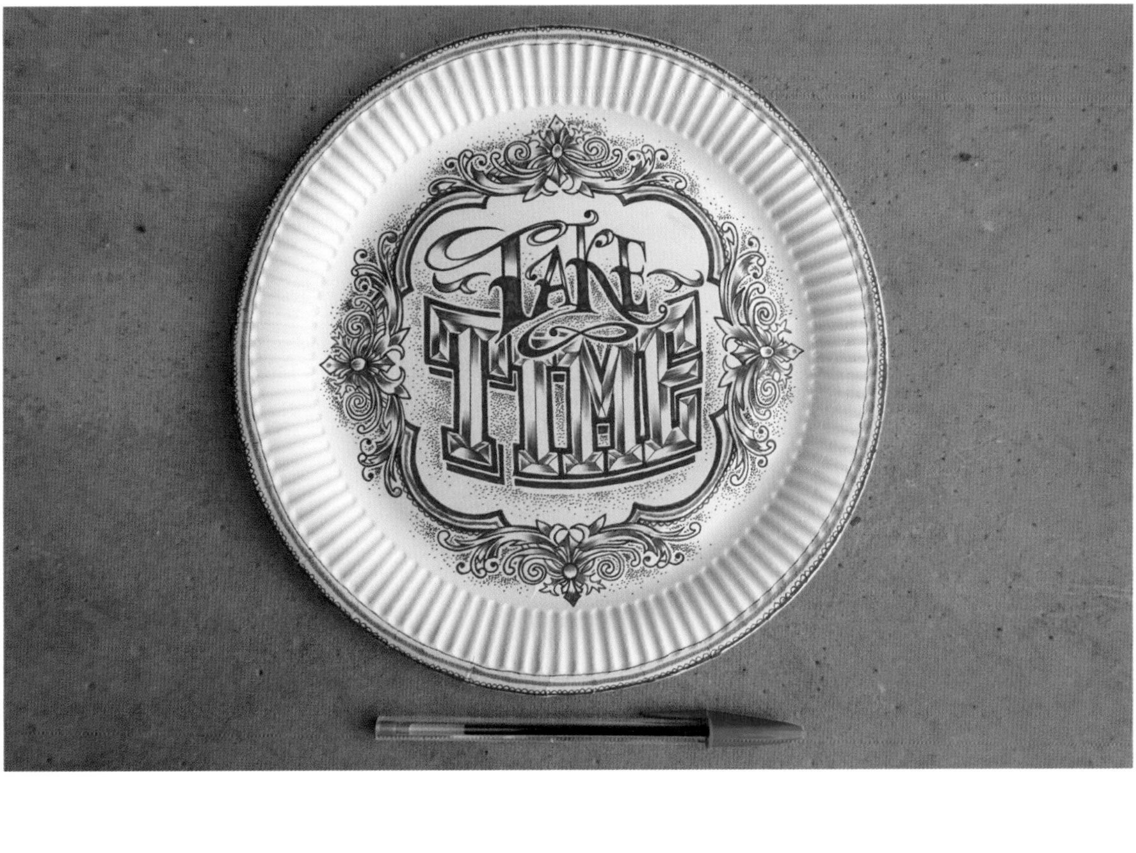
TAKE
TIME

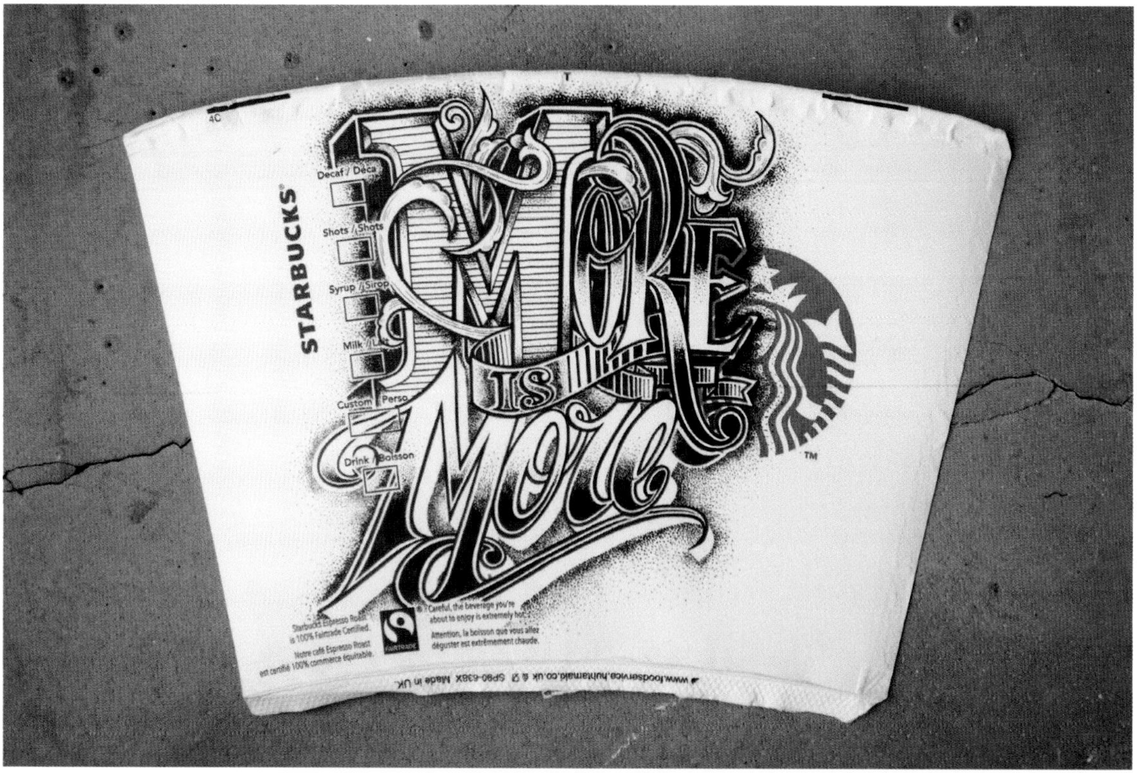
STARBUCKS
Decaf / Déca
Shots / Shots
Syrup / Sirop
Custom / Perso
Drink / Boisson
MORE
IS
More
Starbucks Espresso Roast is 100% Fairtrade Certified.
Notre café Espresso Roast est certifié 100% commerce équitable.
FAIRTRADE
Careful, the beverage you're about to enjoy is extremely hot.
Attention, la boisson que vous allez déguster est extrêmement chaude.

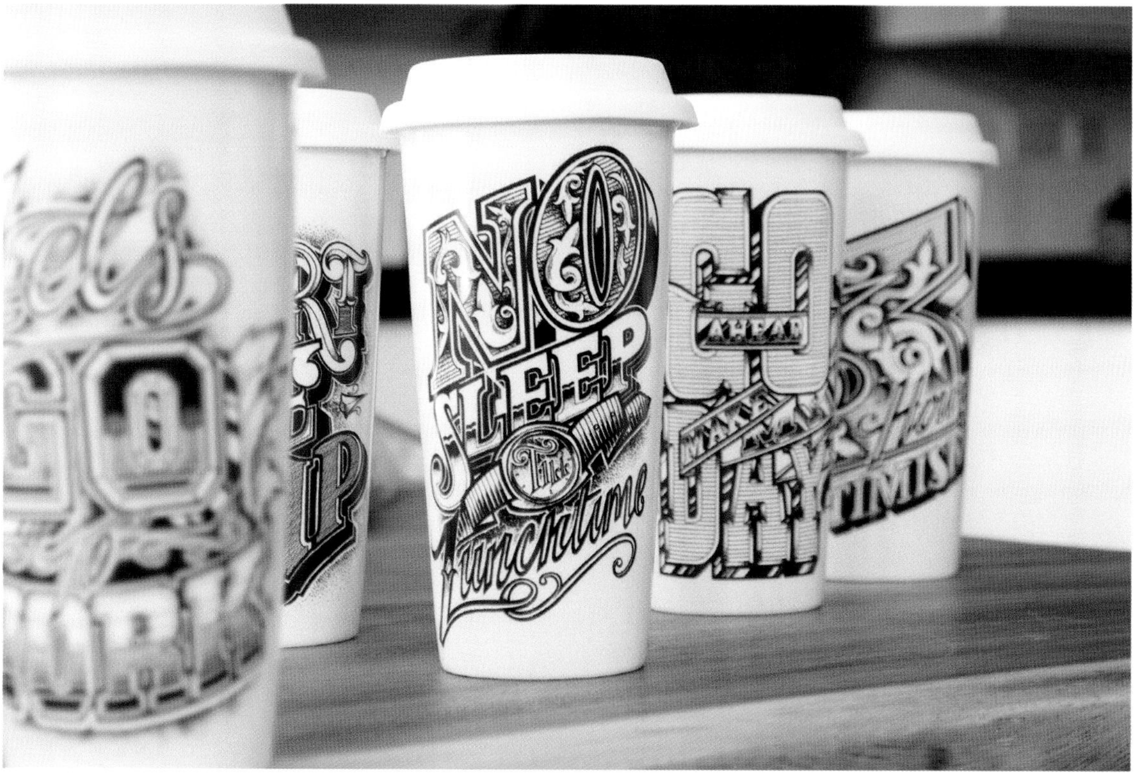
NO
SLEEP
Till
Lunchtime
GO
AHEAD
MAKE
DAY

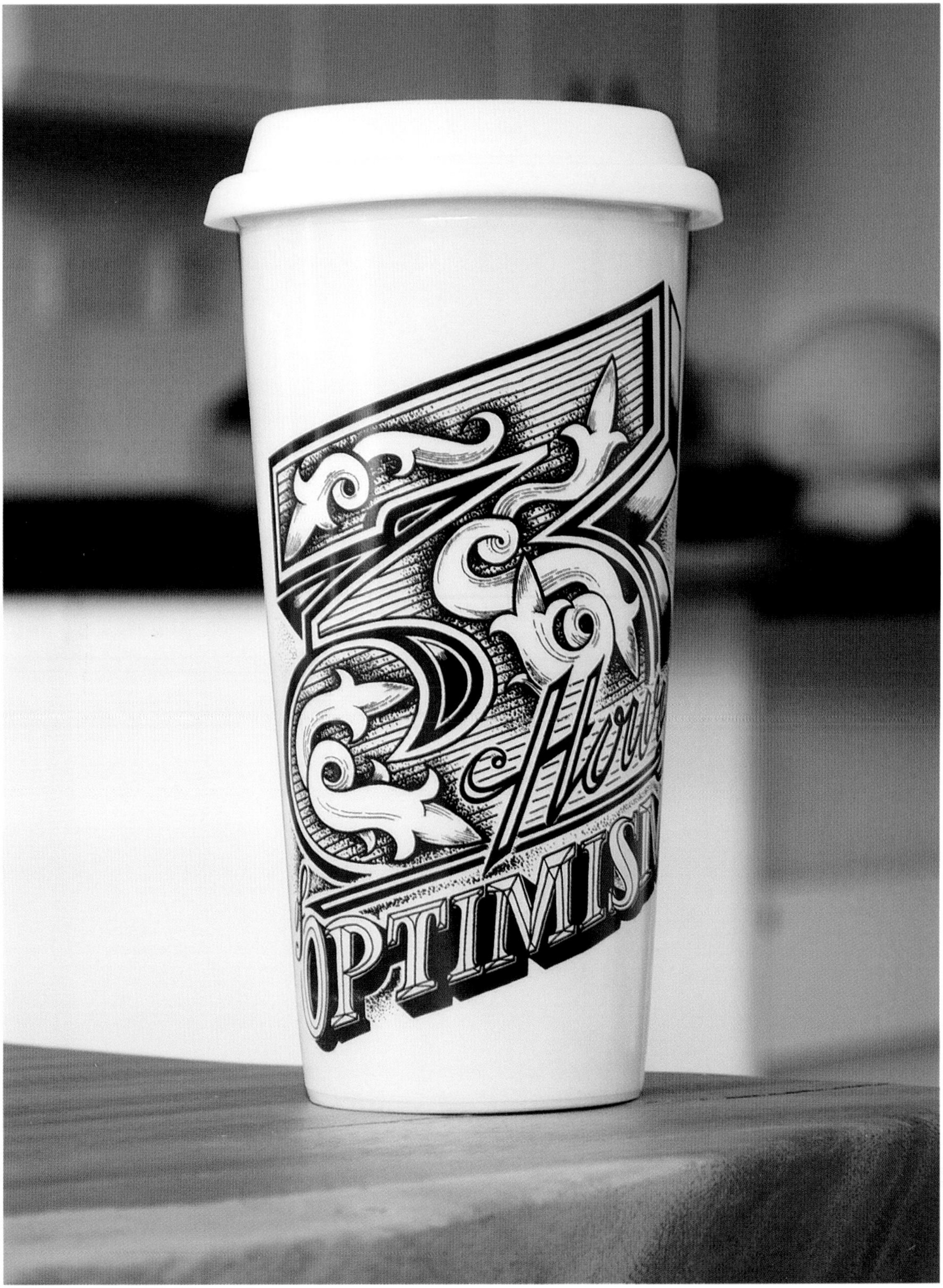

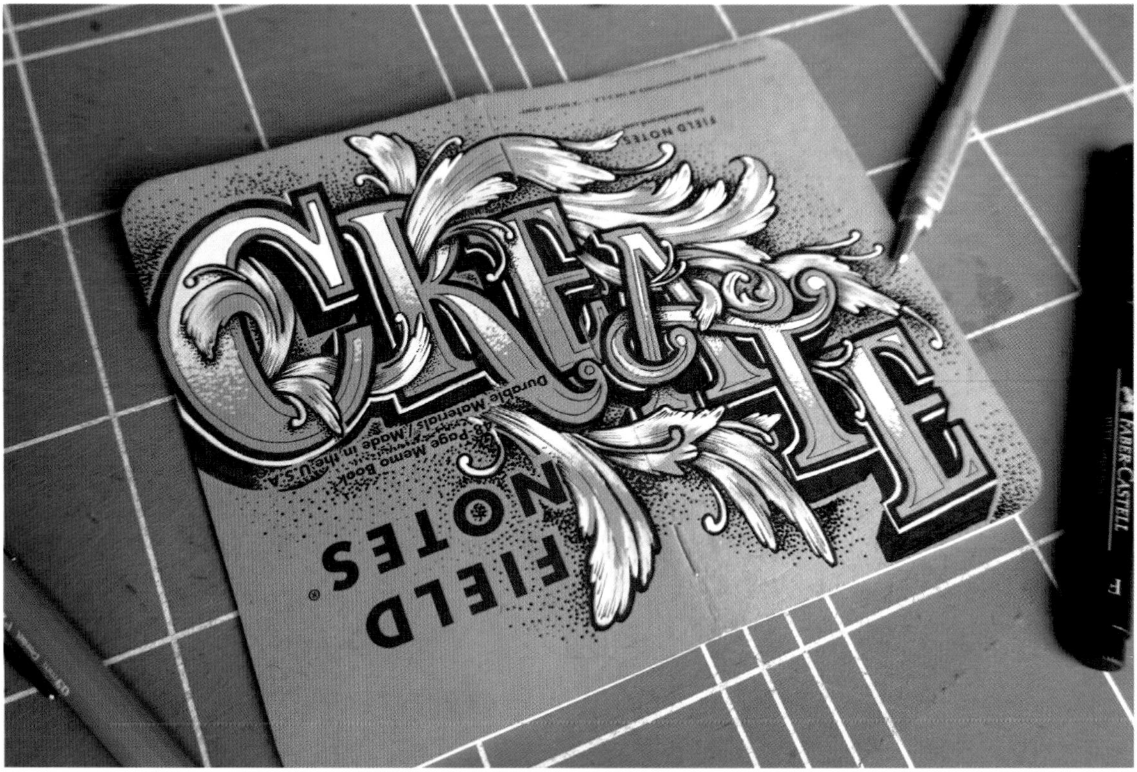
CREATE
FIELD NOTES
48-Page Memo Book
Durable Materials / Made in the U.S.A
FABER-CASTELL

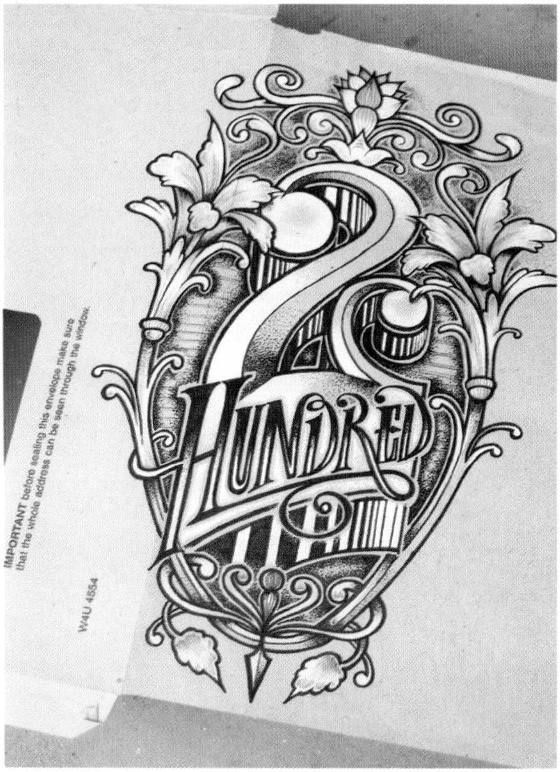
Hundred
IMPORTANT before sealing this envelope make sure
that the whole address can be seen through the window
W4U 4554

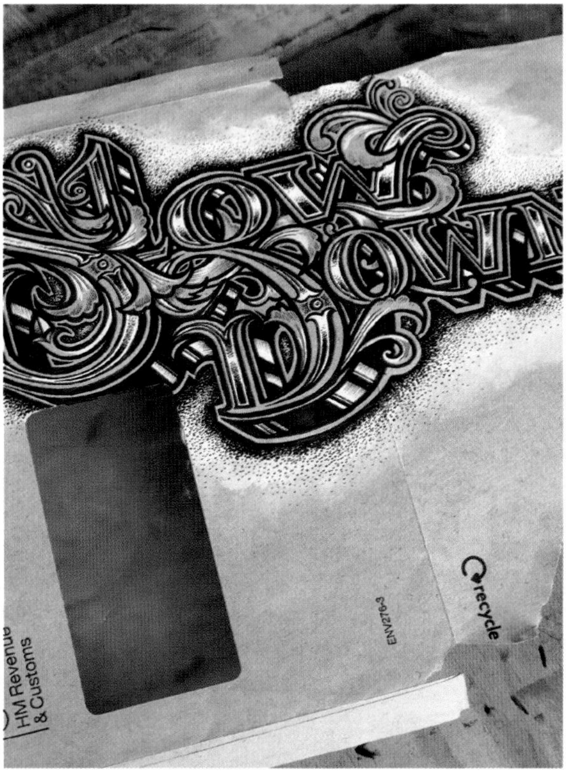
HM Revenue
& Customs
ENV276-3
recycle

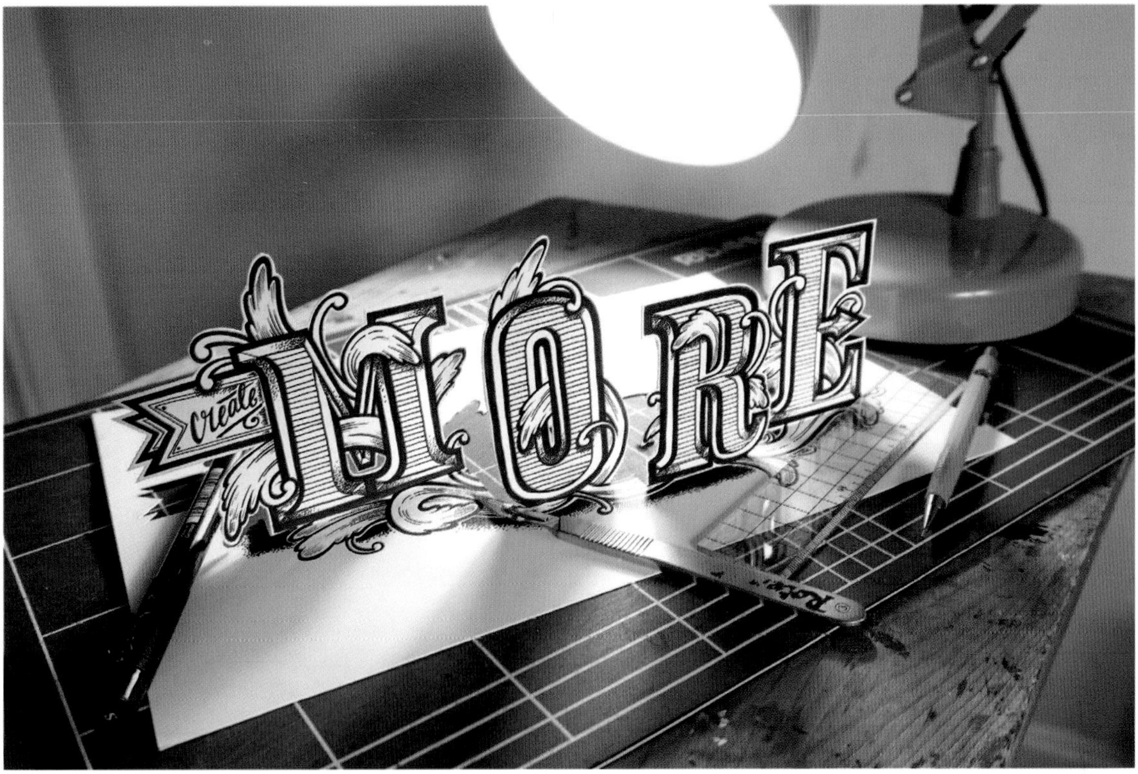
Create
MORE

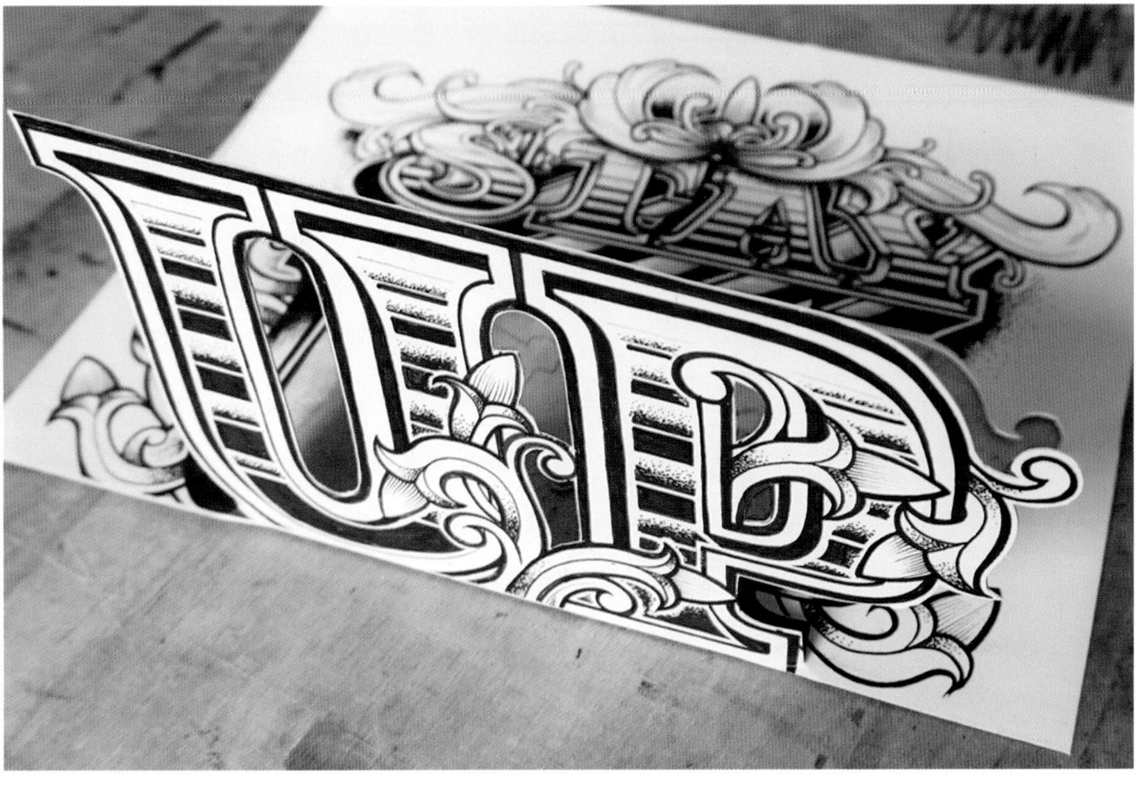
UP

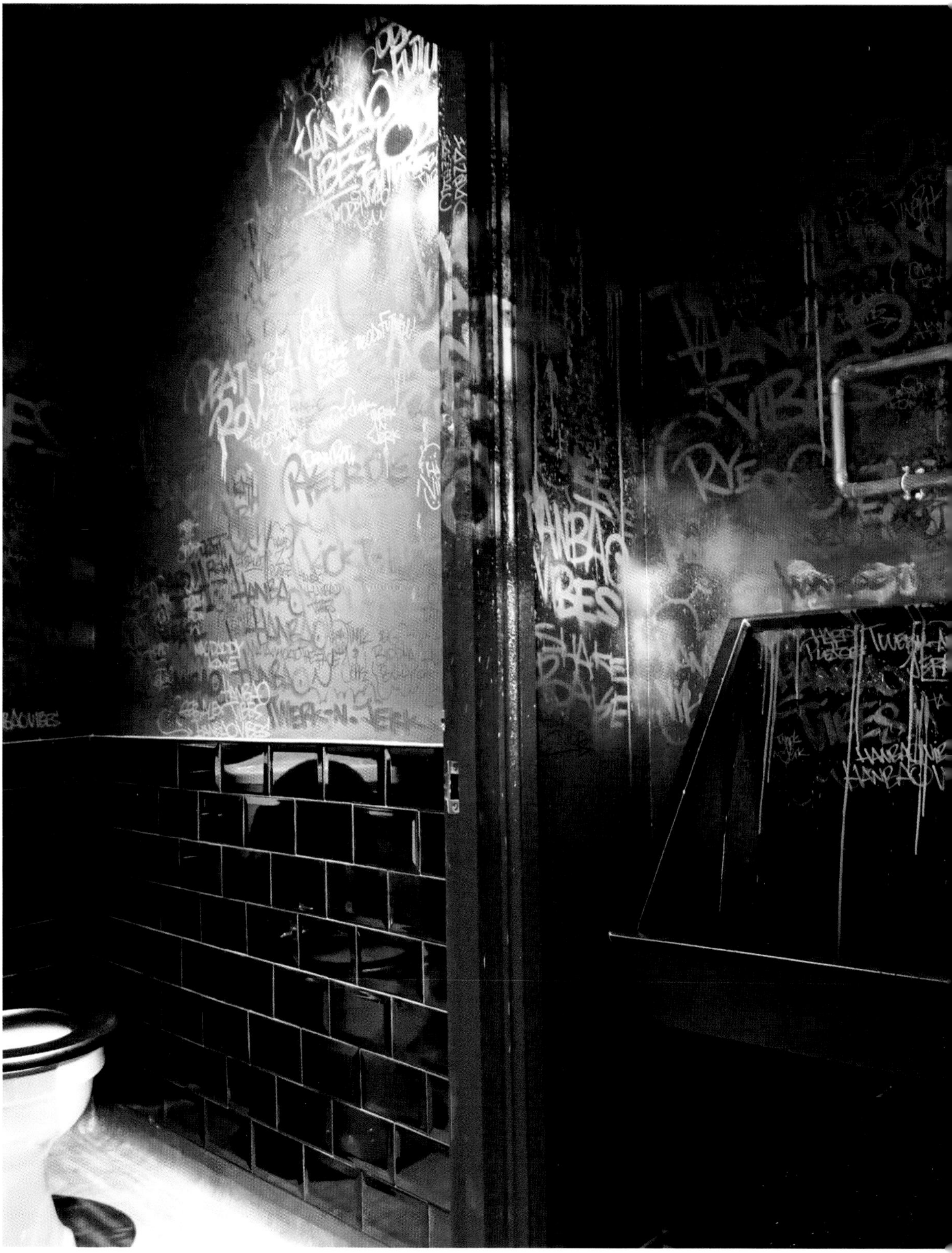

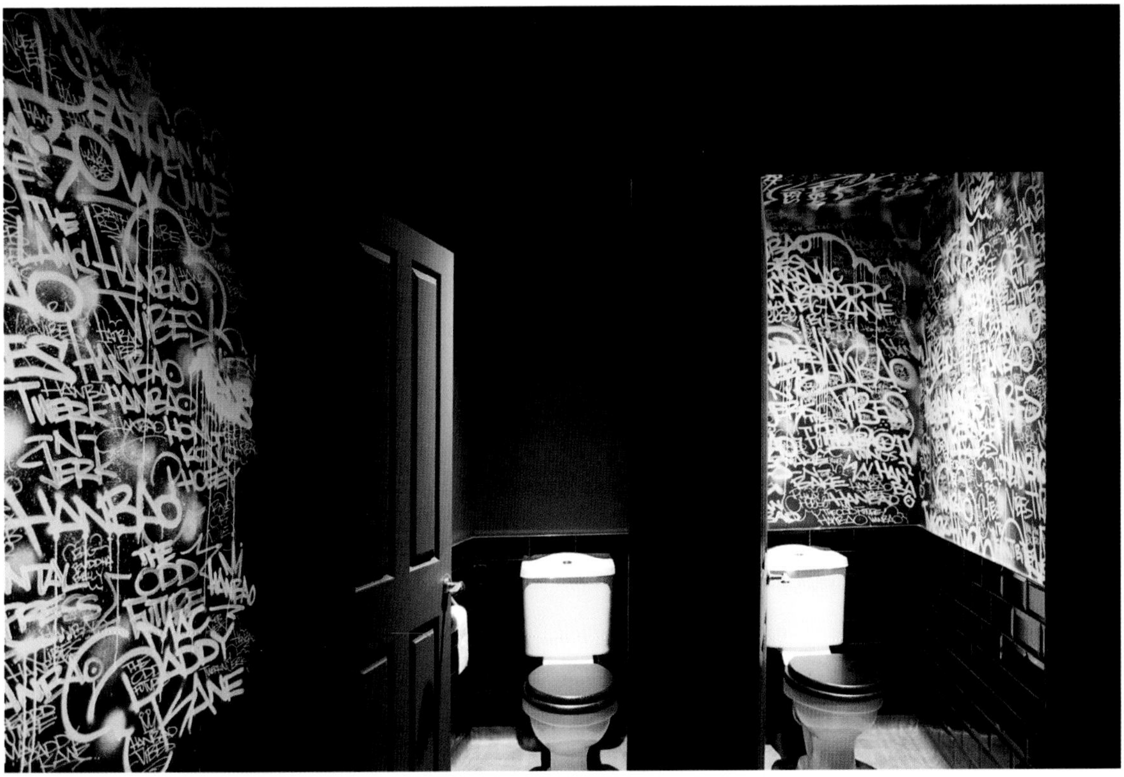

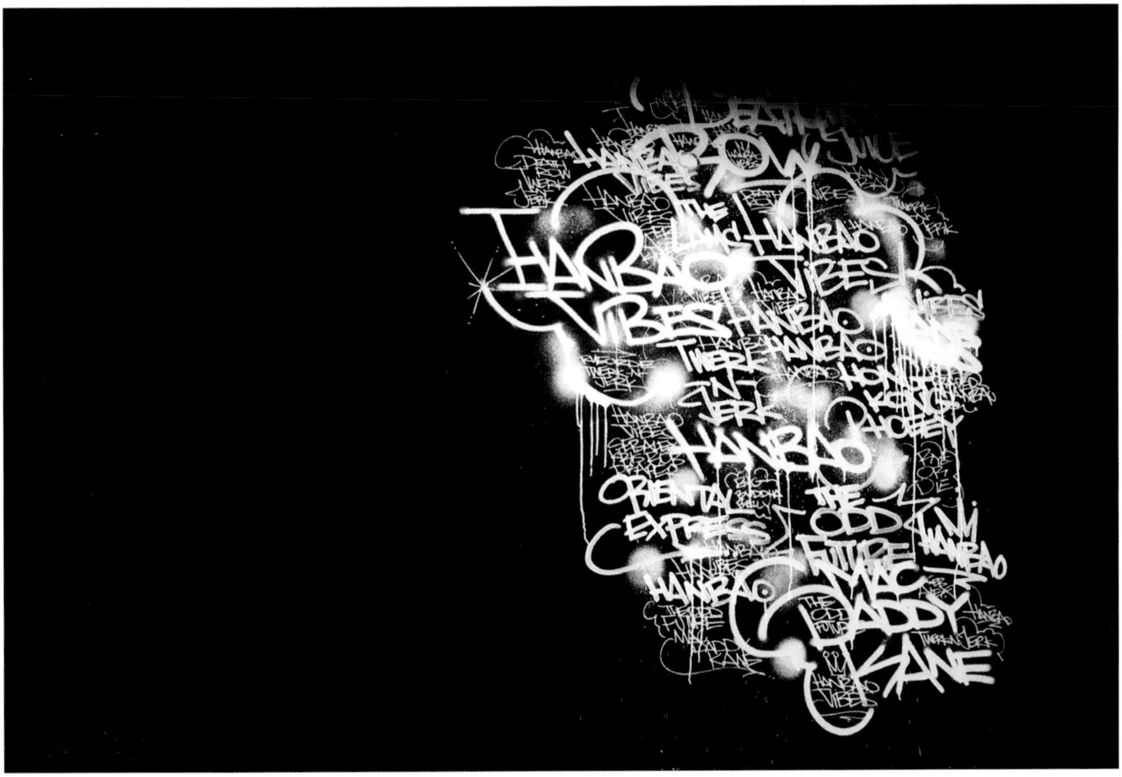
HANBAO
VIBES
ORIENTAL
EXPRESS
THE
ODD
FUTURE
MAC
DADDY
KANE
JUICE

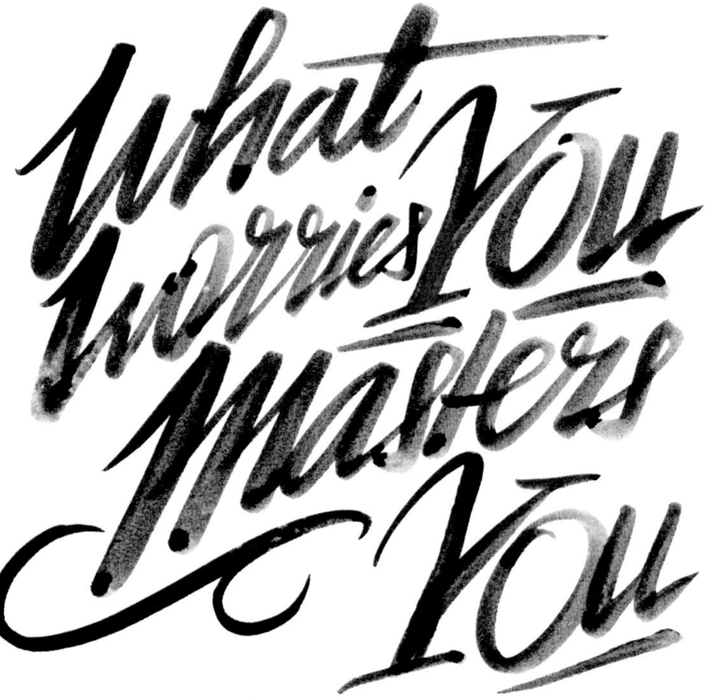
What
worries You
Masters
You

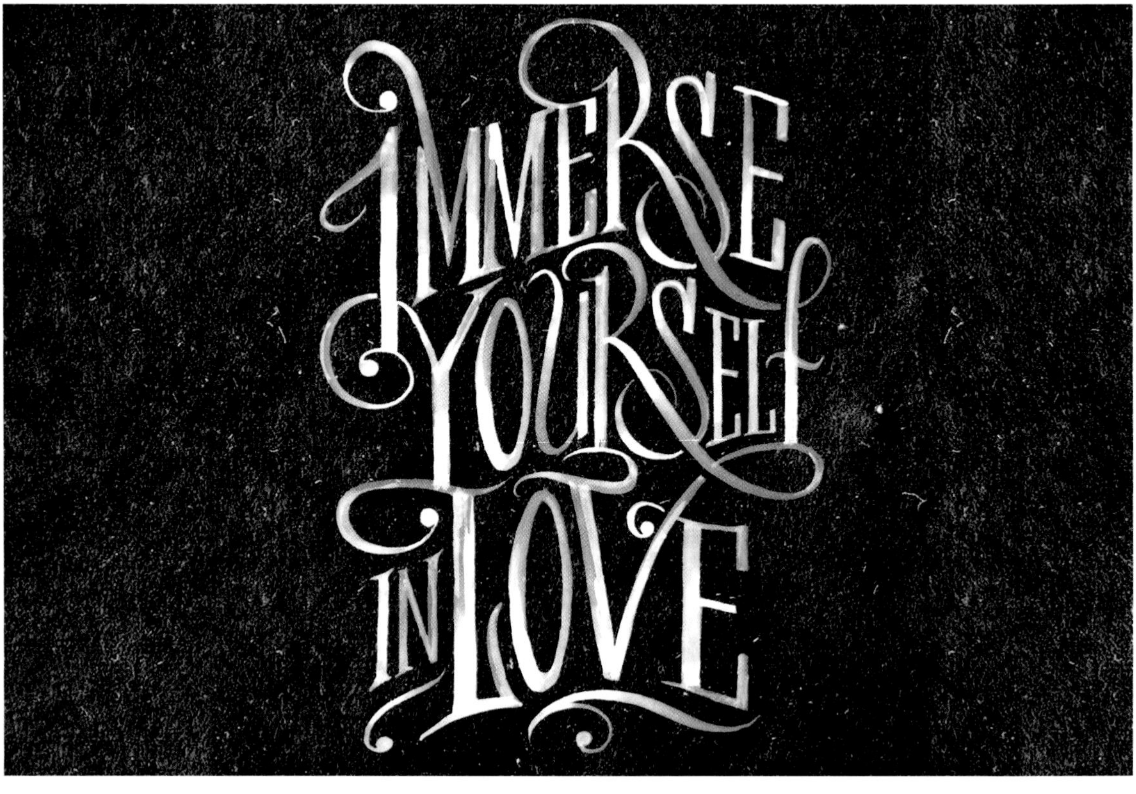
IMMERSE
YOURSELF
IN LOVE

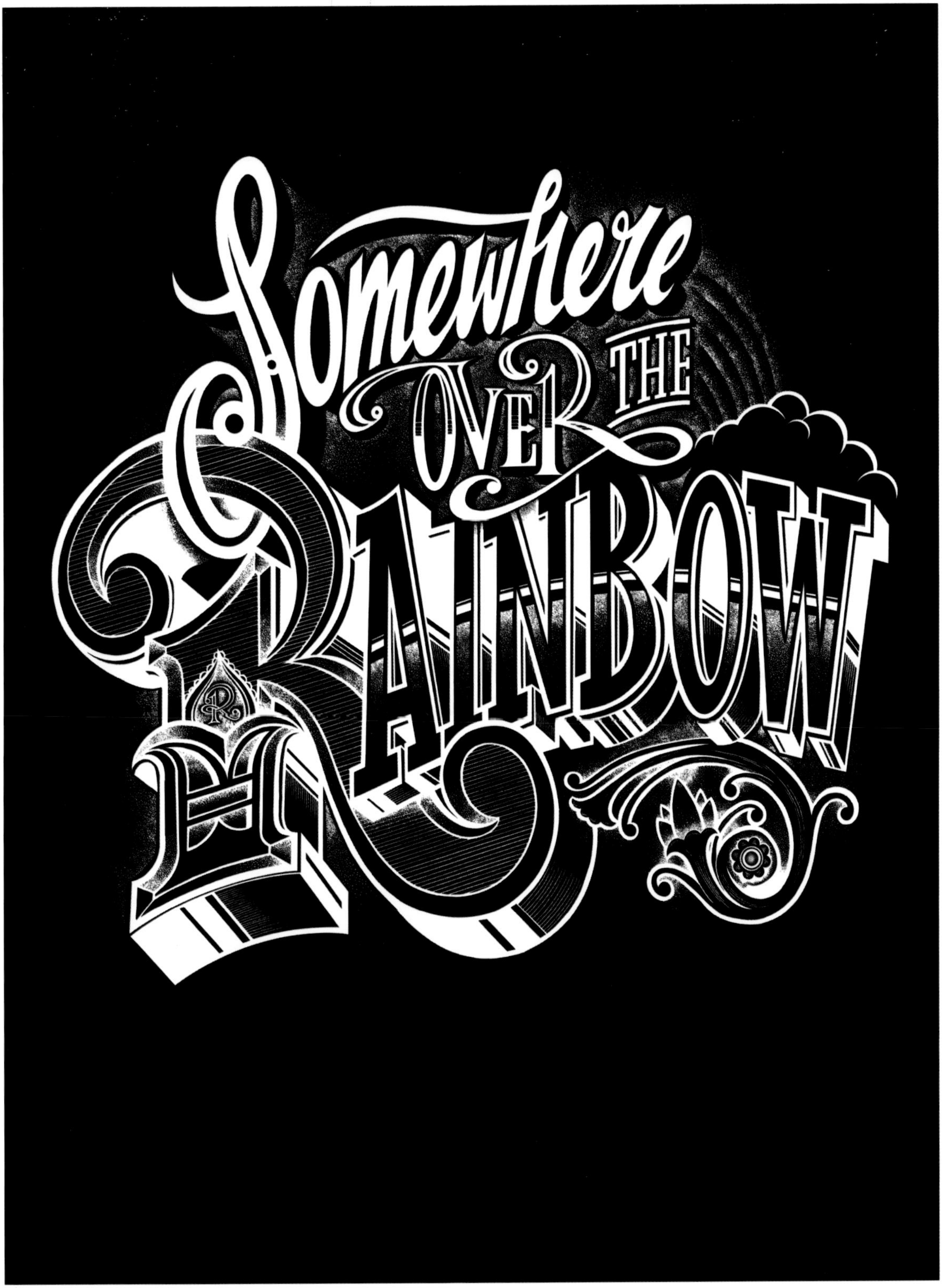
Somewhere
OVER THE
RAINBOW

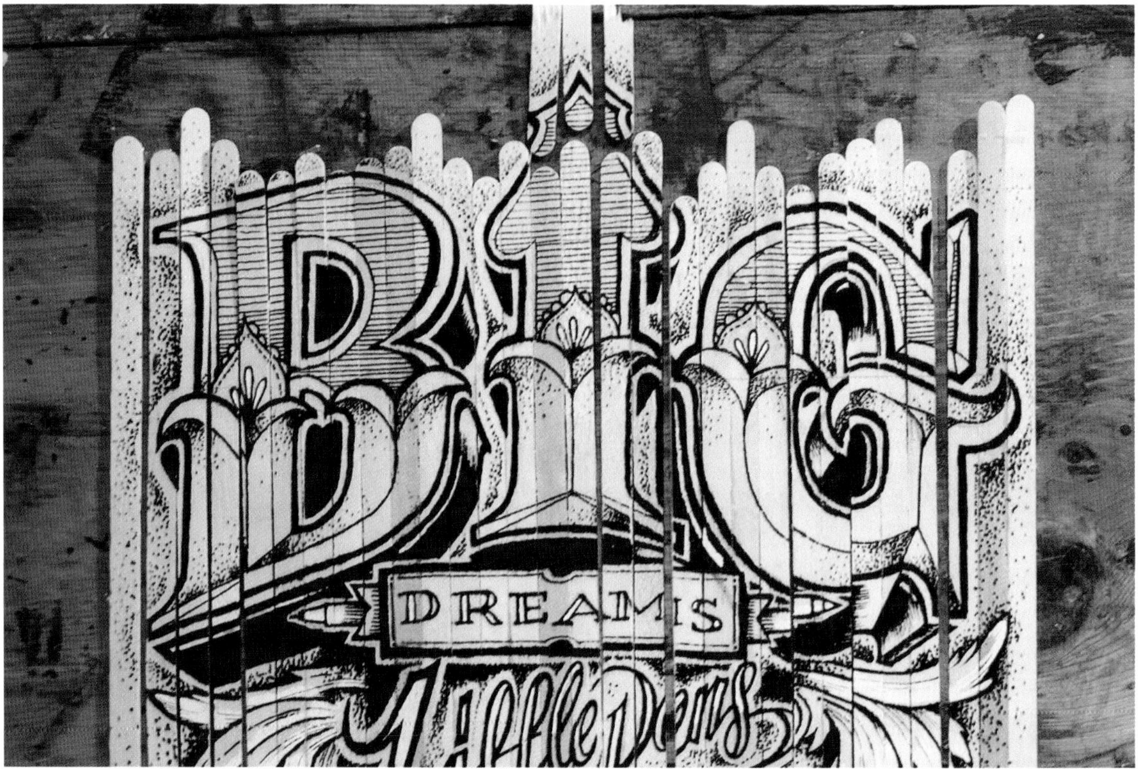
Big
DREAMS

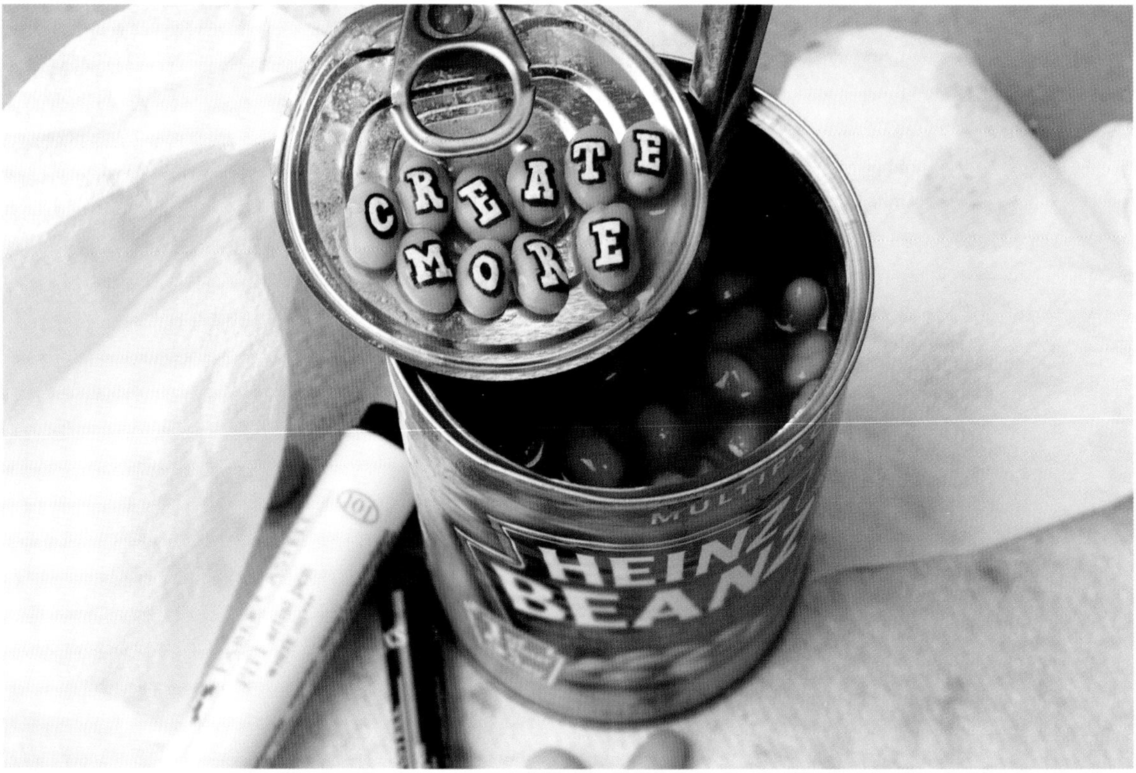
CREATE
MORE
HEINZ
BEANZ

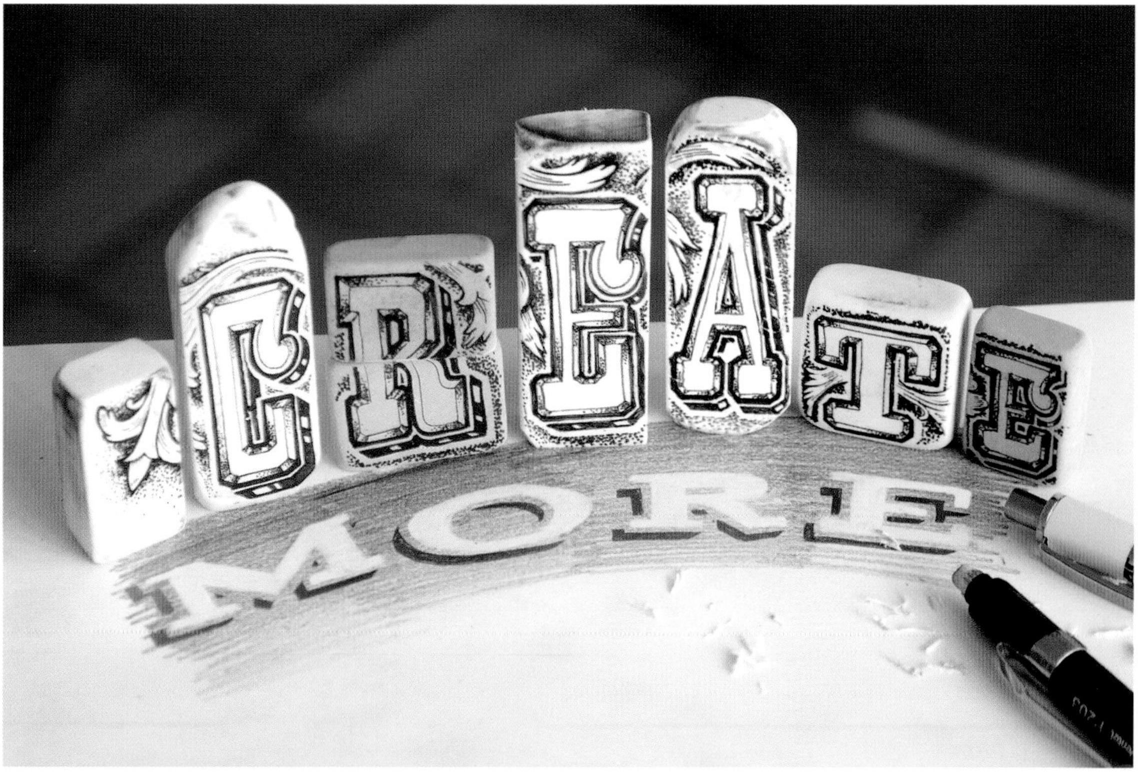
CREATE
MORE

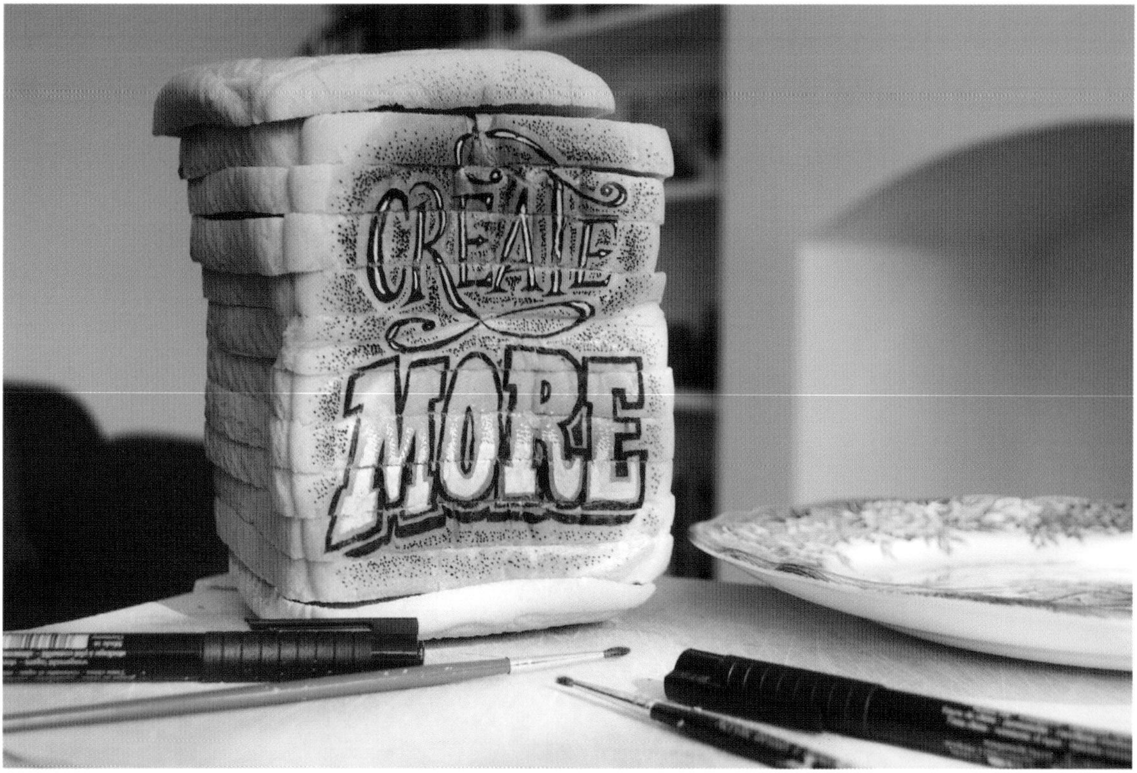
CREATE
MORE

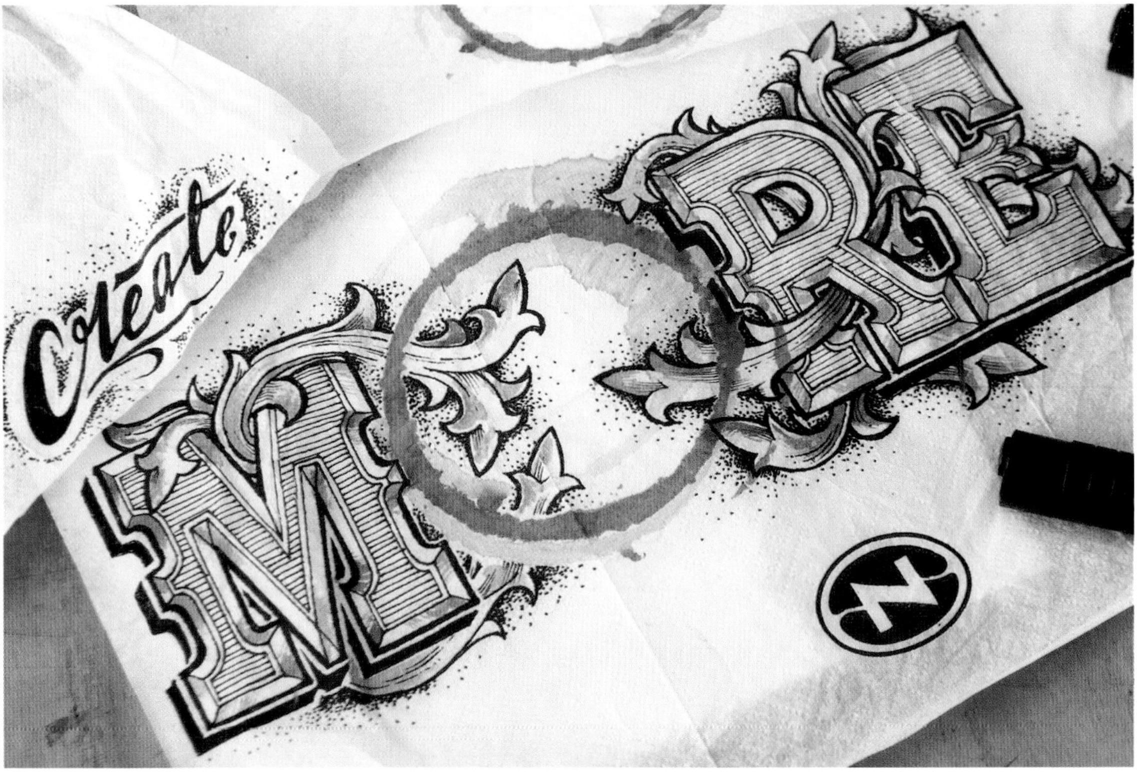
Create

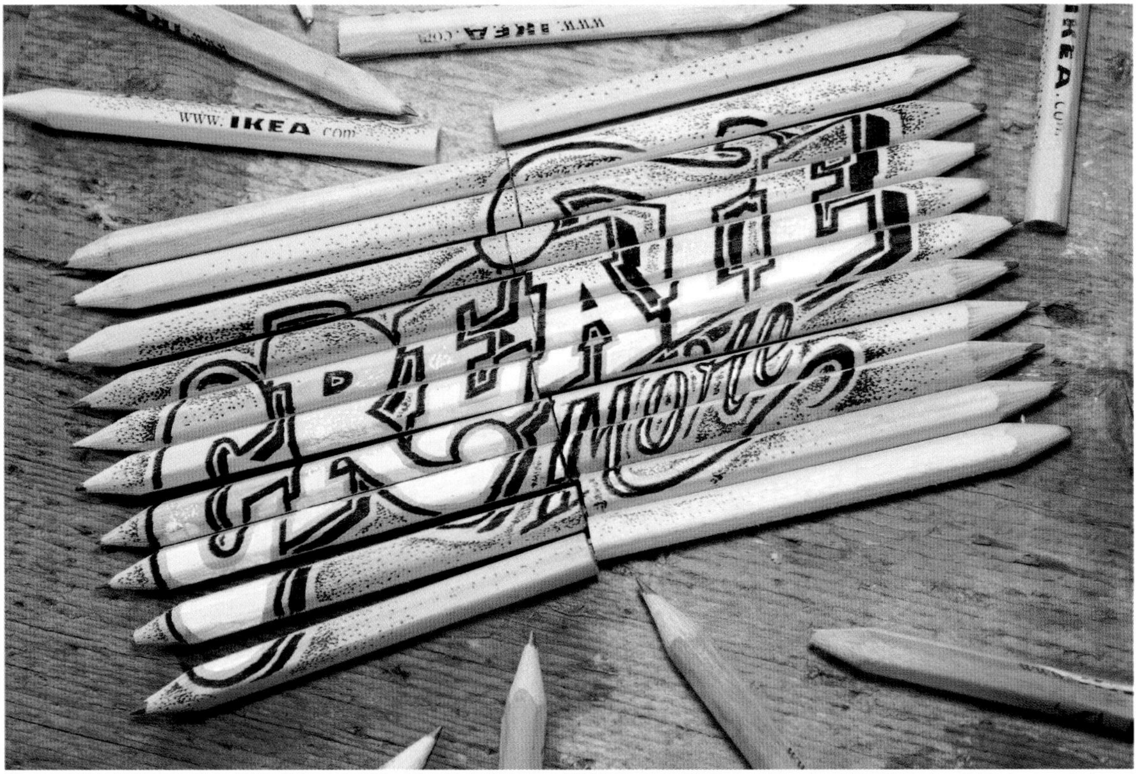
WWW. IKEA .com

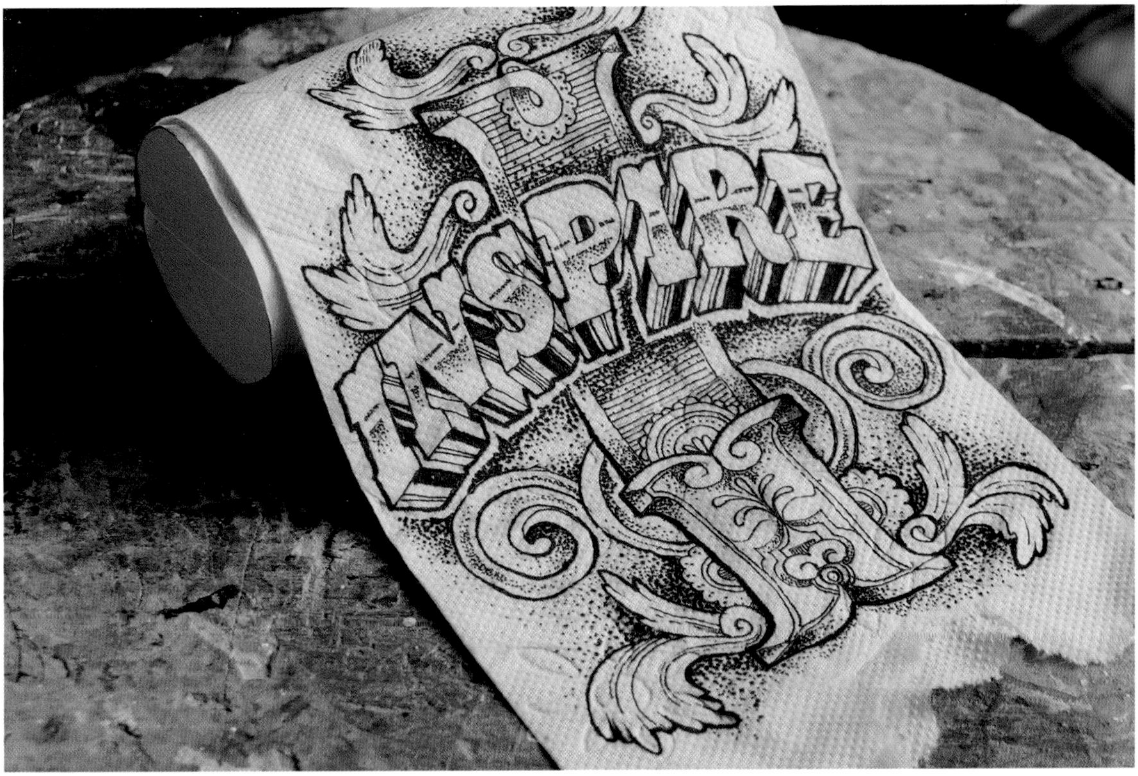
INSPIRE

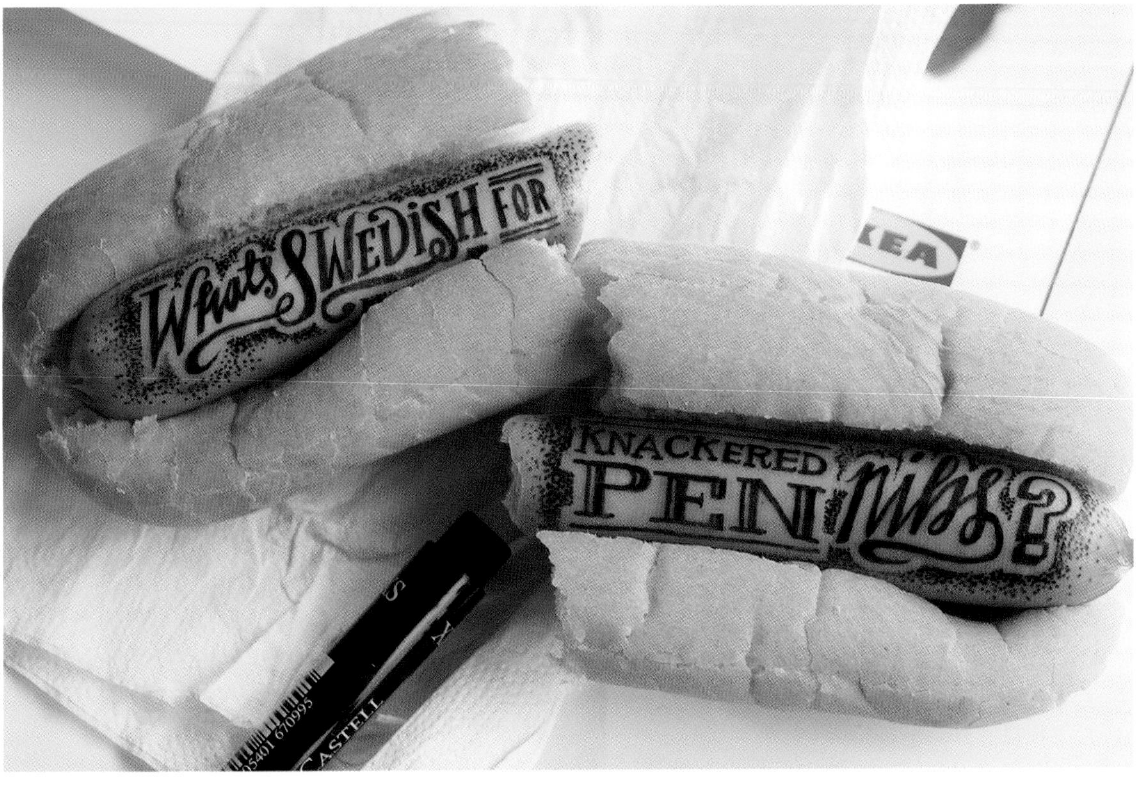
What's SWEDISH FOR
KNACKERED PEN nibs?

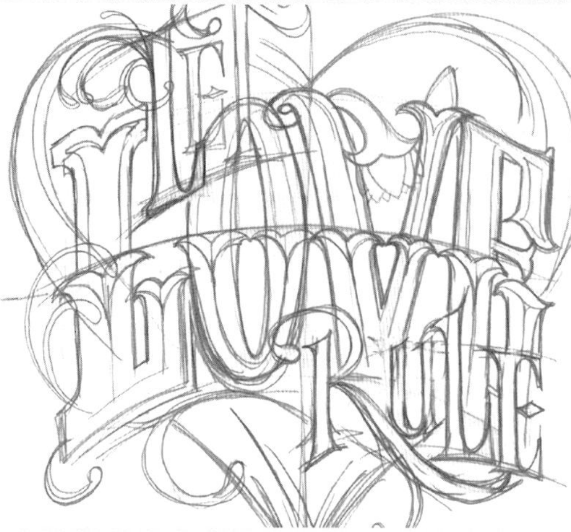

①

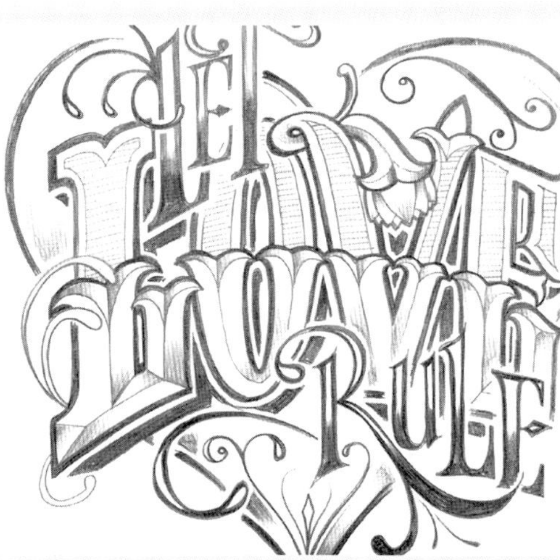

②

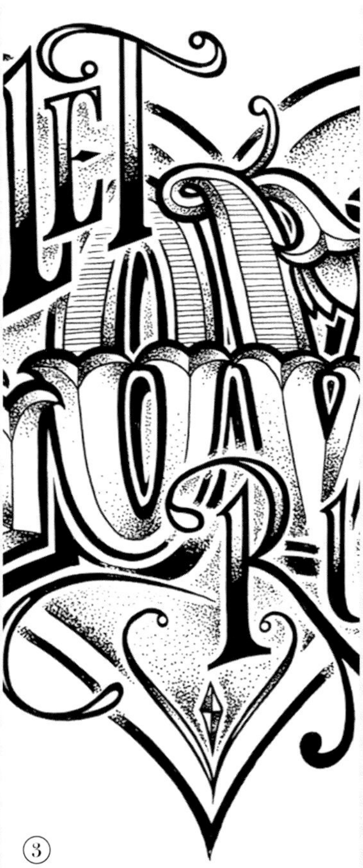

③

Making my lettering

My process often starts very loose, creating a 'shape' for the lettering to fit into. I don't worry too much about detail, at this point its about flow, balance and composition. I tend to think of these rough stages they have to be right or the pieces won't work further down the line. I then use layout paper to sketch over the pervious rough and gradually correct all the areas that need tightening up. This process could take 3 sketches, it could take 20 but I stay in this stage until 100% happy at which point I commit to drawing the final piece in ink.

Creando mi lettering

Mi proceso suele empezar de forma imprecisa, creando una "forma" en la que encuadrar la rotulación. No me preocupan mucho los detalles; en este punto, lo más importante es el equilibrio, la composición, y que la creación fluya. Soy de la opinión de que esta fase inicial tiene que estar bien hecha, o de lo contrario la evolución de la pieza no será la adecuada. Luego utilizo papel de diseño para hacer el boceto e ir corrigiendo poco a poco las zonas que haya que ajustar. Para ello, puedo necesitar 3 bocetos, o incluso 20, pero no doy por concluida esta fase hasta que no estoy 100% satisfecho; solo entonces es cuando empiezo a dibujar con tinta la pieza final.

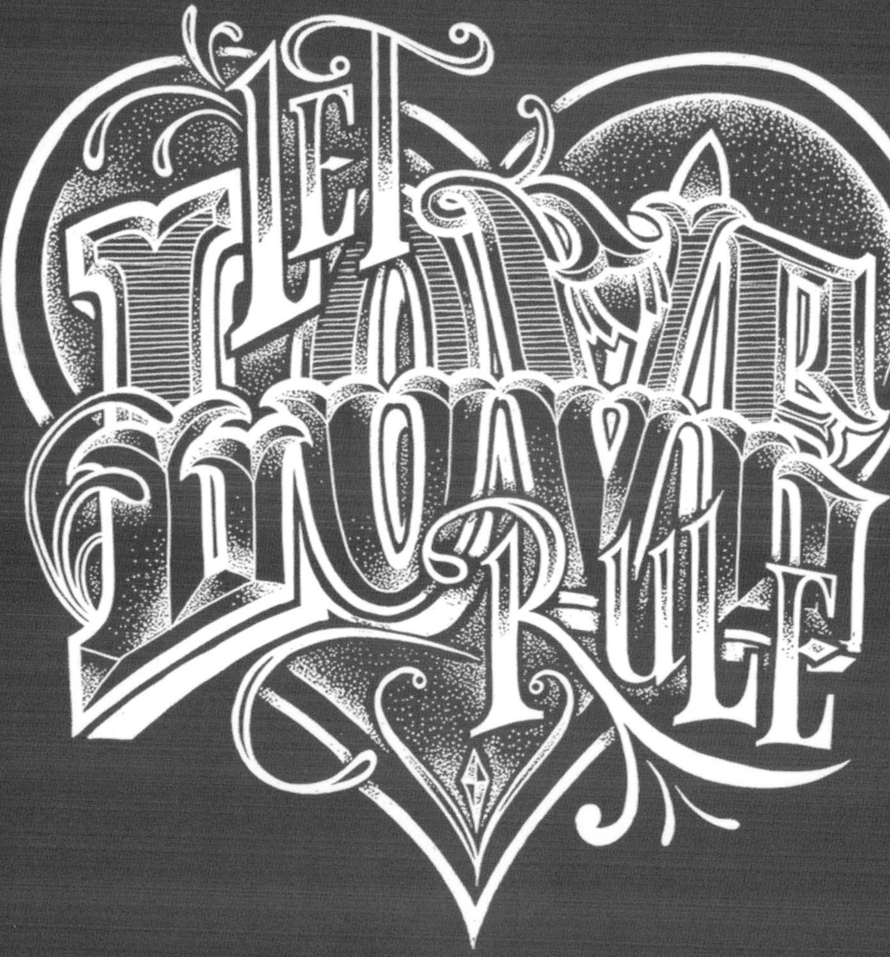
LET
RULE

JEAN CARLOS GARCÍA 'CHAMPOLA'

instagram: champolatype
behance: JeanCarlosG

Jean Carlos García is from Santo Domingo, Dominican Republic.

Currently, he is a Senior Designer at Modafoca. Outside of his graphic design work, he has channeled his passion for lettering and typography by posting his exercises under the pseudonym "Champola". He studied Advertising with a focus on Graphic Design at the Universidad Autónoma de Santo Domingo (UASD). Some time after, he studied Art Director and Copywriting at Brother Escuela de Creativos. These last few years he has been invited to give workshops and lectures about lettering by different institutions in the Dominican Republic.

Jean Carlos has always been really interested in typography, ever since college. He remember he was constantly looking for opportunities to learn how to draw and compose letters perfectly. He started reading books about typography until he stumbled upon the term "lettering". That's when he realized that his interest in typography had become a love for letters. This was the start of his exploration of techniques surrounding typography and lettering, until he found the ones he liked the most, the ones that work best for him.

Jean Carlos García es de Santo Domingo, República Dominicana.

Actualmente, es Diseñador Sénior en Modafoca. Aparte de su trabajo como diseñador gráfico, ha canalizado su pasión por el rotulado y la tipografía publicando sus obras con el pseudónimo "Champola". Estudió Publicidad con especialidad en Diseño Gráfico en la Universidad Autónoma de Santo Domingo (UASD). Posteriormente, estudió Dirección y Edición Artística en la Escuela de Creativos Brother. En los últimos años ha recibido invitaciones para organizar talleres y dar conferencias sobre rotulación por parte de diversas instituciones de la República Dominicana.

Jean Carlos siempre ha estado muy interesado en la tipografía, incluso desde el instituto. Recuerda que siempre estaba buscando oportunidades de aprender a dibujar y componer rótulos a la perfección. Empezó leyendo libros sobre tipografía hasta encontrarse con el término lettering (rotulación). Ahí fue cuando se dio cuenta de que su interés por la tipografía se había convertido en pasión por los rótulos, y cuando empezó a explorar las técnicas que rodean a la tipografía y a la rotulación, hasta descubrir cuáles eran los que más le gustaban y más le convenían.

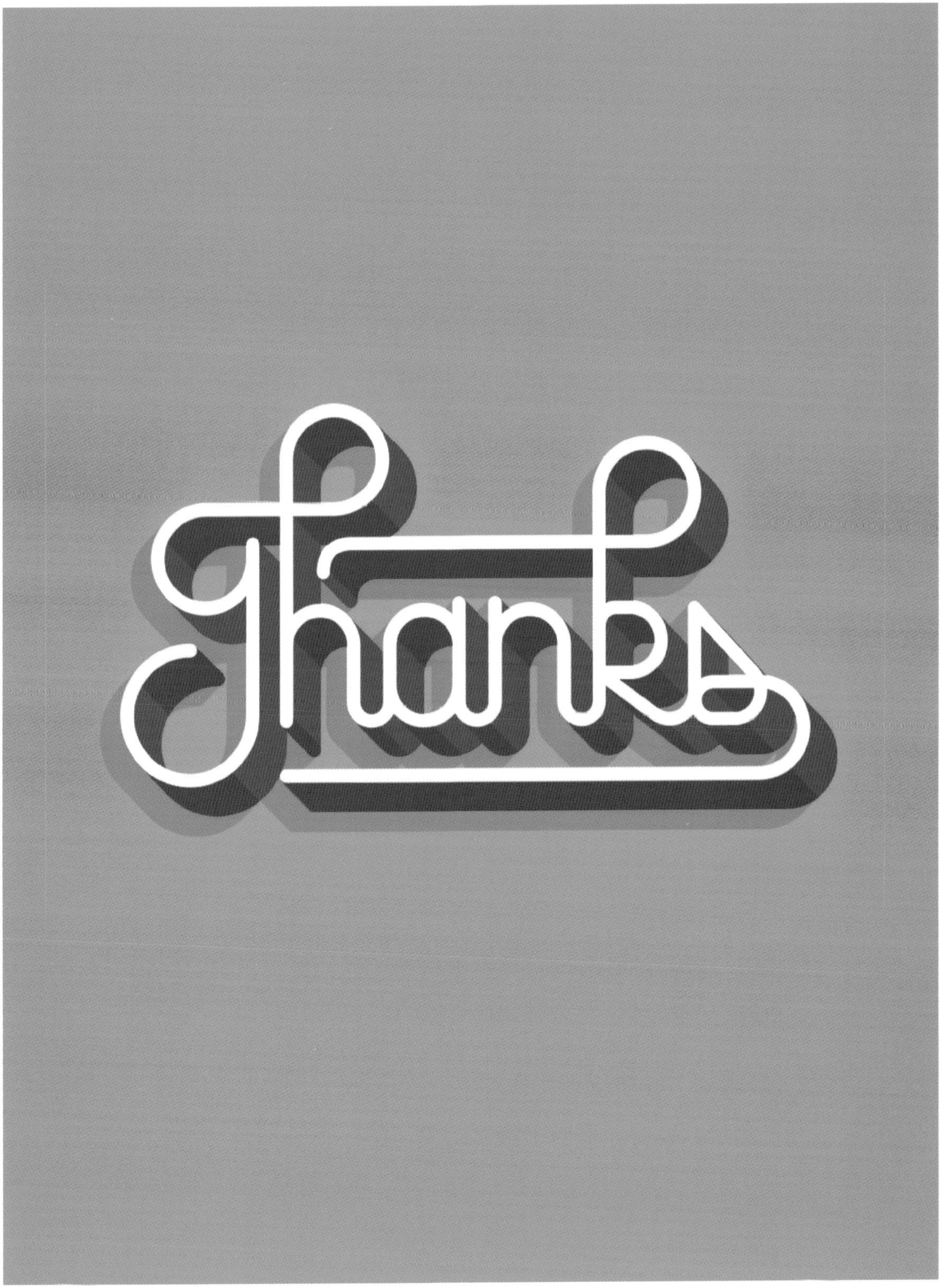
Thanks

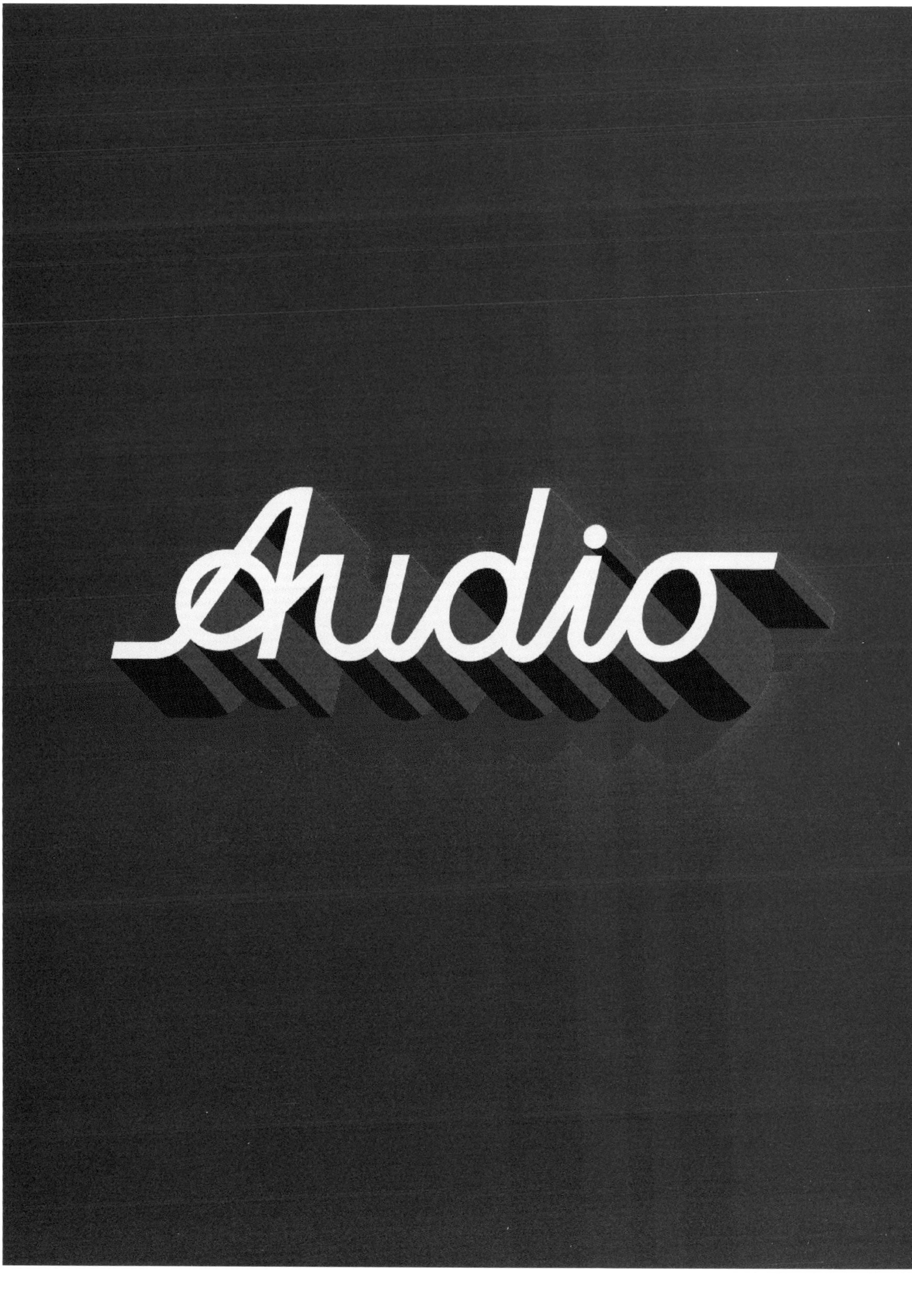
Audio

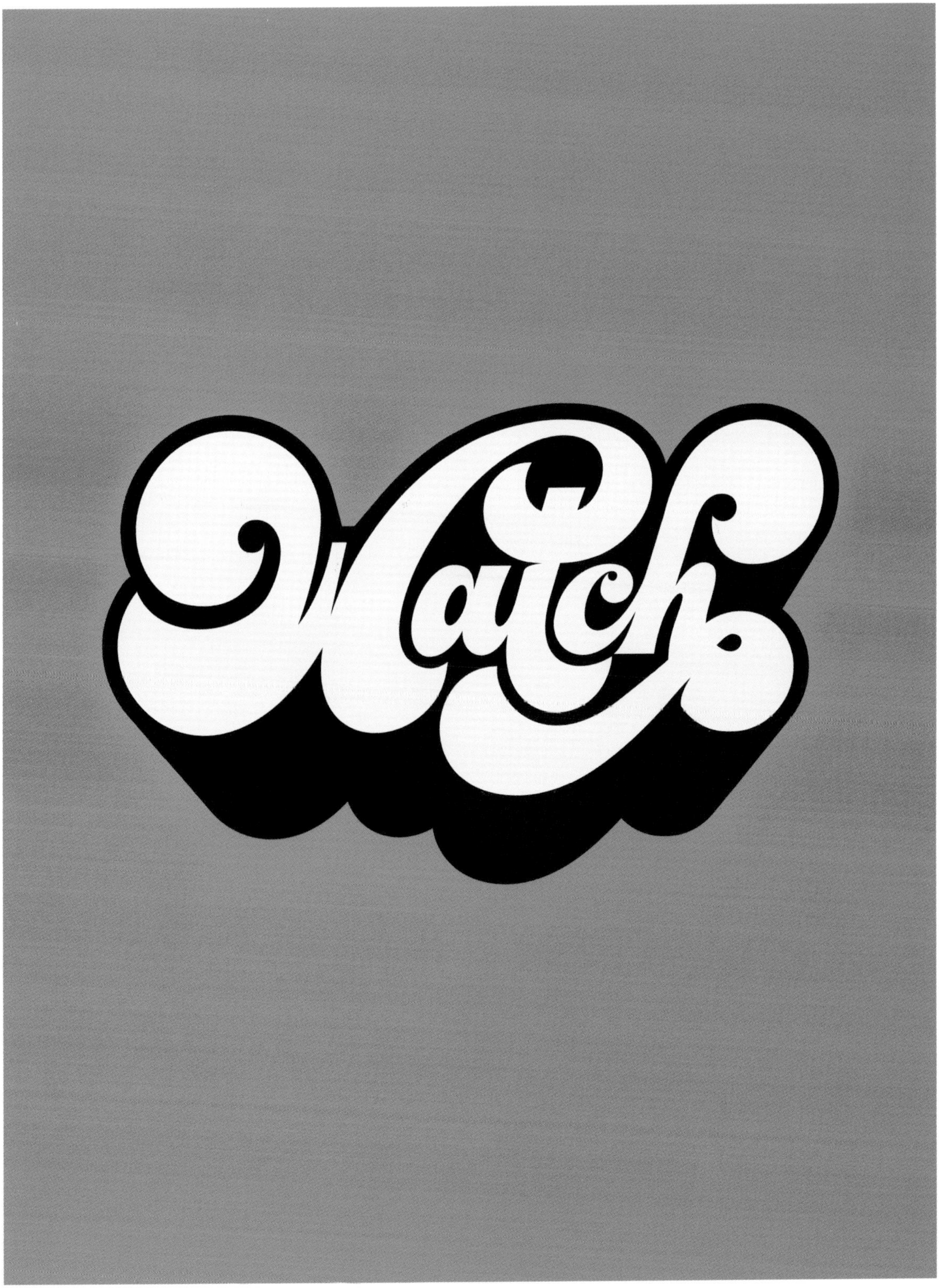
Watch

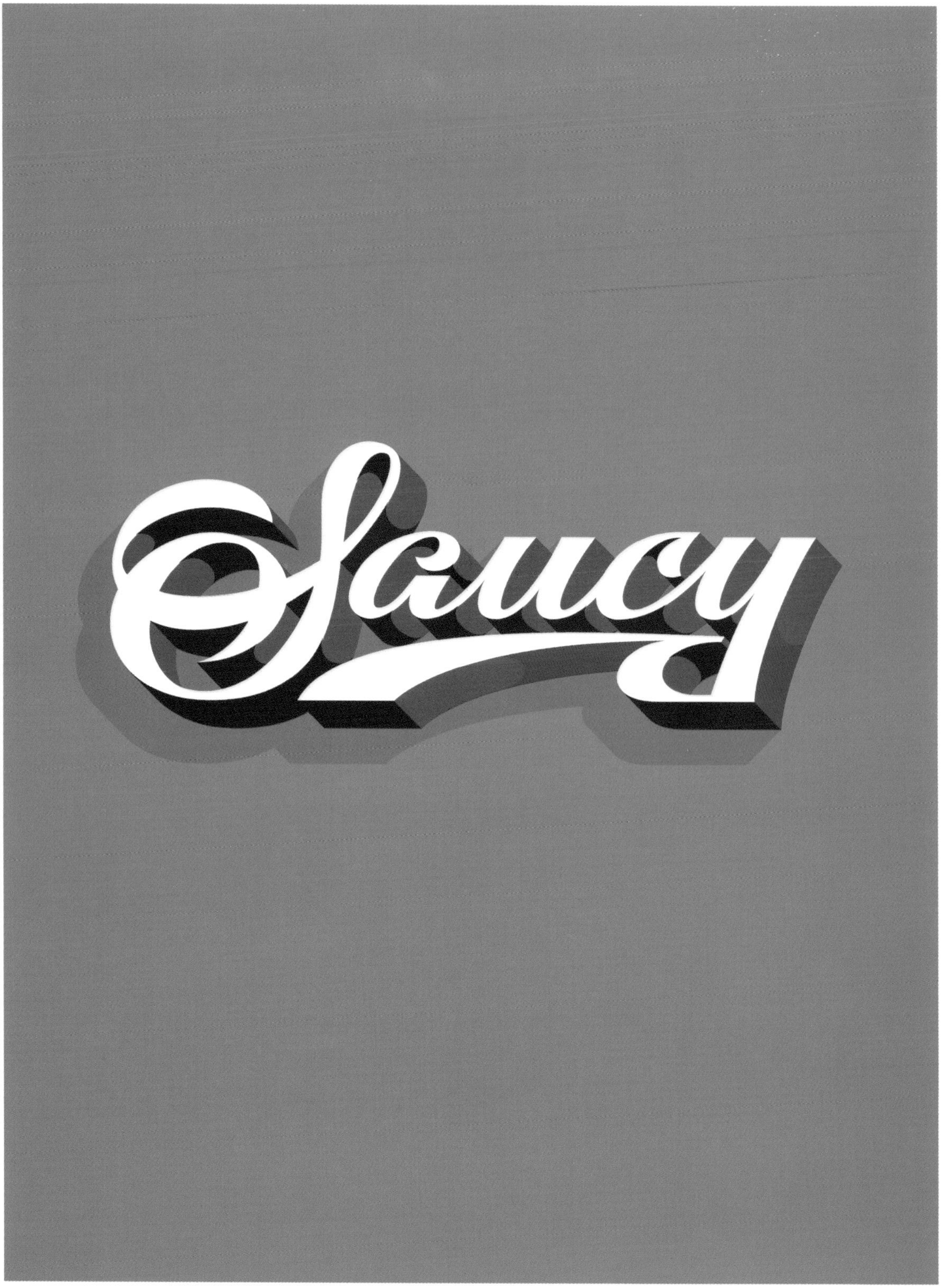
Saucy

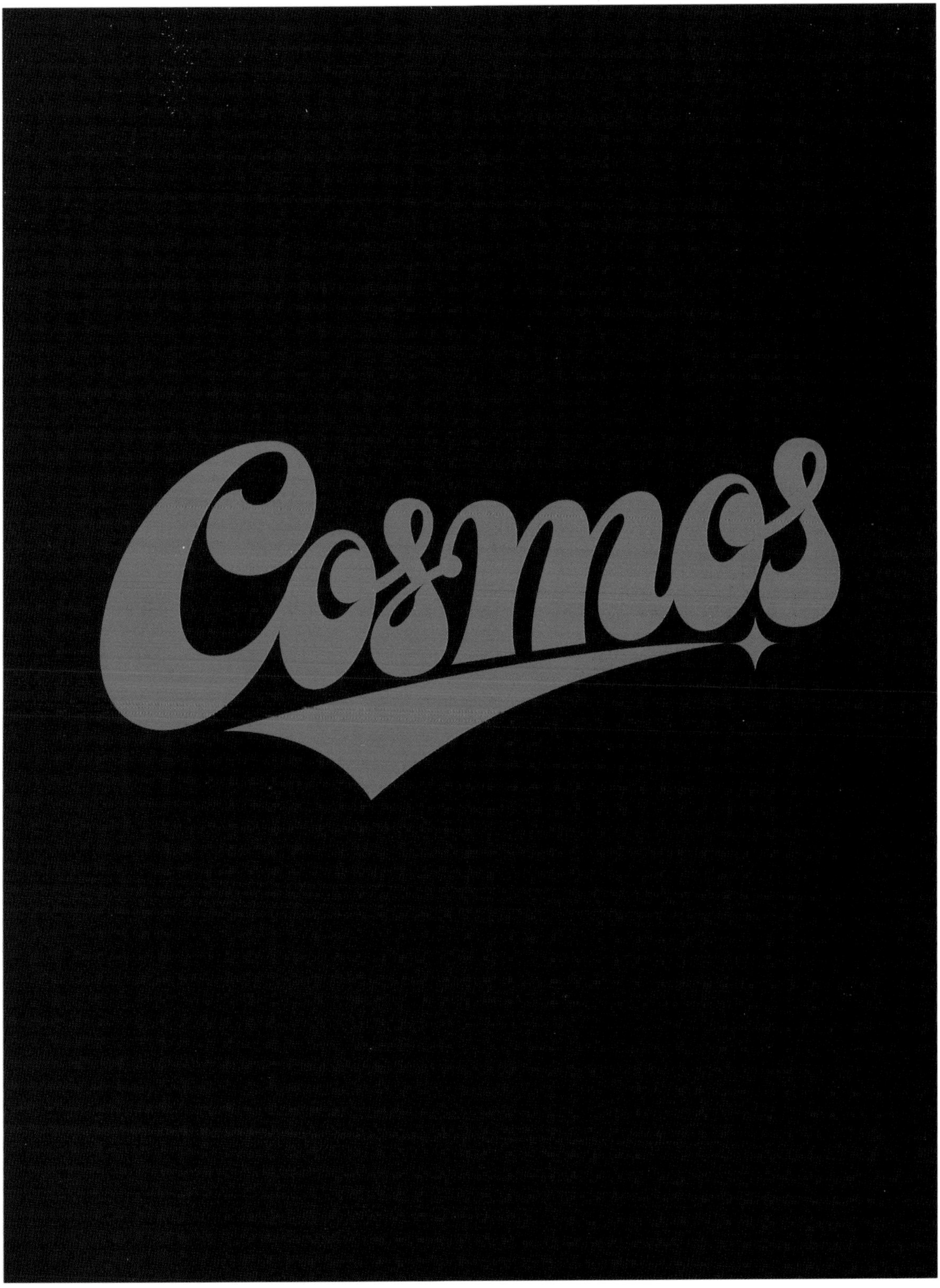
Cosmos

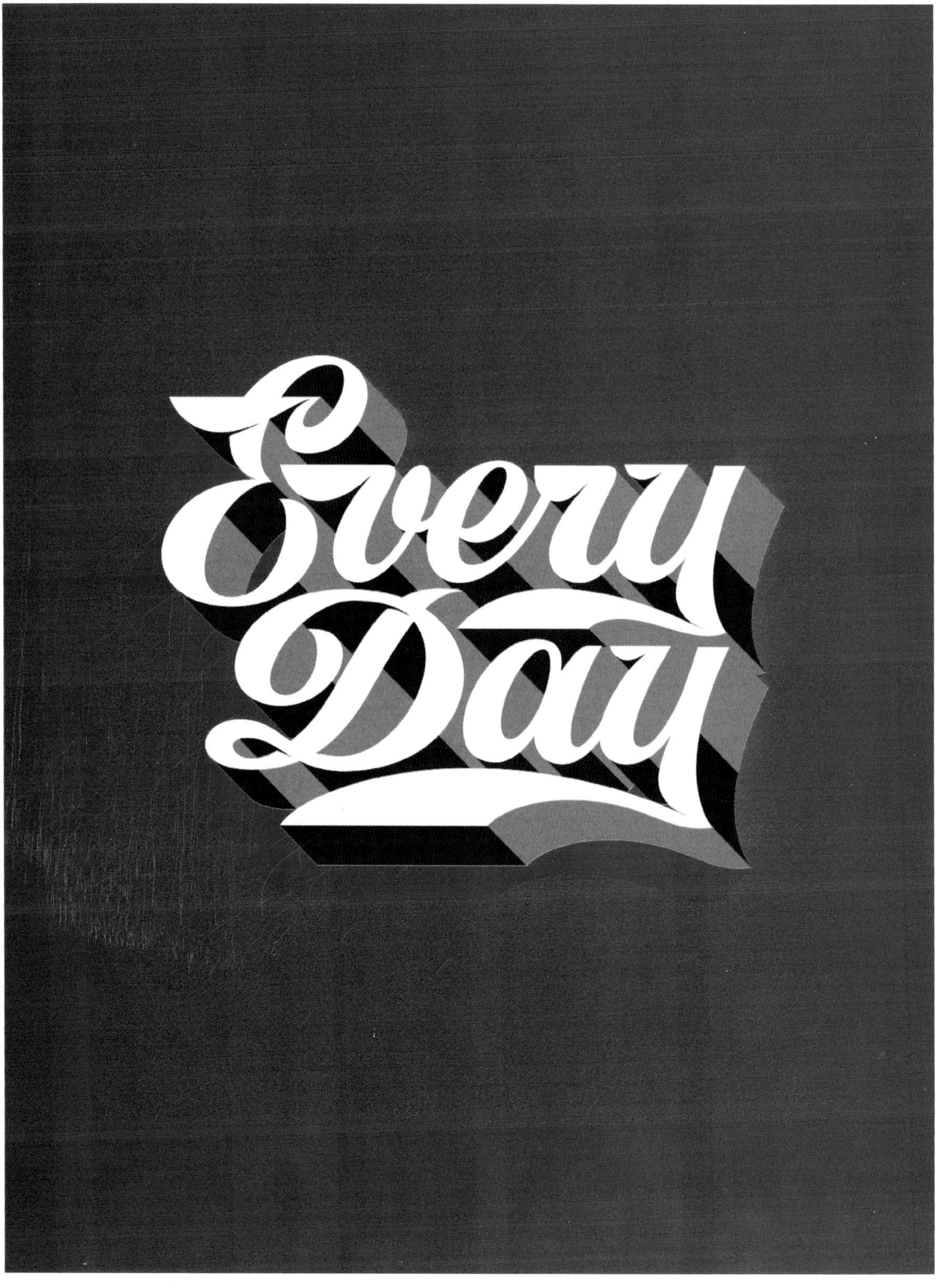
Every
Day

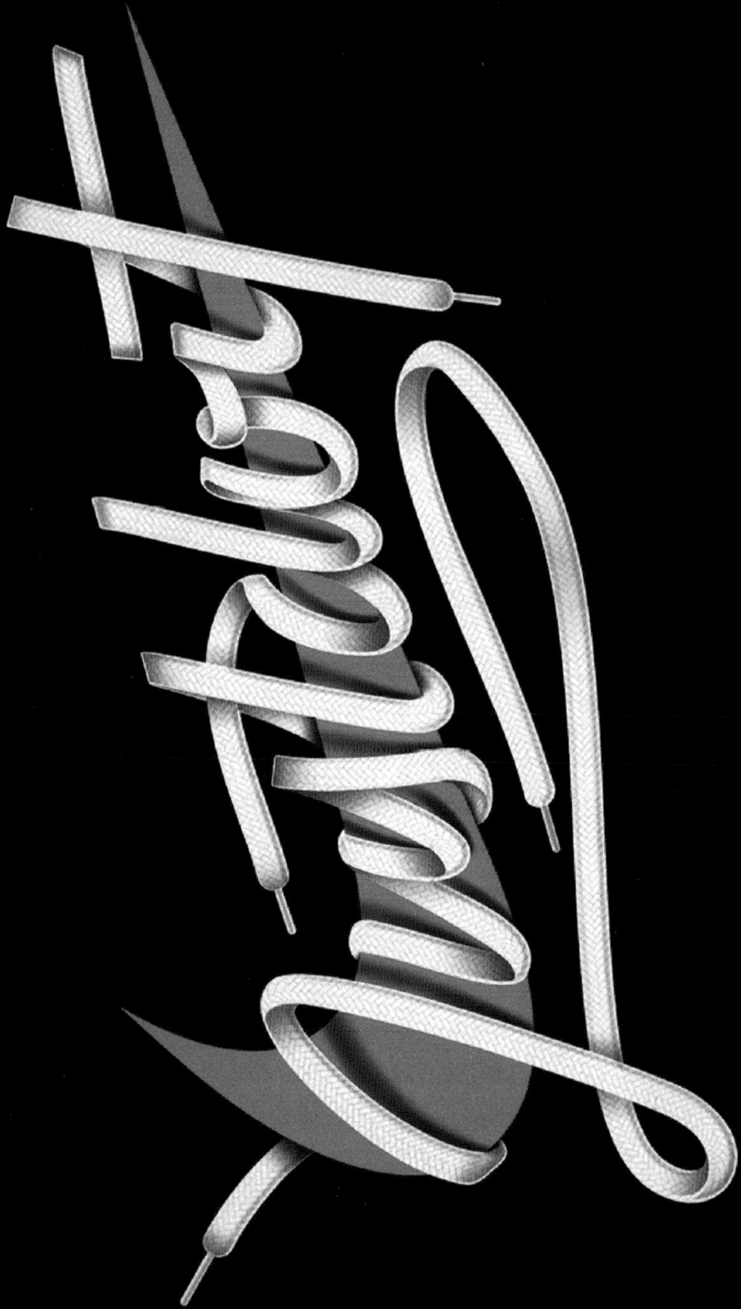

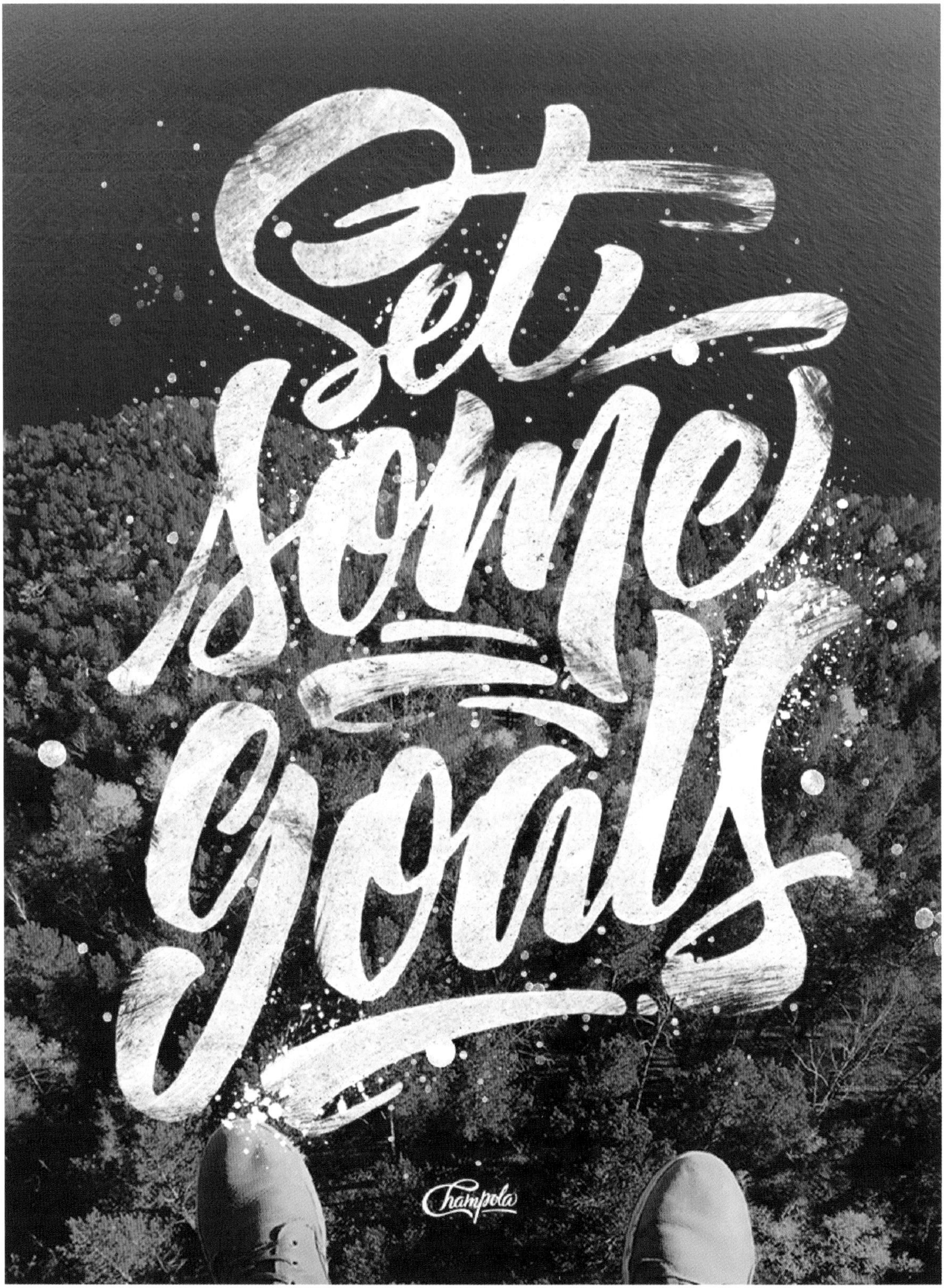
Set some goals
Champola

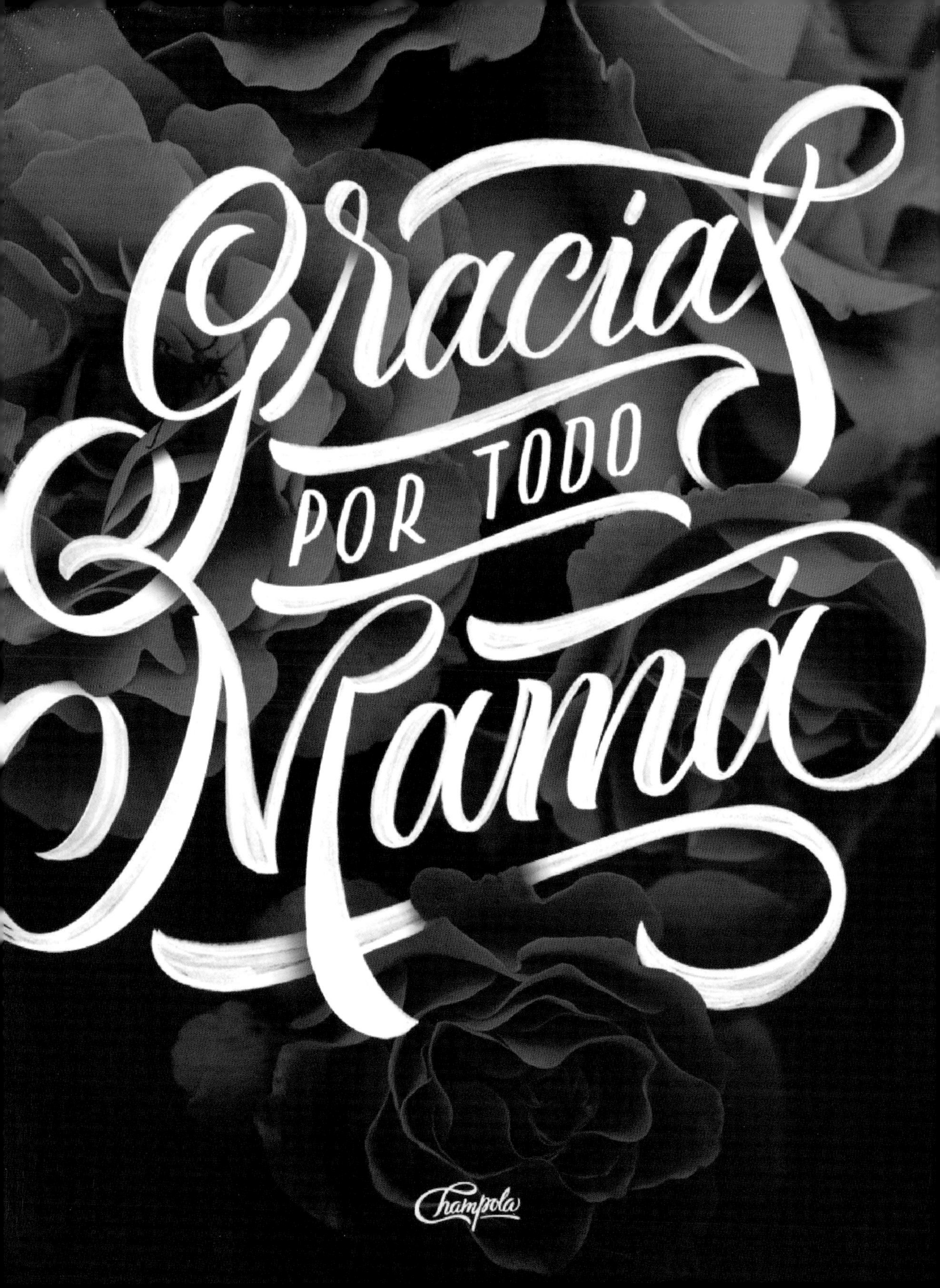
Gracias
POR TODO
Mamá
Champola

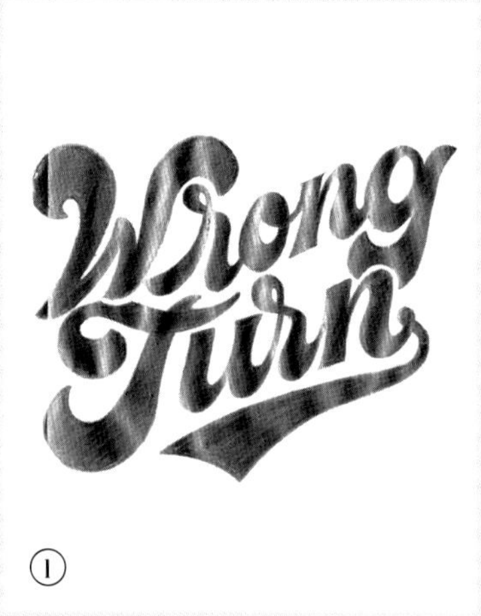

①

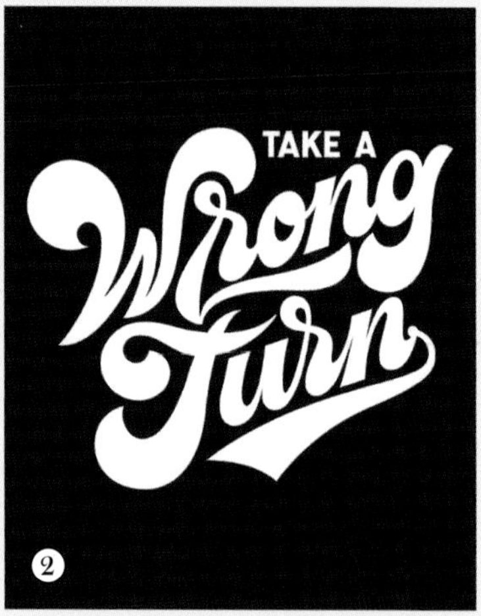

②

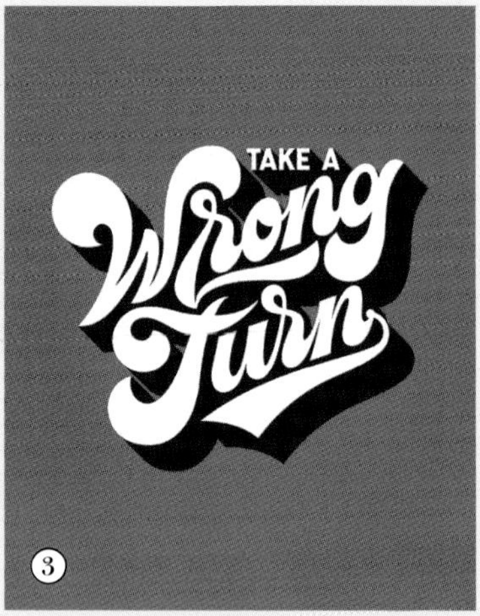

③

Making my lettering

I'd say my lettering process consists in 3 simple things: pencil, paper, computer. Most of the time I don't start working on an idea (for a lettering or a custom type) directly on the screen. Sketches are very important for me because they give me the freedom to let ideas flow unrestricted and I have more control over the strokes and ligatures.

For this lettering, I didn't use too much detail on the sketch because I started working with a very clear idea of how I wanted it to look on Illustrator. When I open a sketch on the software the first thing I do is place my guides and my reference points (in relation to the height and width of my letters). After this, I use the pen tool and redraw the sketch keeping in mind the anchor points. Once I'm done redrawing, I explore the color palette I want to use and start giving the lettering its final touches.

Creando mi lettering

Yo diría que mi proceso de rotulado consta de tres elementos básicos: lápiz, papel y ordenador. Normalmente no suelo empezar trabajando en una idea (para un rótulo o un tipo de línea) directamente sobre la pantalla. Los bocetos me resultan muy importantes porque me dan la libertad de dejar que las ideas fluyan sin restricción y tengo un mayor control sobre los trazos y las ligaduras.

Para este rótulo, no hice un boceto demasiado detallado porque empecé a trabajar con una idea muy clara de cómo quería que quedara en Illustrator. Cuando abro un boceto en el programa, lo primero que hago es colocar mis puntos de referencia (en relación con la altura y la profundidad de las letras). A continuación, utilizo la herramienta de bolígrafo y vuelvo a dibujar el boceto teniendo presentes los puntos de anclaje. Una vez finalizado ese nuevo boceto, exploro la paleta de colores que quiero utilizar y empiezo a darle los retoques finales al rótulo.

TAKE A Wrong Turn

JIMBO BERNAUS

shoutbam.com
instagram: jimbobernaus

Jimbo Bernaus is a letterer and visual designer from Barcelona, Spain. After working for different graphic design studios and agencies, he and his partner Tea Shockats have founded BAM!, a creative studio based in Zagreb, Croatia.

His work has been featured in many international books and well-recognised web pages. At the moment, Jimbo works as an Art Director at BAM! joining his background as a graphic designer with his lettering skills.

Jimbo Bernaus es un rotulista y diseñador visual de Barcelona, España. Después de trabajar para diversos estudios y agencias de diseño, fundó junto con su socio, Tea Shockats, BAM!, un estudio creativo con sede en Zagreb, Croacia.

Sus obras aparecen en muchos libros internacionales y webs de prestigio. Actualmente, Jimbo es Director Artístico de BAM!, aunando su experiencia como diseñador gráfico con sus habilidades como rotulista.

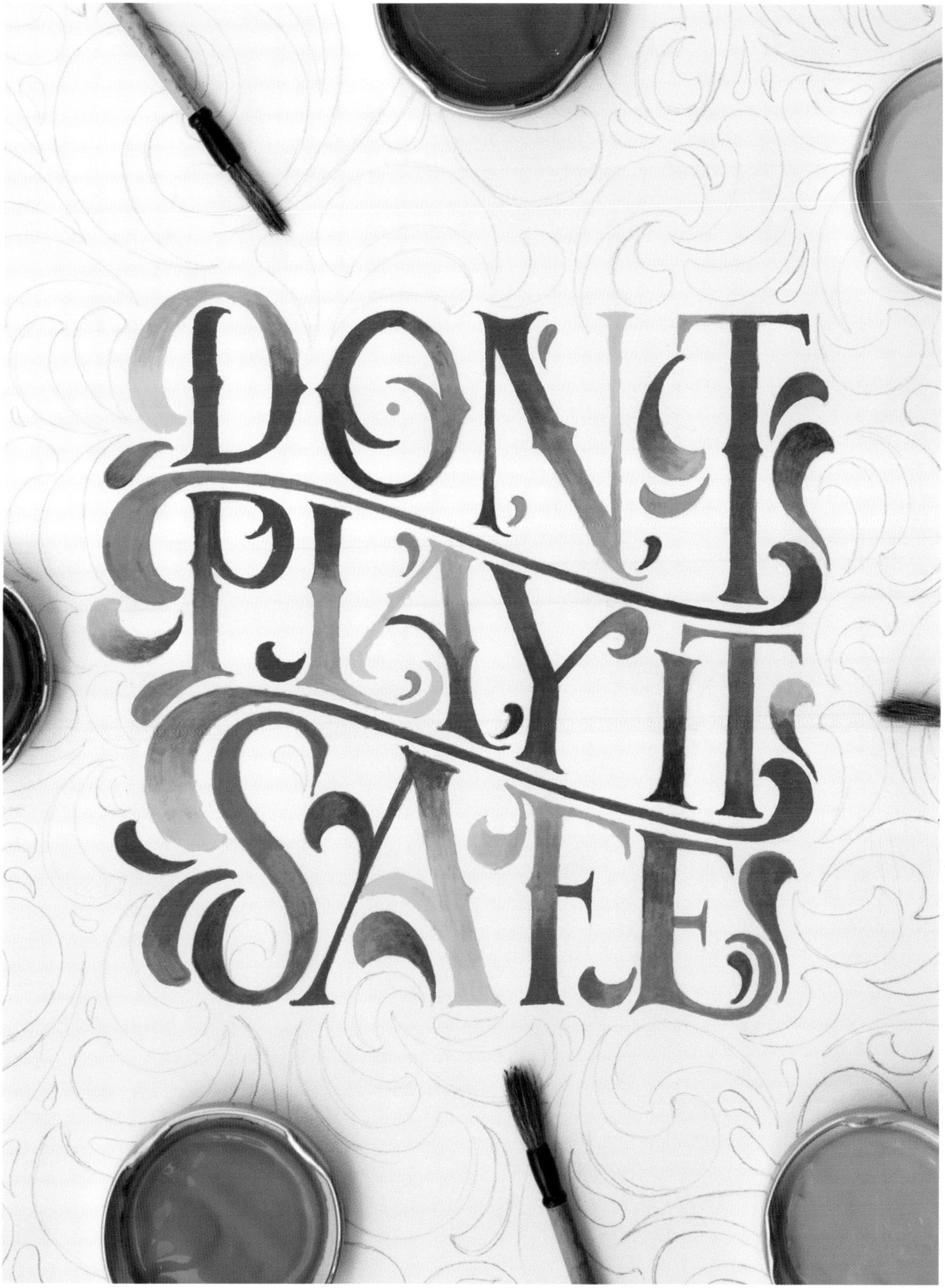
DON'T
PLAY IT
SAFE

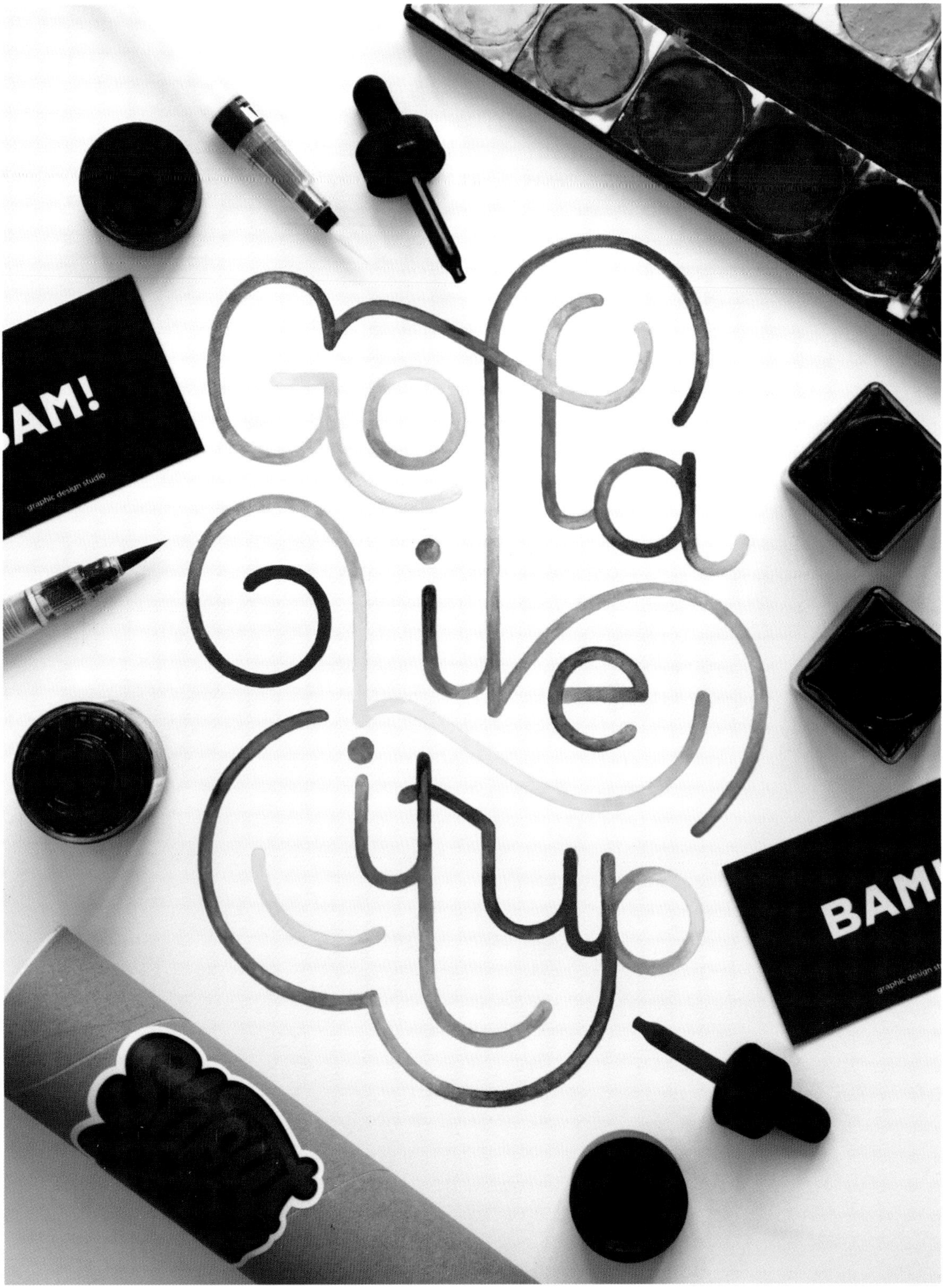
Gotta live it up
BAM!
graphic design studio

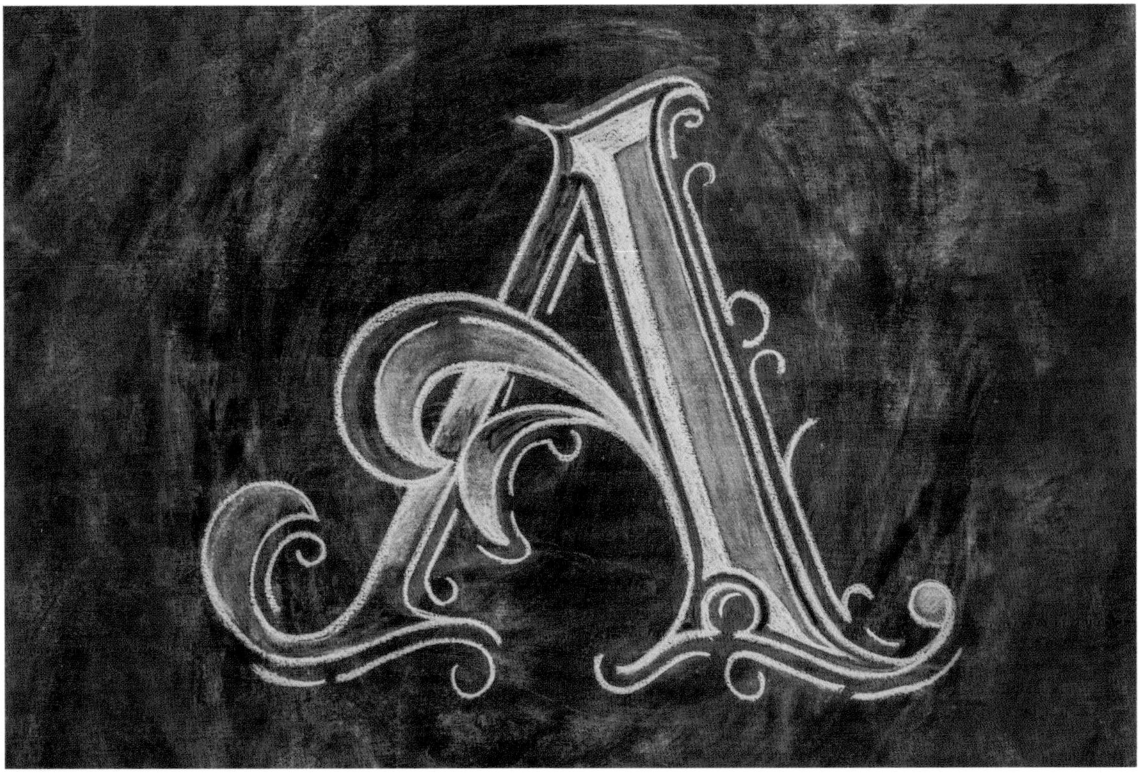

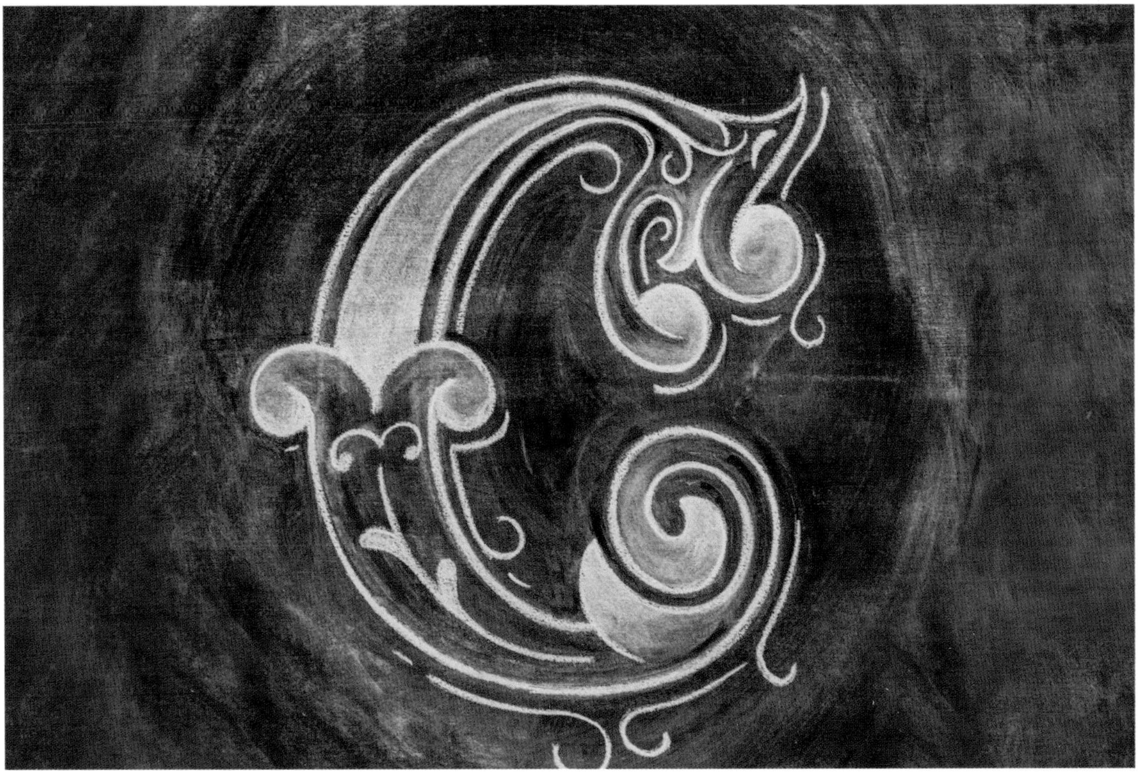

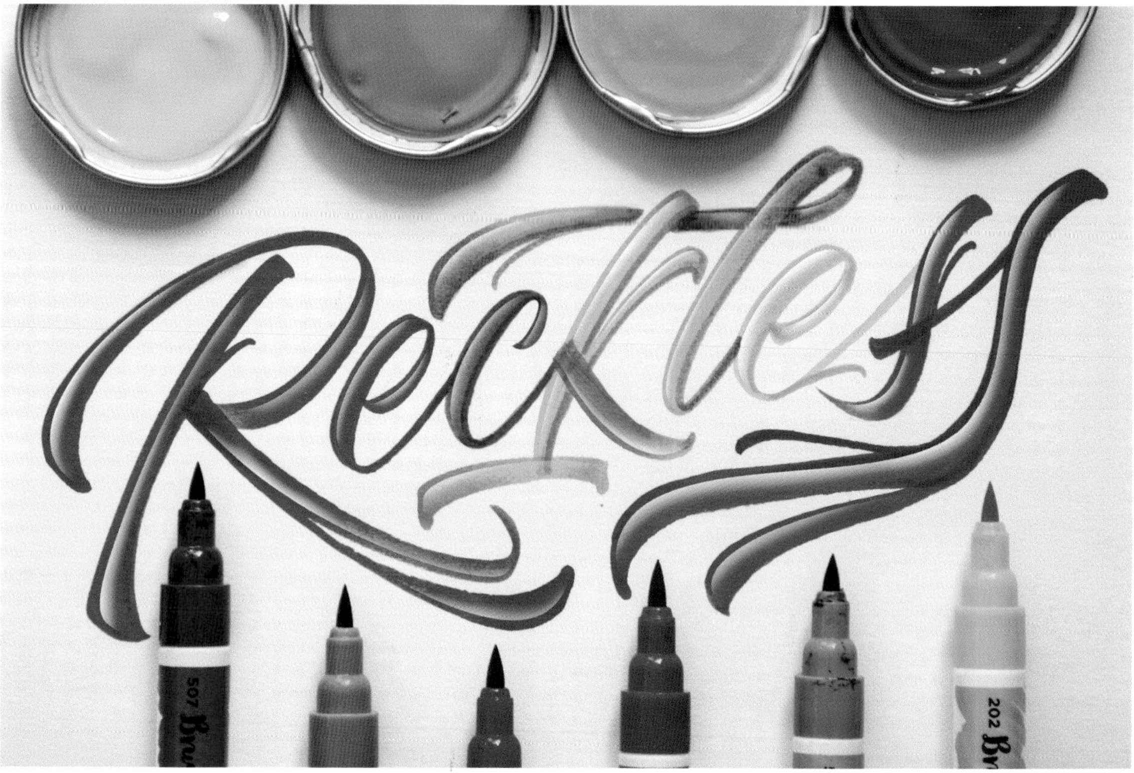
Reckless
507
202

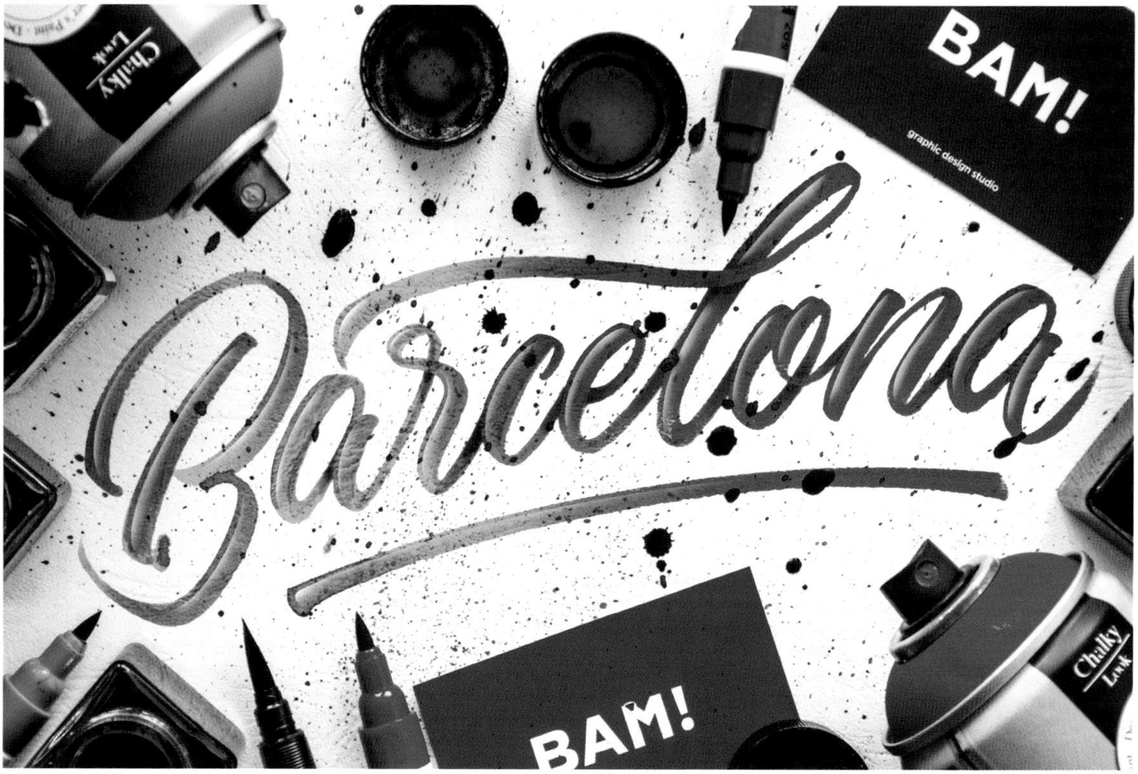
Barcelona
BAM!
graphic design studio
BAM!
Chalky Link
Chalky Link

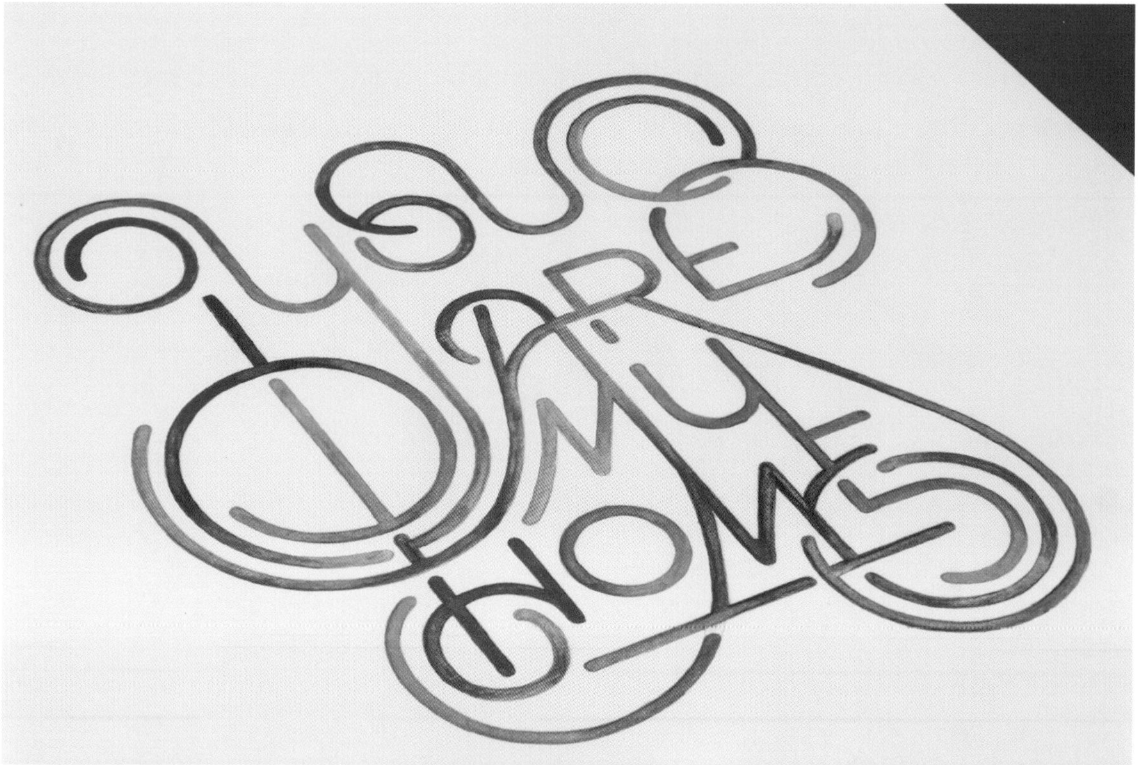

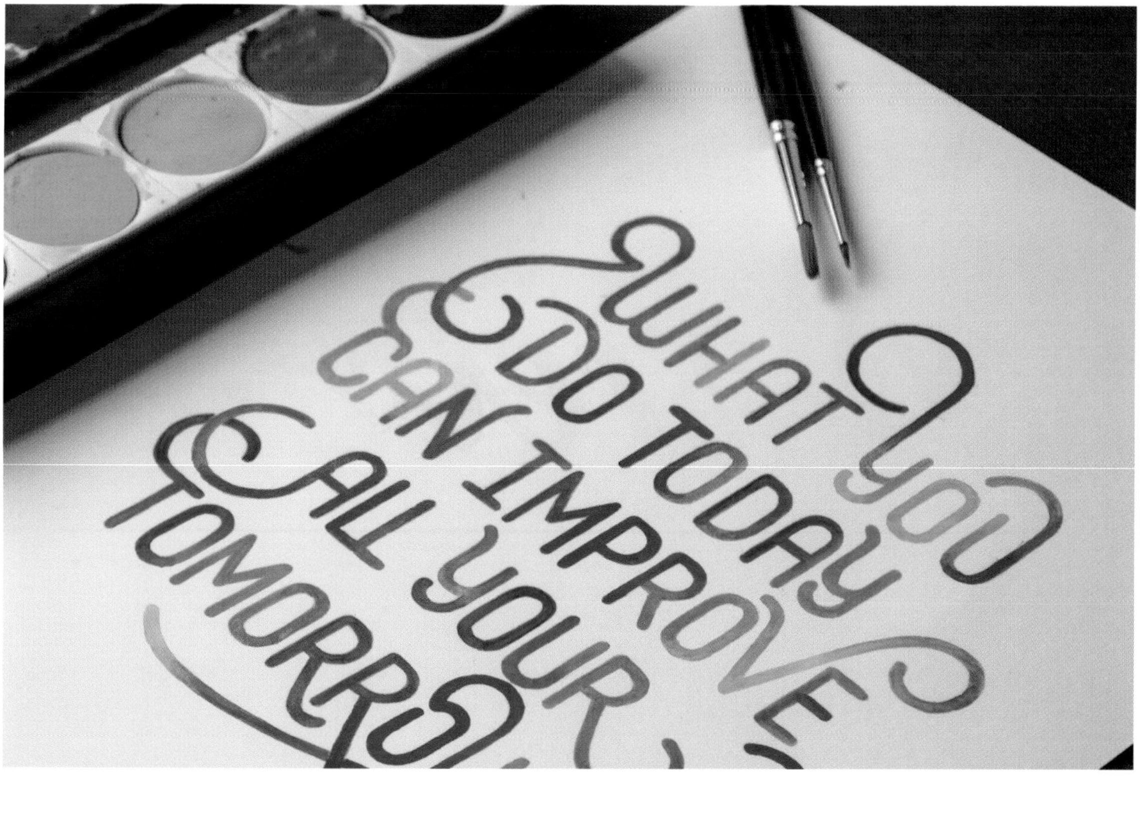
WHAT YOU
DO TODAY
CAN IMPROVE
ALL YOUR

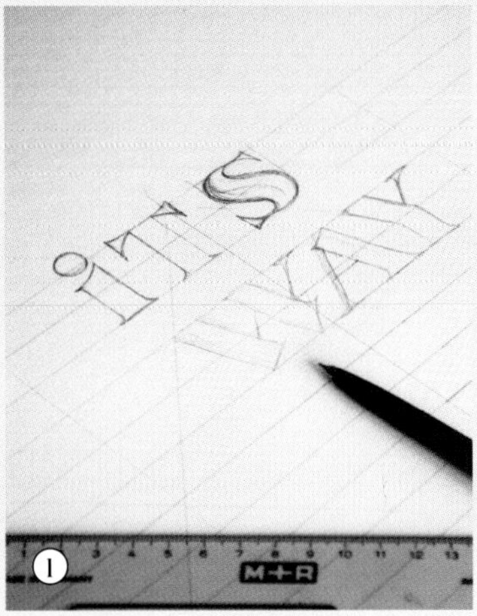

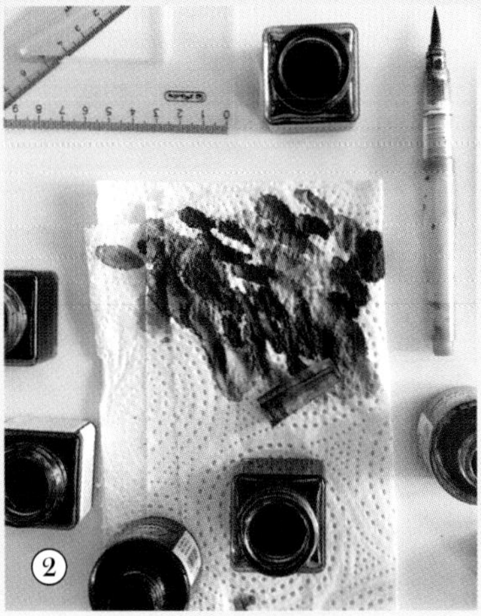

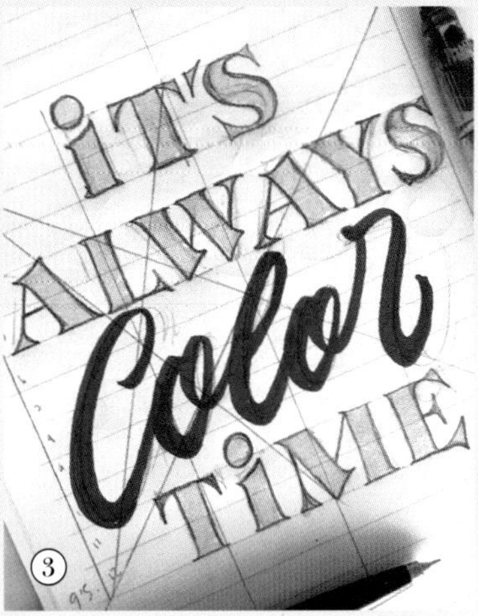

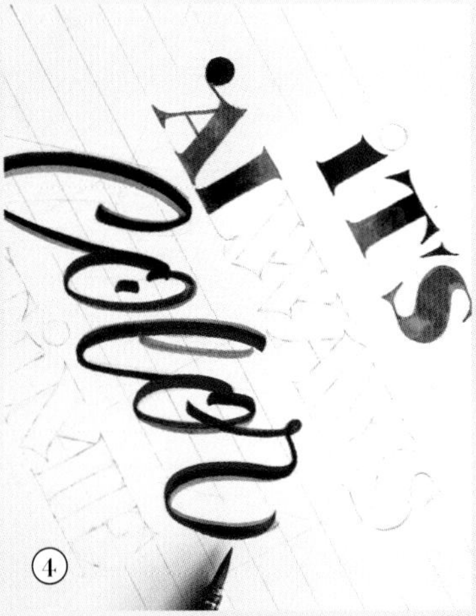

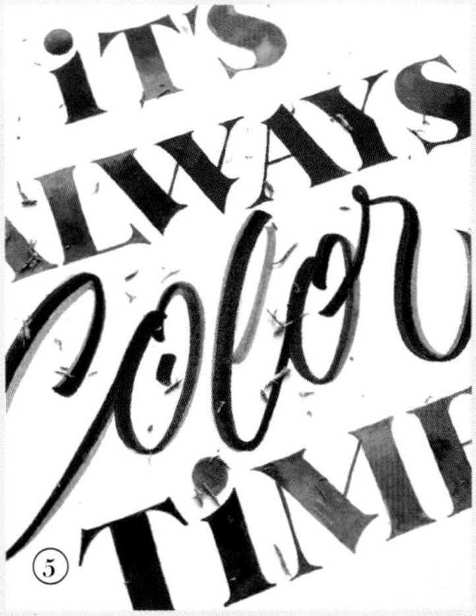

Making my lettering

Every time I do a hand lettered piece I like to experiment using different processes and styles. Starting with very rough sketches I can get the feeling of words, study the style and see what ligatures will suit the artwork perfectly.

In concerned artwork I'm using a basic structure that follows the client's brief. Once I have the letters and its guidelines on a notebook, I transfer the piece onto a larger paper drawing thin lines with a pencil.

This part decides how clean the piece is gonna look like. Lastly I study the color palette I'm going to use and pick the materials and brushes that will work the best. Since the client has given me total freedom regarding the final look, I decided to experiment with gradients and textures using my favourite color scheme.

Creando mi lettering

Cada vez que hago un rótulo a mano, me gusta experimentar y utilizar diversos procesos y estilos. Empezando con bocetos muy aproximados, comienzo a sentir las palabras, a estudiar el estilo y a ver qué ligaduras encajan mejor con la obra.

En esta obra utilizo una estructura básica que se ajusta a las indicaciones del cliente. Cuando ya tengo las letras y sus instrucciones en el cuaderno, paso la composición a un papel más grande, trazando líneas finas con un lápiz.

Esta parte es la que determina hasta qué punto la pieza va a presentar un aspecto limpio. Por último, estudio la paleta de colores que voy a emplear y elijo los materiales y pinceles más convenientes. Como el cliente me dio total libertad para el resultado final, decidí experimentar con gradientes y texturas utilizando mi esquema de colores preferido.

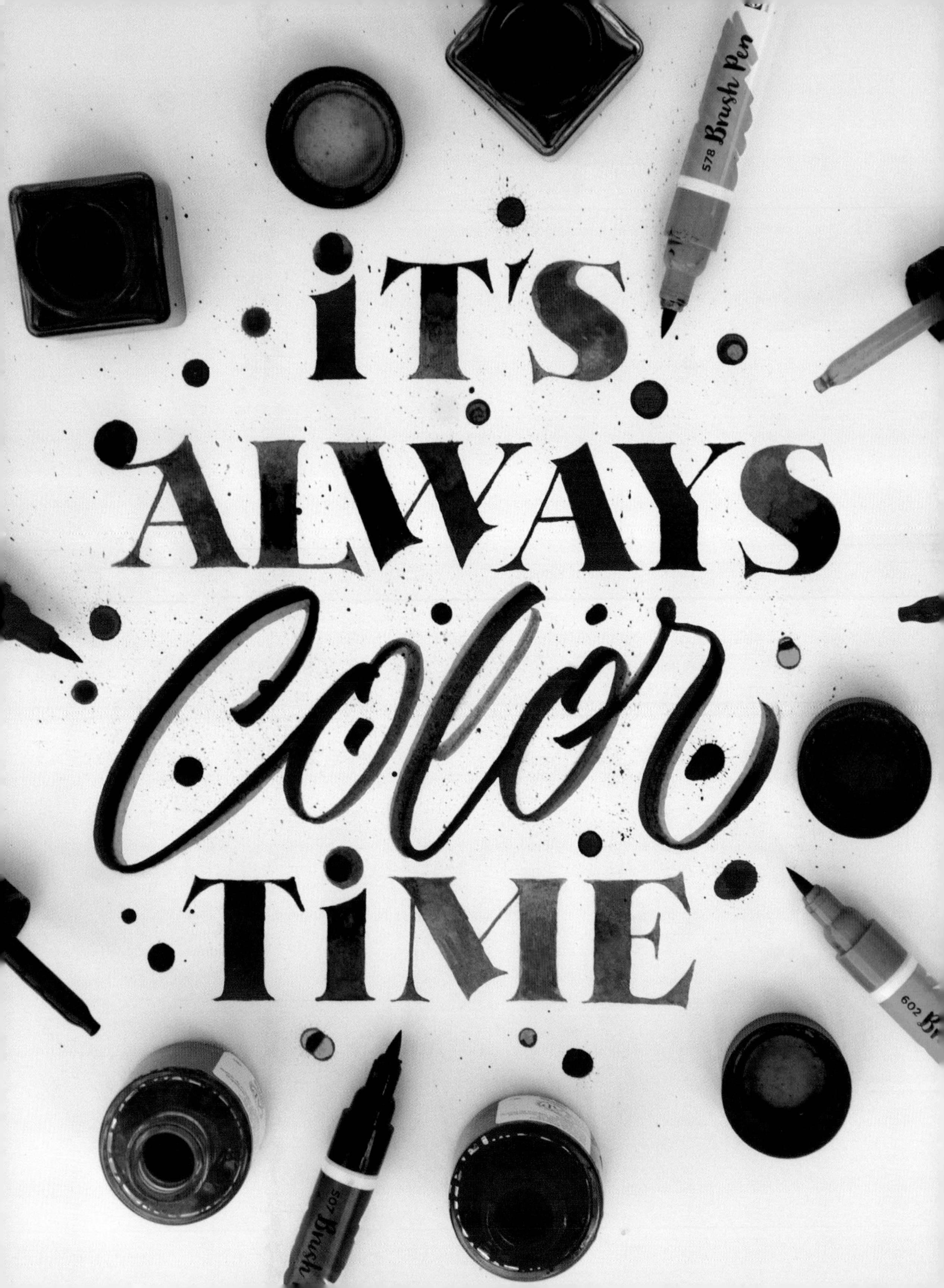
IT'S
ALWAYS
Color
TIME
578 Brush Pen
507 Brush

SAMMIE HO

www.sammieho.com

Sammie Ho is a digital designer and type nerd born and raised in Sydney, Australia. Her love for typography started at a young age, when she was given a lettering book for her birthday. She would hand draw birthday cards and posters, and experiment with different kinds of fonts. During school she would doodle words on her notepad.

She studied design and communications at college, where she developed her skills in custom lettering and type design. Over the years she has broadened her range of typography skills by going to workshops in calligraphy and sign-painting.

What she loves about hand lettering is that it is unique to the artist. You control your letters, your spaces, and your swashes when you draw letterforms. The freedom to be able to put your own personality into lettering makes it a type of signature.

Sammie Ho es una diseñadora digital y amante de la tipografía nacida y criada en Sídney, Australia. Su pasión por la tipografía le llegó siendo muy pequeña, cuando le regalaron por su cumpleaños un libro de rotulación. Dibujaba pósteres y tarjetas de cumpleaños a mano, experimentando con distintos tipos de fuentes; y cuando estaba en el colegio, garabateaba palabras en el cuaderno.

Sammie estudió diseño y comunicaciones en la universidad, donde desarrolló sus habilidades en el ámbito de la rotulación a medida y el diseño tipográfico. Con el paso de los años ha ido ampliando su abanico de destrezas tipográficas asistiendo a talleres sobre caligrafía y rotulado.

Lo que más le gusta de la rotulación a mano es que es exclusiva de cada artista, que es el que controla las letras, los espacios y las salpicaduras cuando dibuja. La libertad de que el artista pueda volcar su propia personalidad en el rótulo lo convierte en una especie de firma característica.

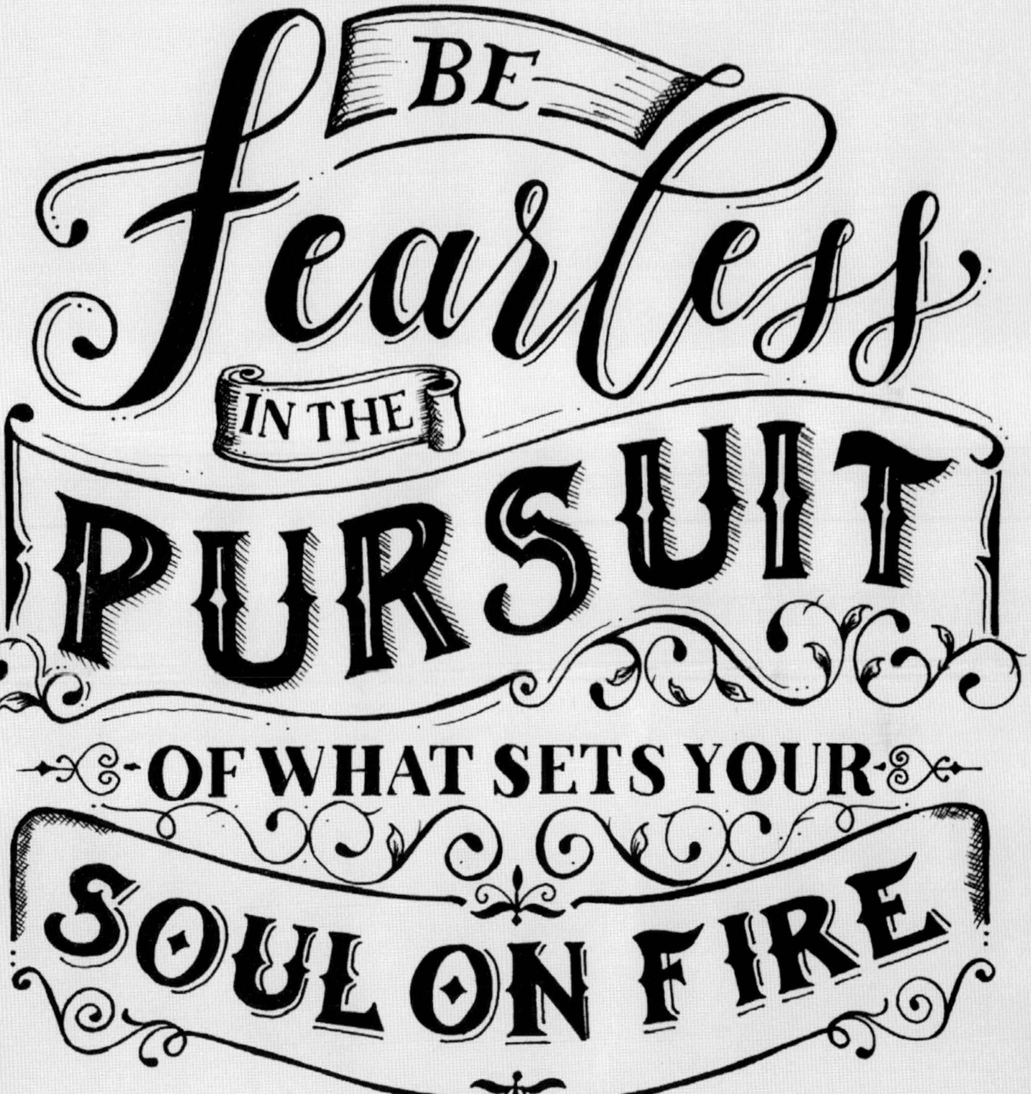
Be
Fearless
in the
Pursuit
of what sets your
Soul on Fire

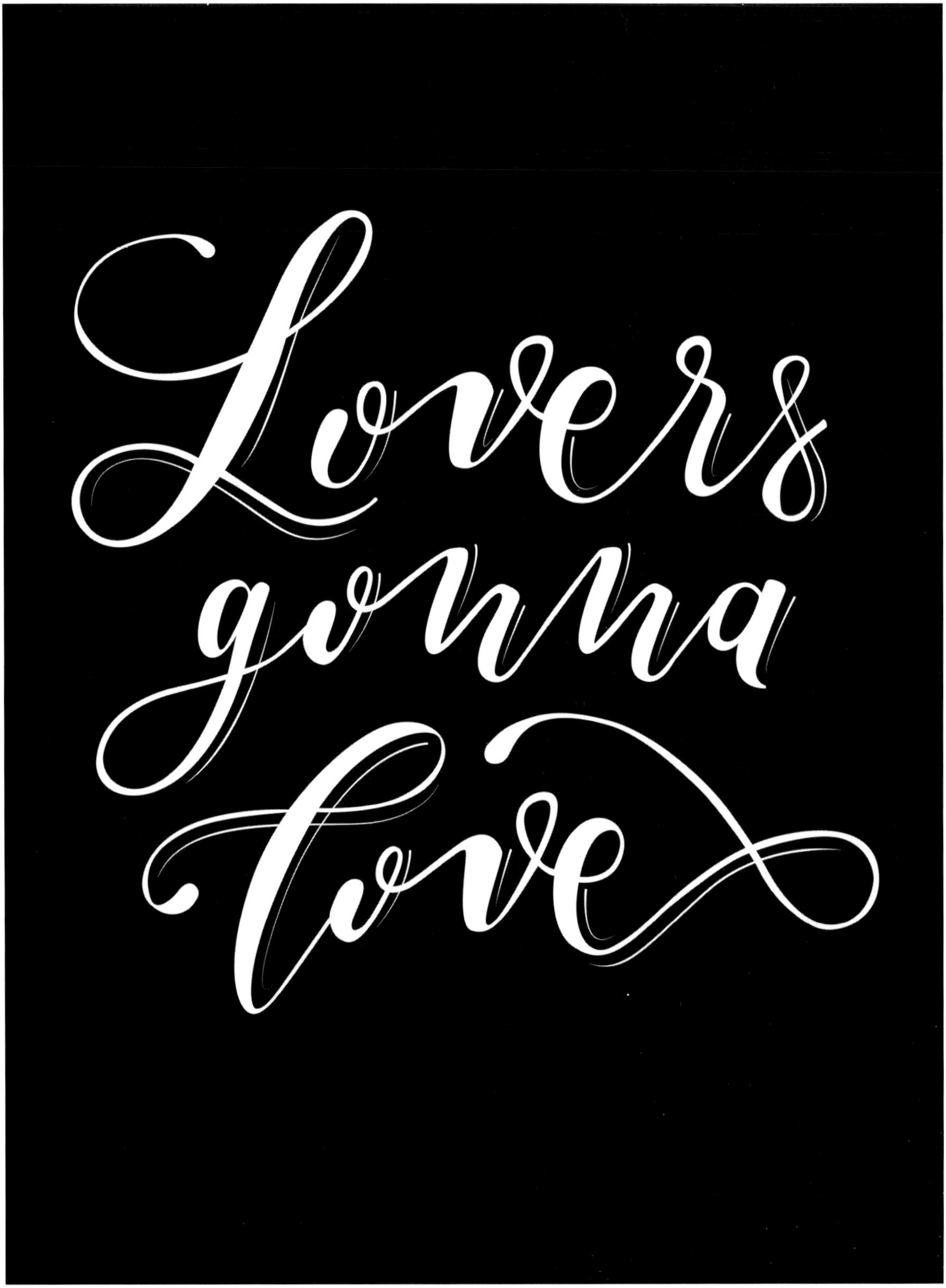
Lovers
gonna
love

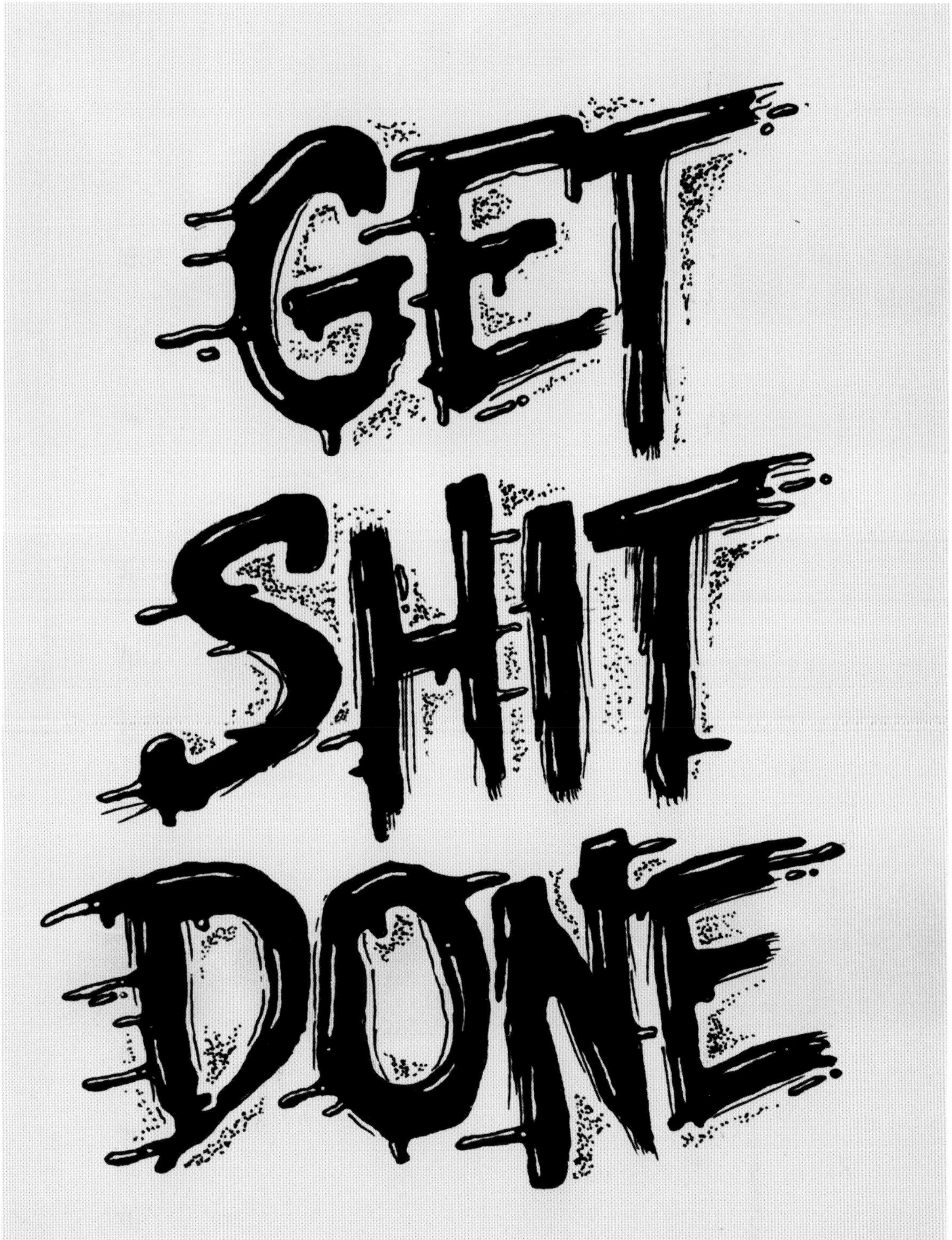
GET
SHIT
DONE

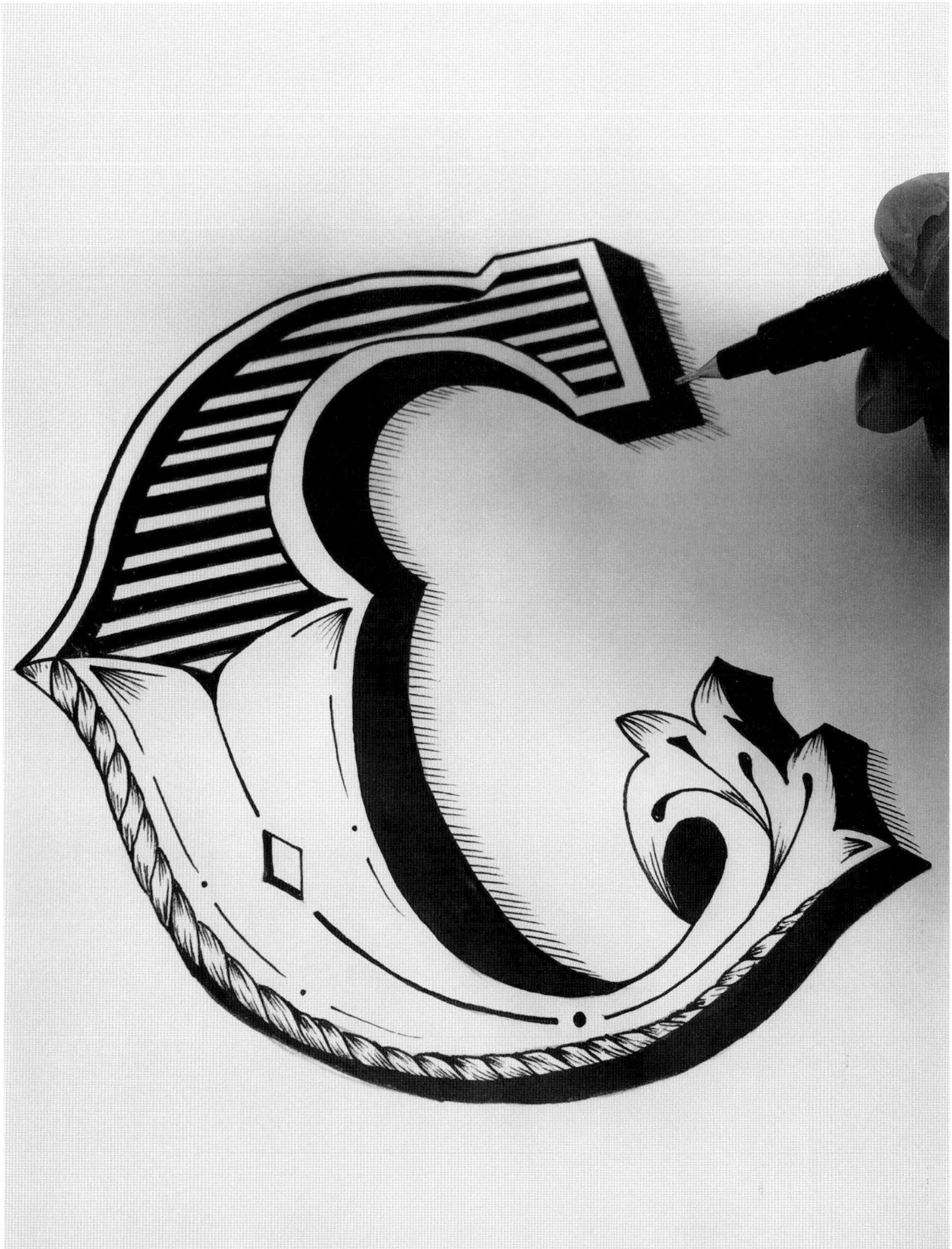

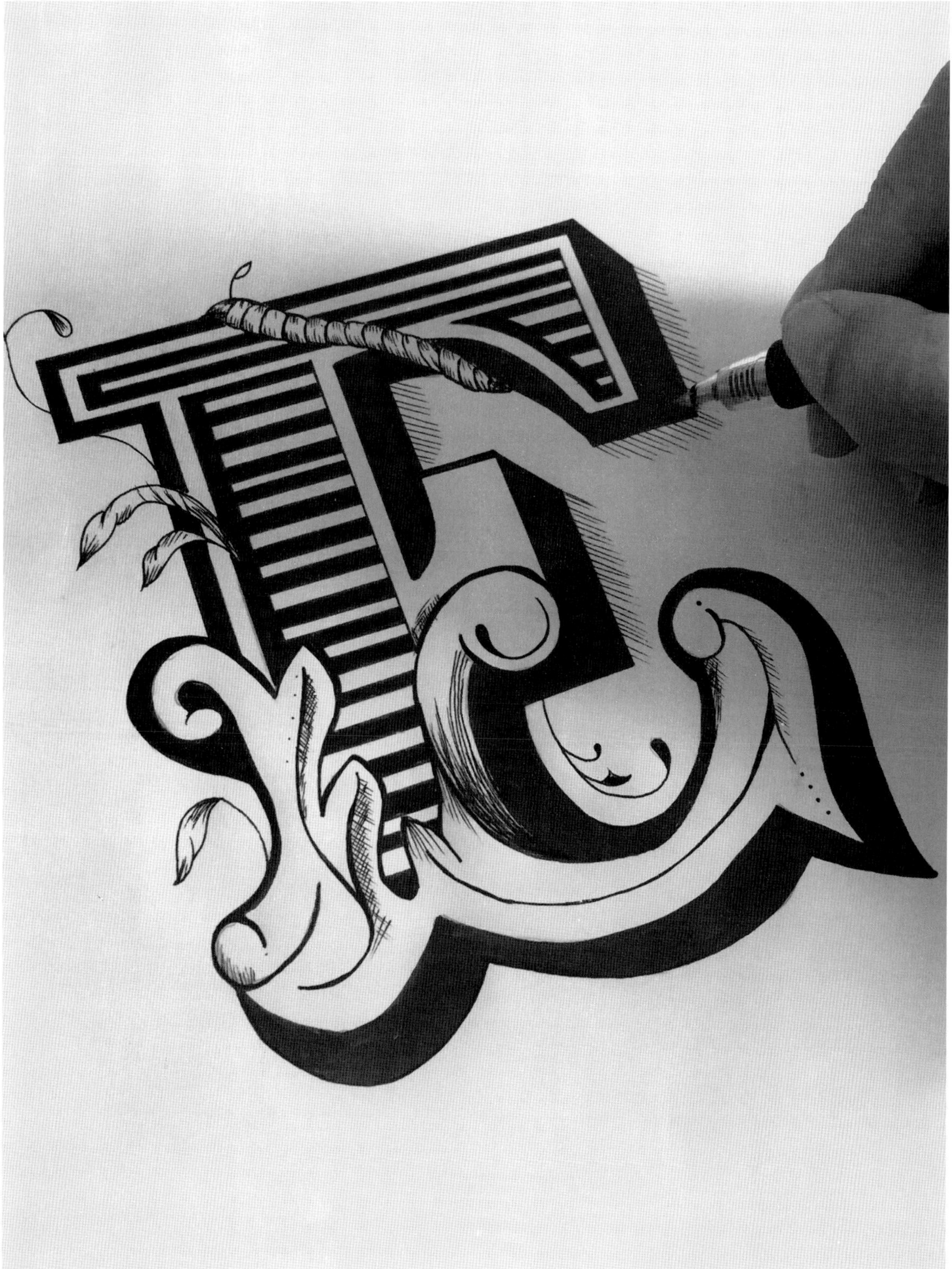

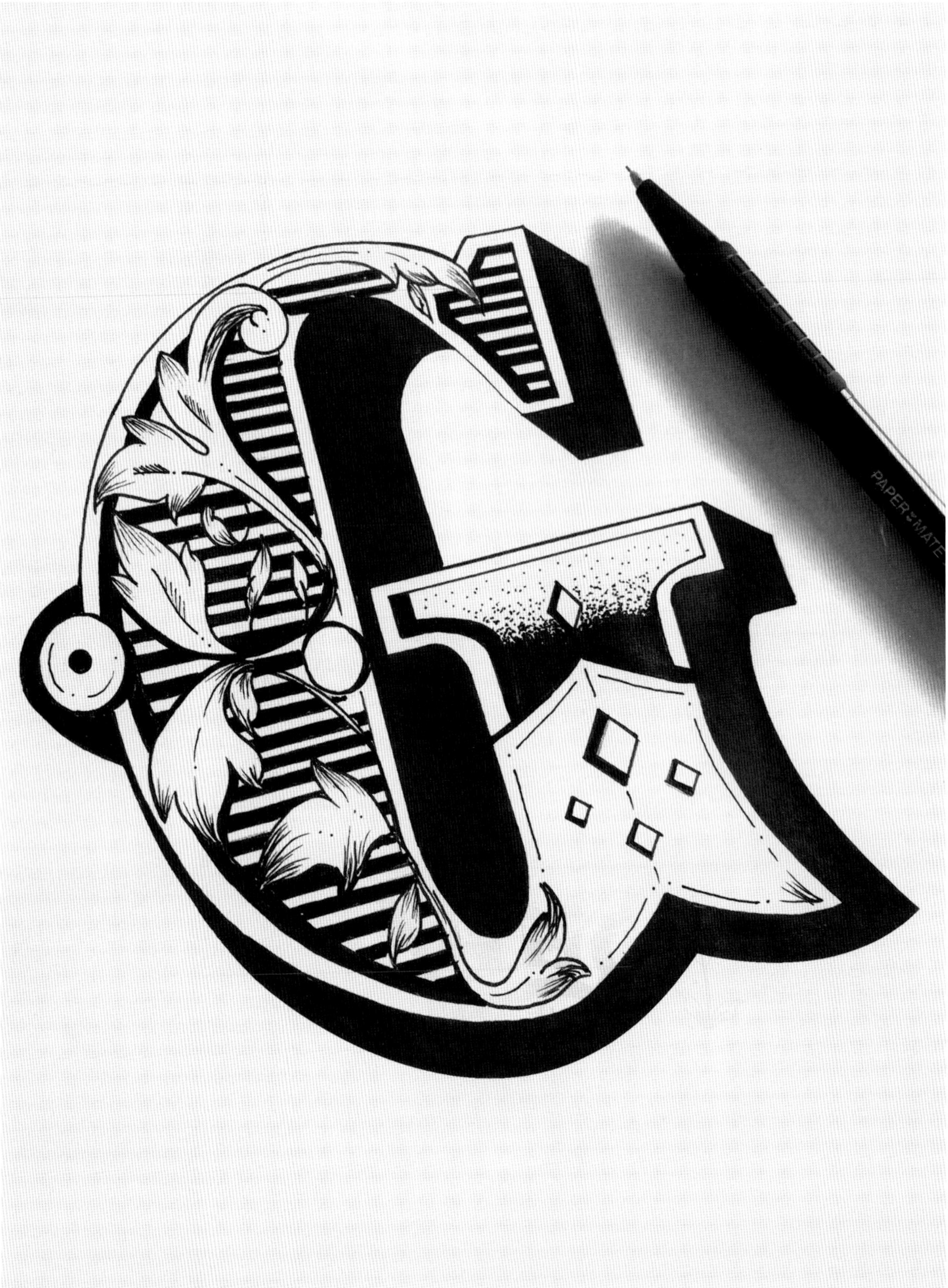
PAPER MATE

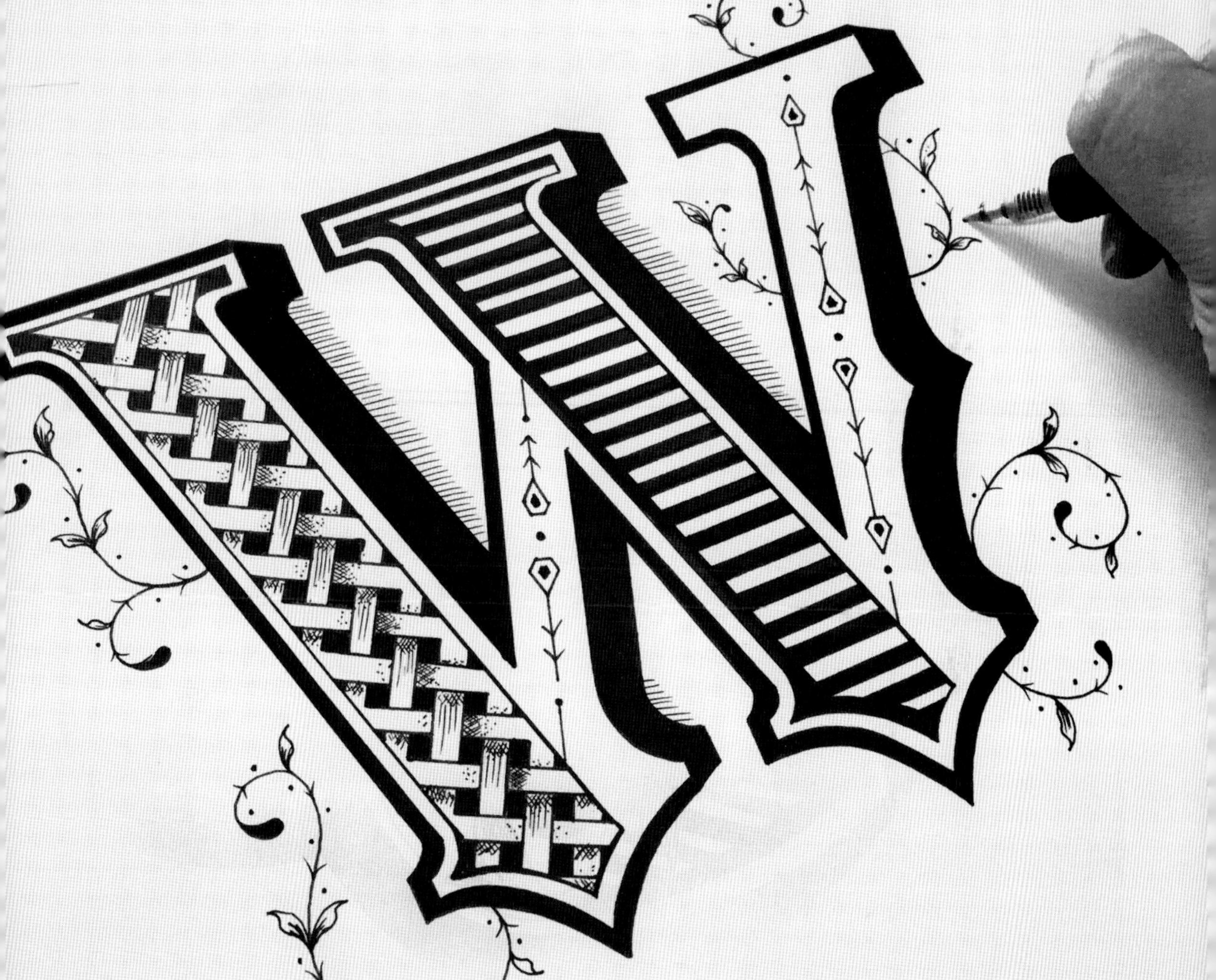

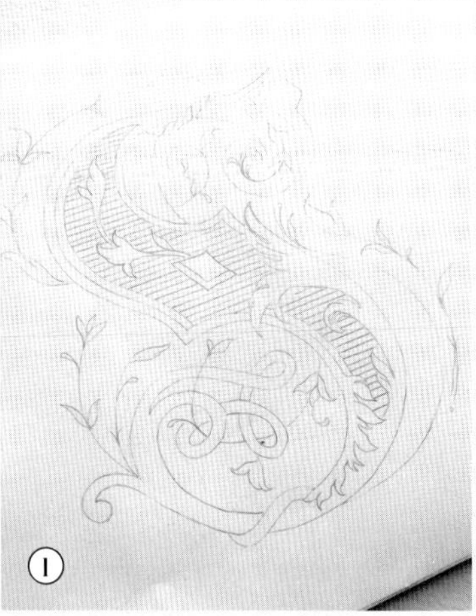

①

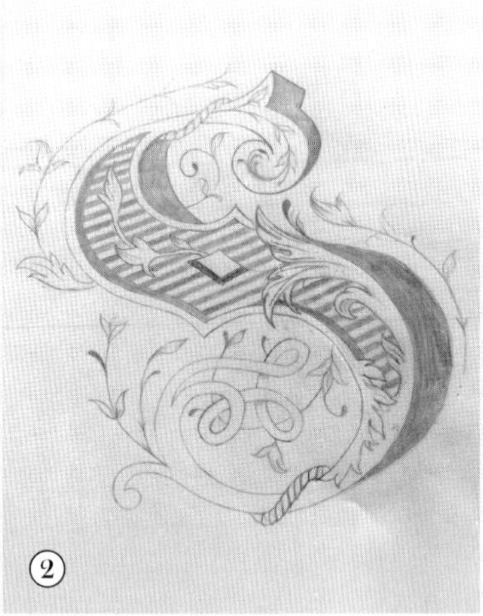

②

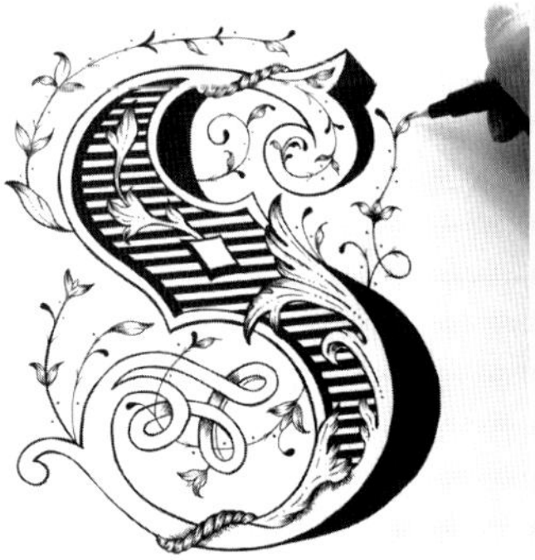

③

Making my lettering

My process always starts with pencil to paper. I love sketching things out freely and experimenting with flows and how the letters all fit together. Once I'm happy with the layout, I fill it in and start adding details. Then I trace it and fill it out with ink. I then scan the work and re-draw it in Illustrator to get a digitised version, where I can explore even further with colours, textures and shadows. I enjoy the blend of traditional freehand work with digital elements.

Creando mi lettering

Mi proceso siempre empieza dibujando con lápiz sobre papel. Me encanta hacer bocetos con total libertad y experimentar con los flujos para ver cómo encajan las letras las unas con las otras. Cuando consigo un resultado satisfactorio, empiezo a completarlo y a añadir detalles. Luego lo trazo y lo paso a tinta. Después escaneo la obra y la vuelvo a dibujar en Illustrator para generar una versión digitalizada en la que puedo jugar aún más con colores, sombras y texturas. Me gusta la mezcla de trabajo tradicional a mano y elementos digitales.

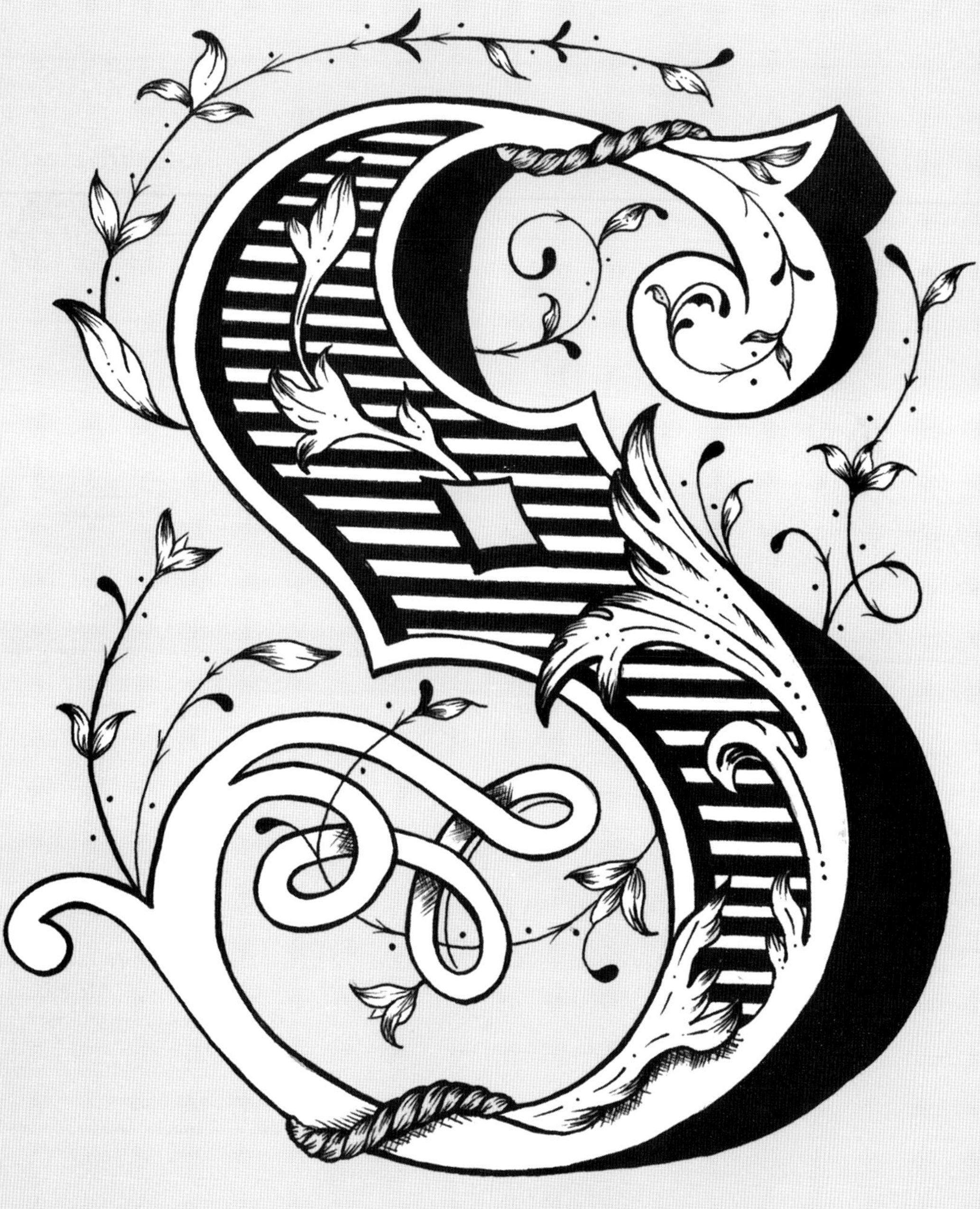

JOEL FELIX

www.joelfelix.com

Joel Felix is a graphic designer and typographer living in Northern California, and is passionate about letters and all things design. He can often be found in his one-man studio sketching out work for a variety of clients, including Jack Daniel's, the San Francisco 49ers, Coach, Sports Illustrated, and many local and national publications. Joel specializes in lettering, logo and identity work, packaging and custom illustration. His work has been featured in Communication Arts magazine, Typism books and a variety of online galleries.

Joel Felix es un tipógrafo y diseñador gráfico con residencia en el norte de California y apasionado por las letras y el diseño de cualquier cosa. Suele pasar el tiempo en su estudio haciendo bocetos para distintos clientes, como Jack Daniel's, los 49ers de San Francisco, Coach, Sports Illustrated y muchas publicaciones locales y nacionales. Joel está especializado en rótulos, logos, trabajos identitarios, empaquetado e ilustraciones a medida. Sus obras han sido expuestas en la revista Communication Arts, en los libros de Typism y en diversas galerías online.

WLT

WORLD LITERATURE TODAY

10 MILESTONES of A DECADE IN CRIME WRITING

THE NSK NEUSTADT PRIZE

For Children's Literature

CELEBRATING The FIRST TEN YEARS

Plus → NATIVE LIT IN THE 21ST CENTURY

WRITERS FROM AUSTRALIA, ERITREA, MONGOLIA & MORE

$4.95 US / £3.25 UK

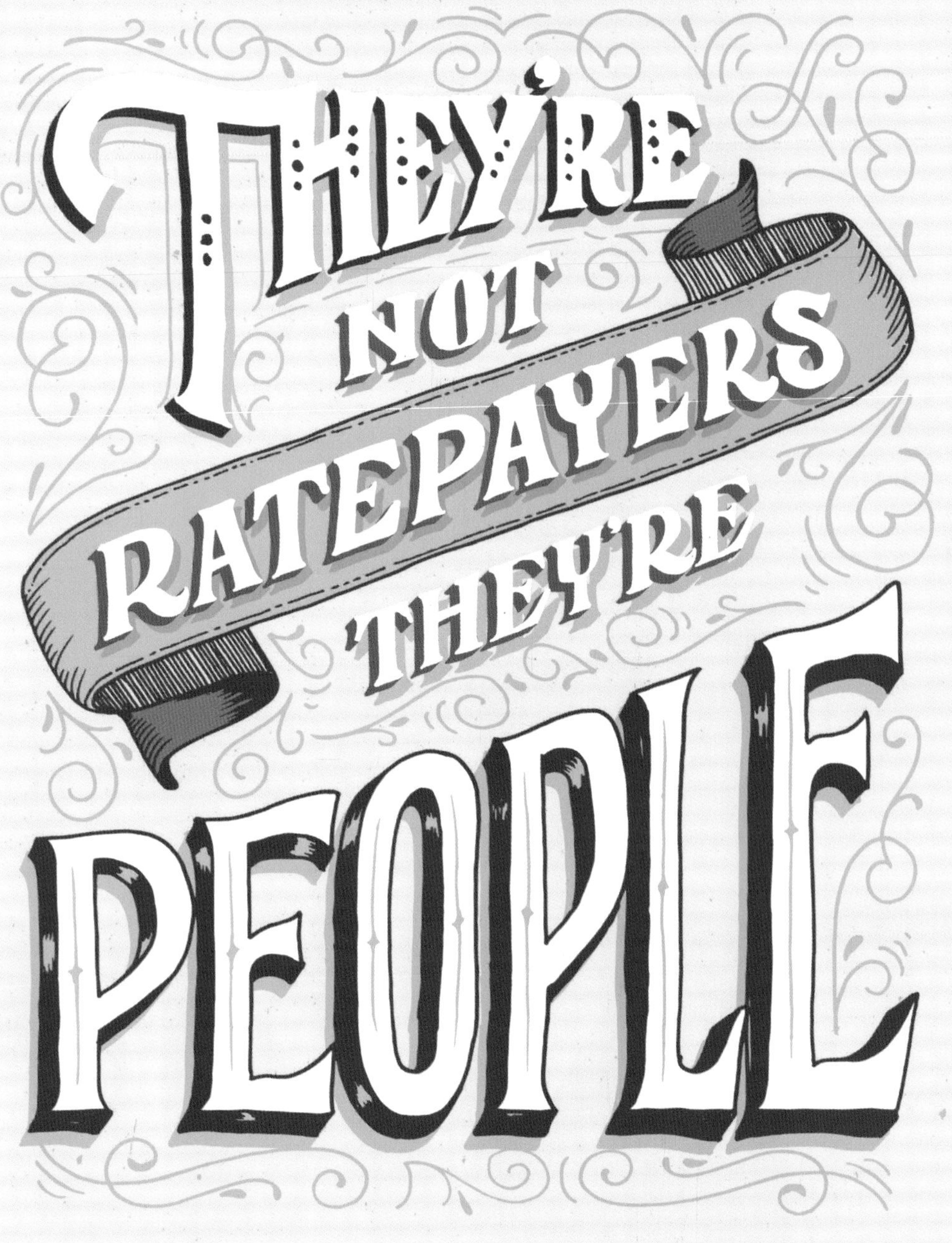
THEY'RE
NOT
RATEPAYERS
THEY'RE
PEOPLE

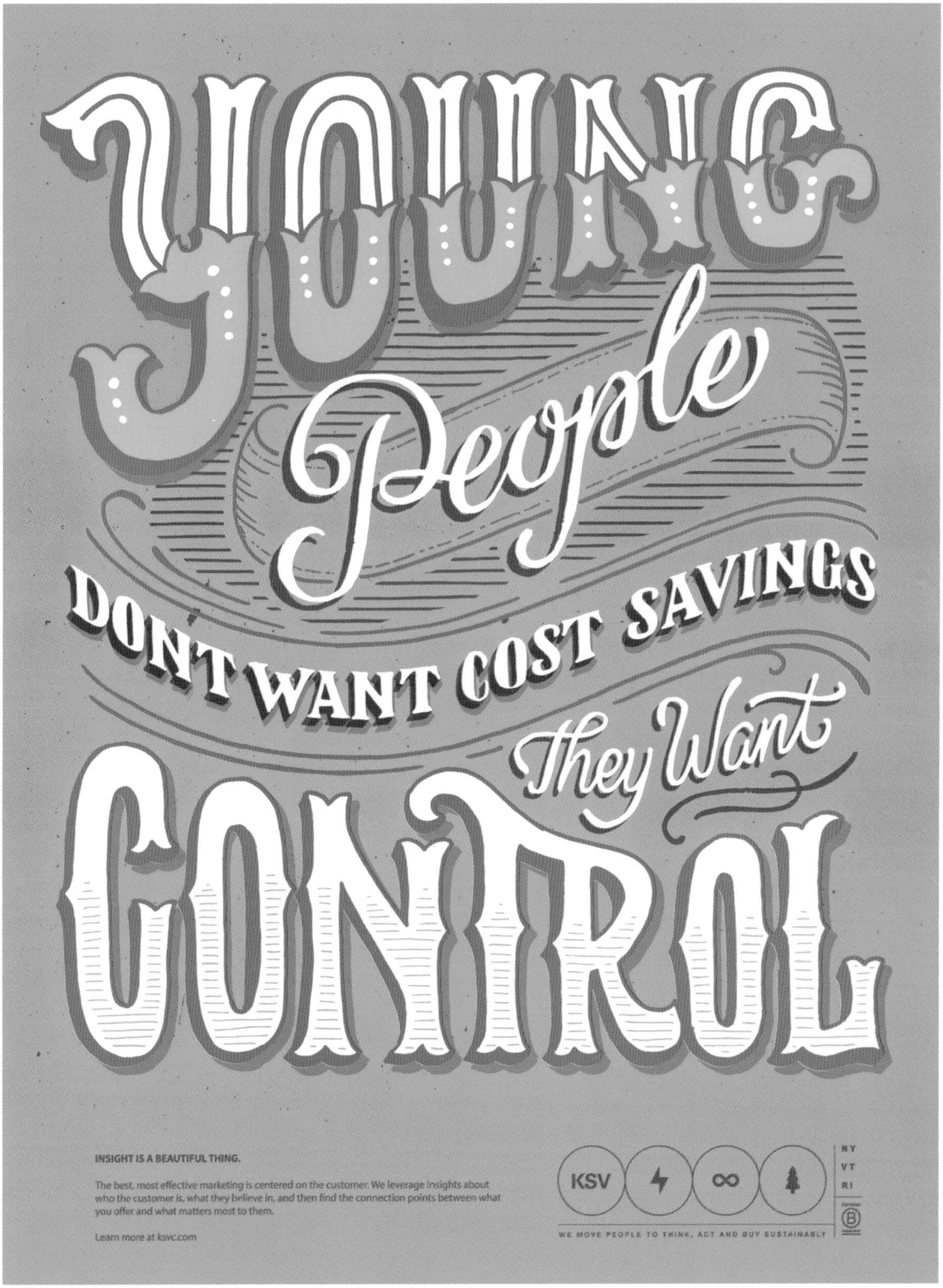
YOUNG
People
DONT WANT COST SAVINGS
They Want
CONTROL
INSIGHT IS A BEAUTIFUL THING.
The best, most effective marketing is centered on the customer. We leverage insights about who the customer is, what they believe in, and then find the connection points between what you offer and what matters most to them.
Learn more at ksvc.com
KSV
NY
VT
RI
WE MOVE PEOPLE TO THINK, ACT AND BUY SUSTAINABLY

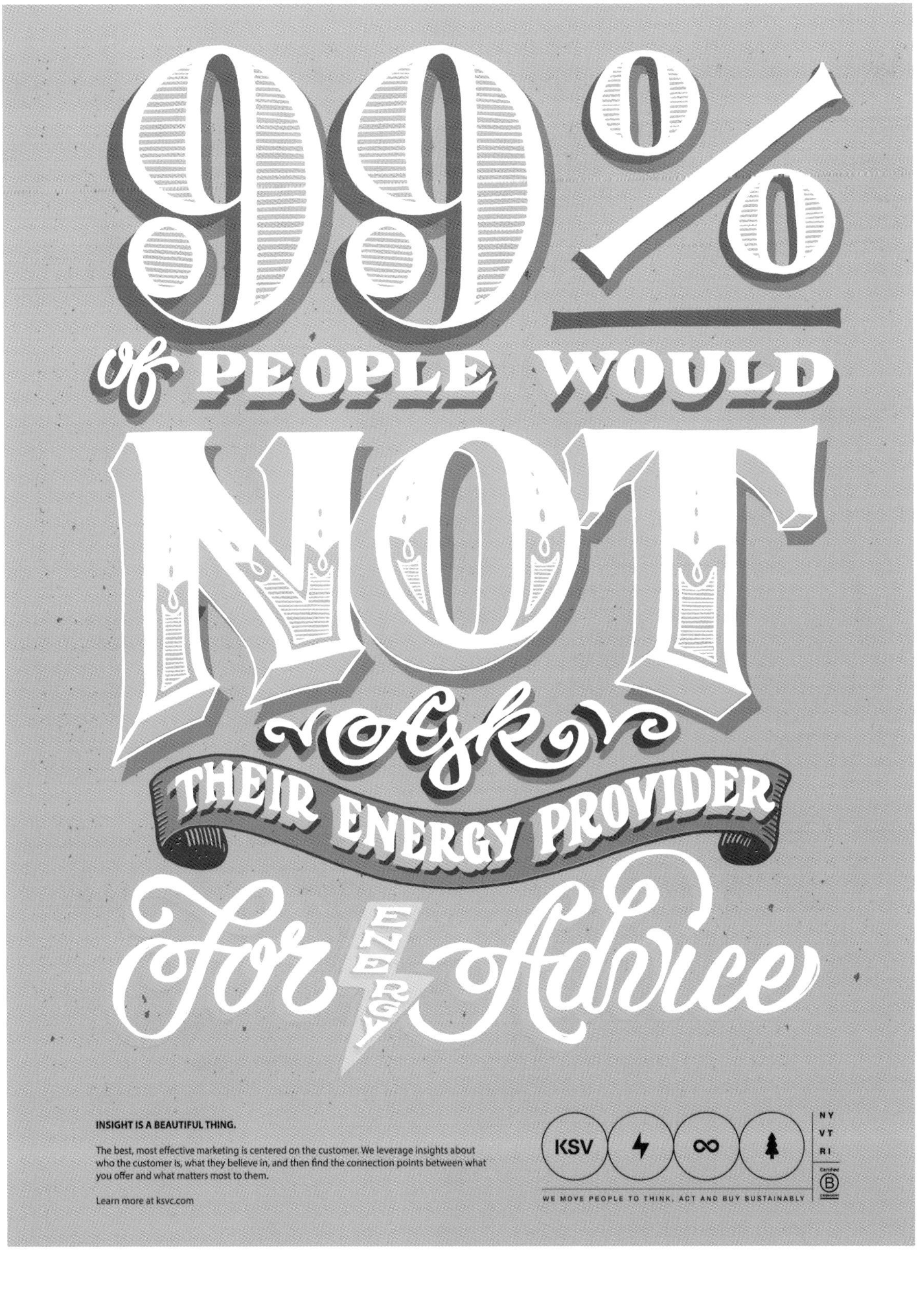
99%
of PEOPLE WOULD
NOT
Ask
THEIR ENERGY PROVIDER
For ENERGY Advice
INSIGHT IS A BEAUTIFUL THING.
The best, most effective marketing is centered on the customer. We leverage insights about who the customer is, what they believe in, and then find the connection points between what you offer and what matters most to them.
Learn more at ksvc.com
KSV
NY
VT
RI
WE MOVE PEOPLE TO THINK, ACT AND BUY SUSTAINABLY

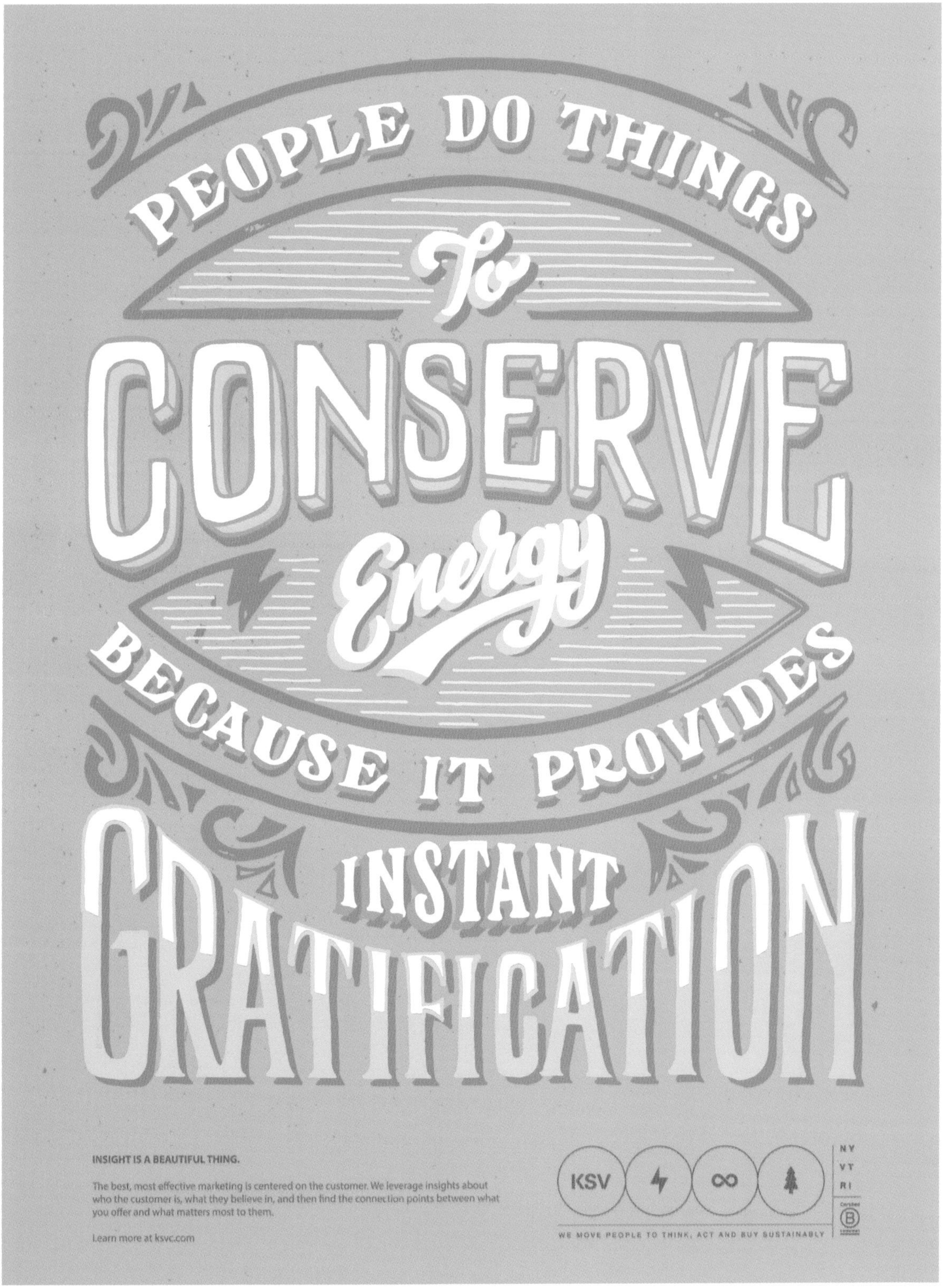

PEOPLE DO THINGS
To
CONSERVE
Energy
BECAUSE IT PROVIDES
INSTANT
GRATIFICATION
INSIGHT IS A BEAUTIFUL THING.
The best, most effective marketing is centered on the customer. We leverage insights about who the customer is, what they believe in, and then find the connection points between what you offer and what matters most to them.
Learn more at ksvc.com
KSV
NY
VT
RI
WE MOVE PEOPLE TO THINK, ACT AND BUY SUSTAINABLY

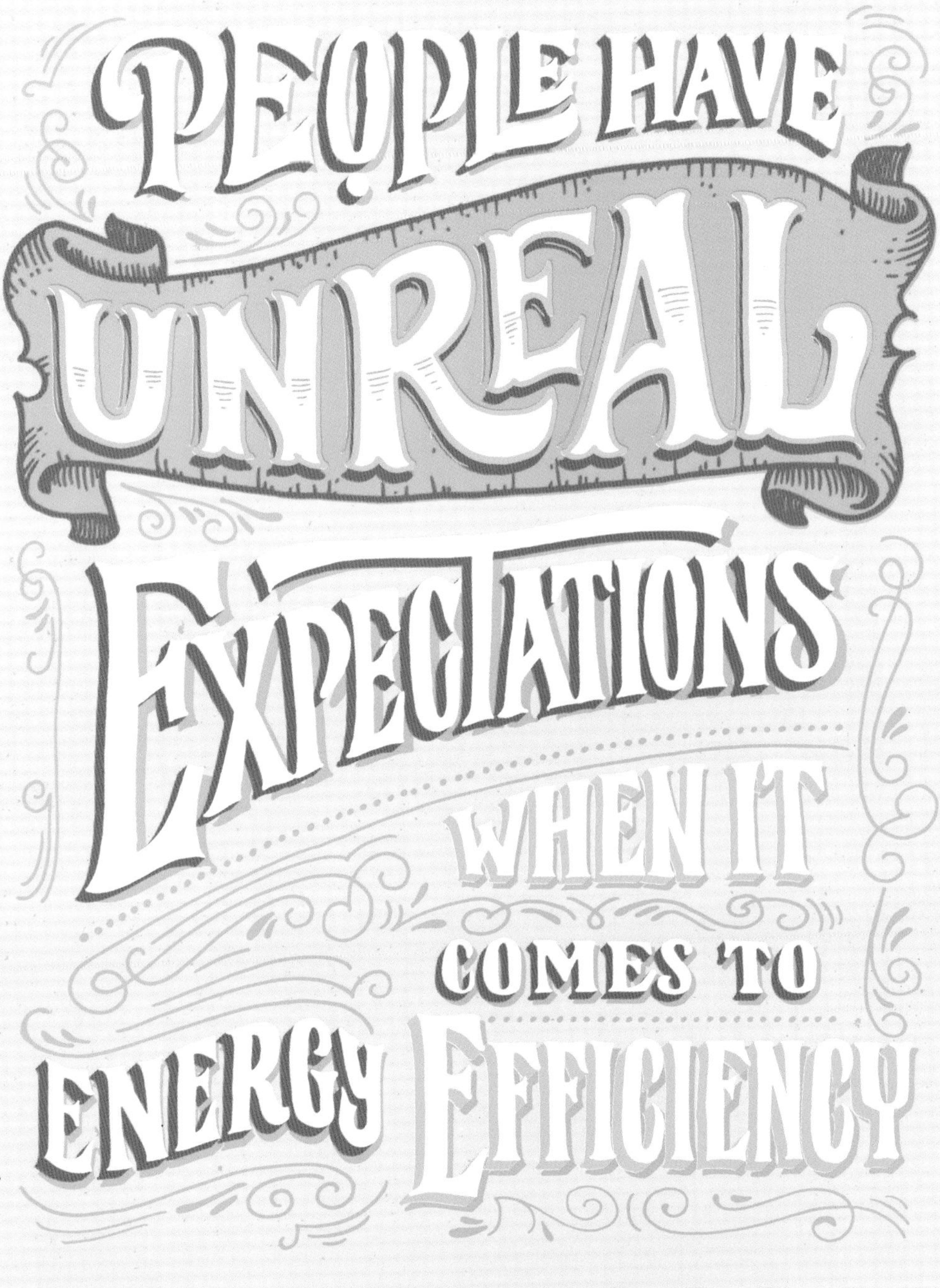

INSIGHT IS A BEAUTIFUL THING.

The best, most effective marketing is centered on the customer. We leverage insights about who the customer is, what they believe in, and then find the connection points between what you offer and what matters most to them.

Learn more at ksvc.com

KSV

NY
VT
RI

WE MOVE PEOPLE TO THINK, ACT AND BUY SUSTAINABLY

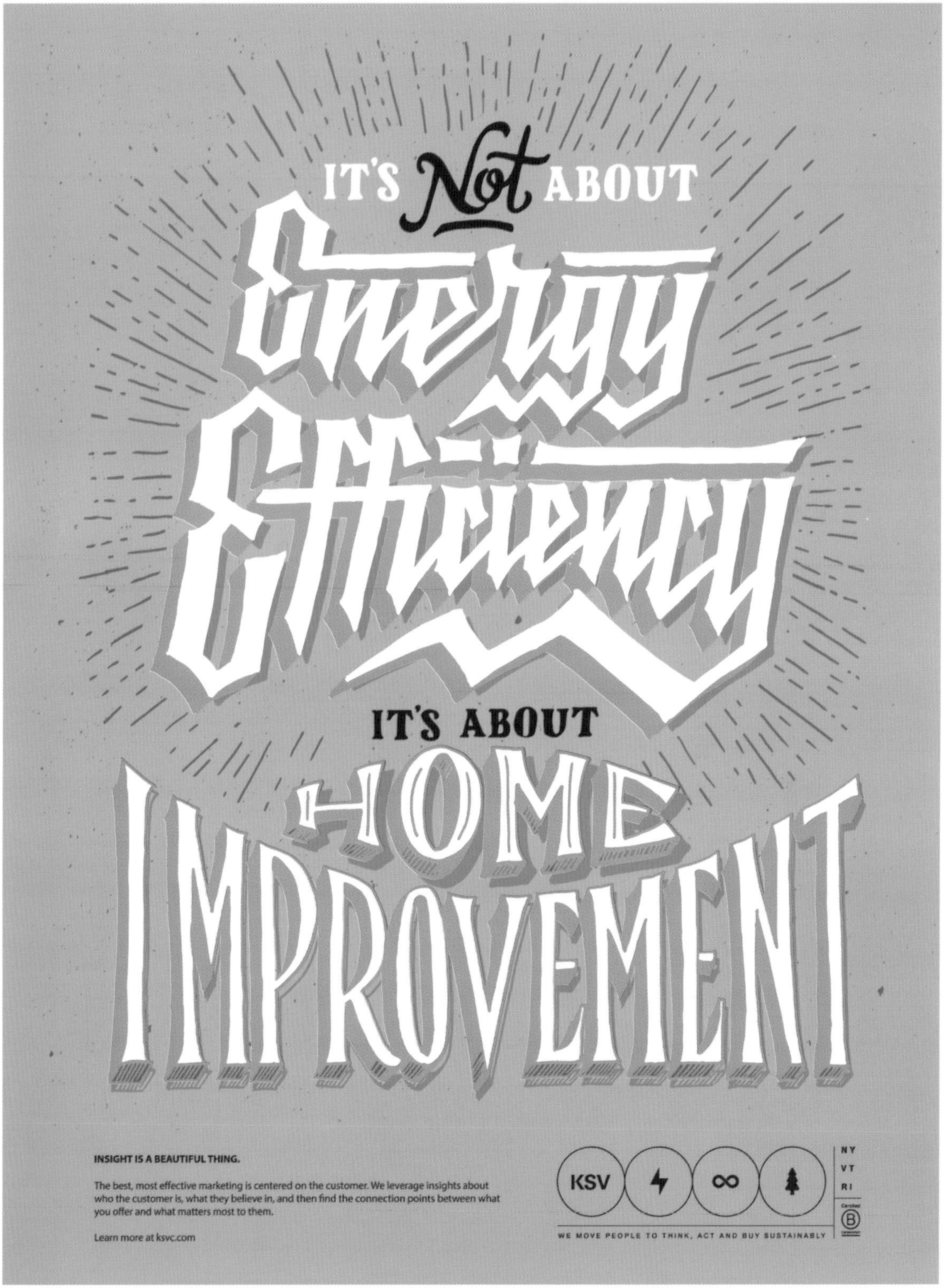
IT'S Not ABOUT
Energy Efficiency
IT'S ABOUT
HOME IMPROVEMENT
INSIGHT IS A BEAUTIFUL THING.
The best, most effective marketing is centered on the customer. We leverage insights about who the customer is, what they believe in, and then find the connection points between what you offer and what matters most to them.
Learn more at ksvc.com
KSV
NY
VT
RI
WE MOVE PEOPLE TO THINK, ACT AND BUY SUSTAINABLY

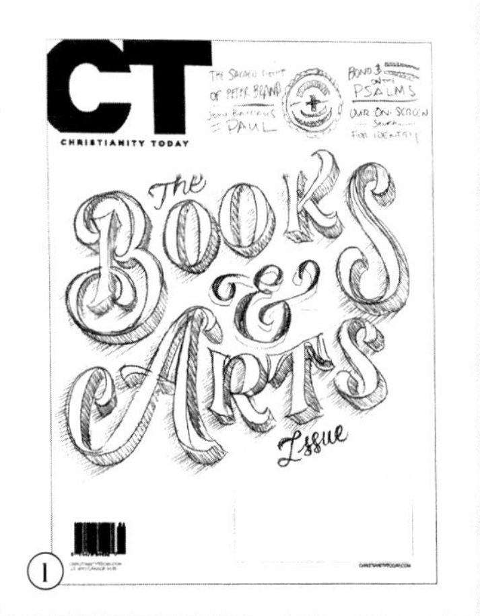

1

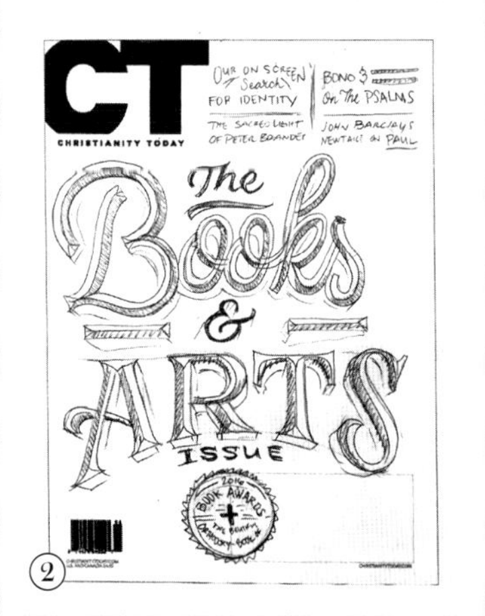

2

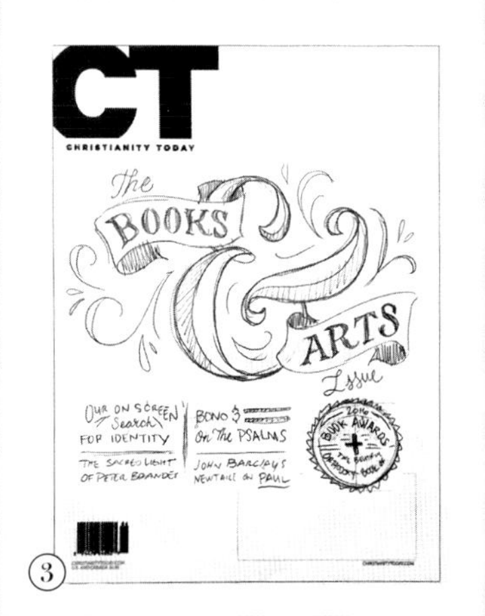

3

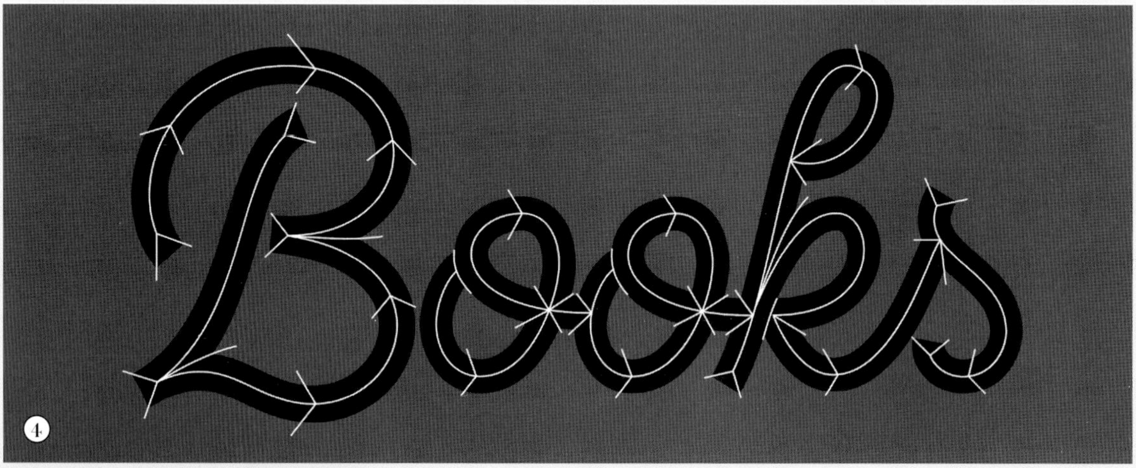

4

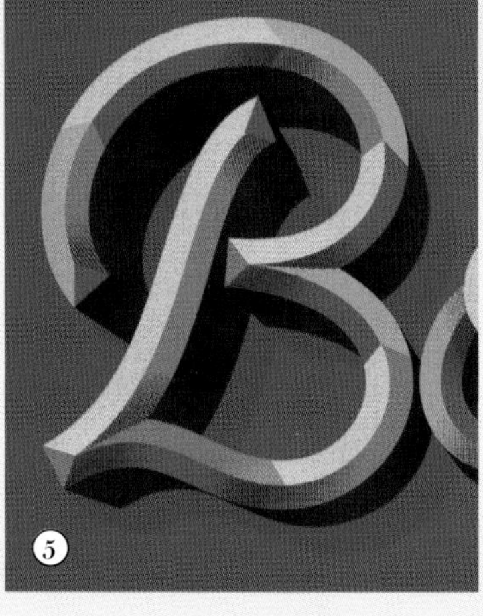
5

Making my lettering

For this commissioned project I started working with the art director on style directions then I went about sketching out very rough composition of the primary headline. The direction was to create a very stylized 3d effect on the typography to add depth and visual interest. I also added a bevel effect to the typography in illustrator and gave it some subtle color variation to give the type that chiseled look.

Creando mi lettering

Para este proyecto que me encargaron, comencé trabajando con el director artístico sobre las indicaciones de estilo, para empezar creando un boceto lo más aproximado del titular principal. Me habían pedido que creara un efecto 3D muy estilizado sobre la tipografía para añadir profundidad e interés visual. También añadí un efecto bisel a la tipografía en Illustrator y le di una sutil variación cromática para atribuirle a la tipografía ese aspecto cincelado.

CT

CHRISTIANITY TODAY

2016

BOOK AWARDS

+

THE BEAUTIFUL ORTHODOXY

BOOK OF THE YEAR

The Books & ARTS Issue

OUR ON-SCREEN Search FOR IDENTITY

THE SACRED LIGHT OF Peter Brandes

JOHN BARCLAY'S New Take ON PAUL

10

0 74470 84052 7

Thanks